COMPARATIVE POLITICS AND POLITICAL THEORY

THE UNIVERSITY OF

NORTH CAROLINA PRESS · CHAPEL HILL

COMPARATIVE
POLITICS
AND
POLITICAL
THEORY

ESSAYS WRITTEN IN HONOR OF
CHARLES BASKERVILL ROBSON

EDITED BY

EDWARD L. PINNEY

Editor's Preface

The past two generations of political scientists have witnessed the separation of factual-institutional description from theoretical speculation, and then their reunion in a vigorous restatement of the discipline. In some sense this reunion represents no more than the restoration of theory to apropriate status in the ordering of political data. Perhaps also, however, it represents the ultimate victory of the new political theory over arid abstraction on the one hand and trivial empiricism on the other.

The initial departure from historicism and normative polemics was under the influence of the German idealistic tradition and its American adherents, most notably John W. Burgess and W. W. Willoughby. American political science became more or less synonymous with the study of structural and institutional arrangements, but underlying this factual orientation was a determination to integrate somehow the unrivaled world prestige of German theory and scholarship with appropriate attention to constitutional forms and legal analysis. This "retreat to factual description," as the late Sigmund Neumann put it, allowed American political scholarship to develop along lines that made recourse inevitable to objective fact-finding on a broad comparative base.

If the first stirrings of a theory for political science were German in origin, the take-off phase was thoroughly American. What appeared to be a self-effacing abandonment of the speculative tradition of political inquiry and a "retreat to factual description" represented in effect a new—one may say more ambitious—statement of purpose for political science. The new political science turned away from easy generalities and untested assumptions and placed new emphasis on a total social science approach, on the functions and processes of political life, and on the continuing need for unraveling an entangled reality by steady reliance on theoretical orientation, and a hard-bitten insistence on sticking close to empirical reality.

The odyssey of change in our discipline during this century is largely a matter of the developing course of its links with other social sciences. The gradual breakdown of hard and fast departmental borderlines was again mainly an American effort, beginning in the 1920's and 1930's. The breakdown was speeded by such wartime emergencies as the Office of Strategic Services, which required a great deal of inter-disciplinary borrowing. Political science began to enlist findings from auxiliary fields, especially economics, psychology and psychiatry, sociology, anthropology and linguistics. To avoid the pitfalls of inter-disciplinary borrowing and lending associated with comparative politics, such as the all too glib application of inappropriate concepts and nomenclatures, there has been an auspicious revival of theory. The restoration of theory demonstrates the loyalty of present-day political science to its Greek antecedents. The political science scholar, no less than Aristotle, must confront and examine the existing political habits in efforts to confirm or to discard current theoretical postulates by reference to the stubborn realities of contemporary politics.

This volume in honor of Charles Baskervill Robson is put together to acknowledge with gratitude the intellectual and personal profit each contributor has gained from knowing Professor Robson; and to acknowledge his broader contribution in the furtherance of political knowledge as teacher and colleague, as challenger, defender, innovator. It is our hope that these essays taken together constitute an appropriate testimony to the influence Professor Robson has had, as well as to the rich and varied material of politics as a field of study. The essays are organized to reflect the diffuseness of comparative and theoretical political study and to present the major dimensions of comparative politics: normative, conceptual, institutional, behavioral, and methodological. Underlying each contribution is the assumption that, intrinsically, every theoretically relevant unit of political life is comparable, and every reliable agency of comparison in politics possesses theoretical significance. This assumption has lain at the heart of Charles B. Robson's role in the discipline—reflected in the orientation of his own teaching, in his own writing, and in the writings of his students which in turn reflect the subtle influence of a great spirit. Giving further expression to this assumption we are here suggesting that the study of political science is ultimately the study of political theory and unavoidably the study of comparative politics.

E. L. P.

Lexington, Virginia
July, 1966

Contents

Charles Baskervill Robson

An Introduction

This collection of essays has been written in honor of Charles Baskervill Robson—or "Pat" Robson as all of us know him. The contributors include some who were privileged to study with him and others who have been privileged to work closely with him as faculty and professional colleagues. What unites us is the rewarding experience of knowing this man in the fullness of his personal and professional life; and each of us is the richer for it— richer for the warmth and compassion of his friendship, richer for his gentle wisdom liberally sprinkled with humor, and for the penetrating insights of his mind.

Charles B. Robson, the teacher-scholar, in his generation has spanned revolutionary changes within the discipline of political science. He came of age intellectually in the normative tradition of American political science in the 1920's, as a graduate student at Princeton University and The University of North Carolina. His mind found lasting enrichment and stimulation through exposure to German idealistic political thought in advanced study at Heidelberg and Bonn in 1926 and 1927. As with every true scholar, graduate study was only the first impetus to his intellectual development, and through almost four decades as teacher, department head, Kenan Professor and practicing political scientist, he has grown steadily with his students and with the discipline.

Charles Robson, as department faculty member and leader, in his tenure at The University of North Carolina at Chapel Hill, has spanned the development of the institution from a state and regional educational center of modest size to a great university of national and international stature. Teaching at first within a department of history and government, he helped to establish an independent department of political science in 1935 and from the beginning was its principal architect and builder. He served successively as its executive secretary for seven years, as head for sixteen years, and since 1959 in the indispensable role of "older statesman." In this period, and largely shaped by his leadership and his example, the department has increased many-fold in size, has developed a doctoral training program of national distinction, and has built a tradition of scholarship and criticism in a contagious atmosphere that embraces students and faculty as teammates in the exciting search to understand the political ways of man.

Among the most important contributions to scholarship has been his service to scholarly publishing as a member of the Board of Governors of The University of North Carolina Press. Since his appointment in 1939, he has served continuously and has been a member of both its Manuscript Committee and its Finance Committee. His advice on manuscripts in the field of political science and his active scouting among colleagues, old and young, have been the major factor in building the Press's publishing strength in the political science field. But perhaps even more important has been his influence on the general policy of the Press. During a period when it, like many other university presses, was changing from a small publishing operation firmly encased within its local academic community into a complex and professionally staffed publishing organization, he has been a strong and unswerving force toward keeping its publishing purpose focused on scholarship. And he has insisted on the Press's right and duty to promote freedom of inquiry by exercising the concomitant right of freedom to publish. The Press's reputation as a southern center of liberal publishing has been largely the creation of a handful of Chapel Hill scholars, and prominent among them is "Pat" Robson.

As a practicing political scientist and man of letters, he has found creative ways to contribute out of his professional skills to the world of public affairs. First as a social science analyst for the Strategic Bombing Survey in Germany, and later as consultant on higher education to the United States military government and as Foreign Service Staff Officer in Bonn, he found useful application for the intimate knowledge he commanded of German political traditions and institutions. His efforts in those years were bent towards helping re-establish competent teaching and research in the social sciences at West German universities. He has continued his close association with a number of these institutions over the past decade, serving as guest professor and lecturer from time to time at the Free University in West Berlin, and at the University of Cologne. Through these associations, and through his regular contributions to social science journals and scholarly series in West Germany, he has helped to build and maintain a more substantial bridge for the interpenetration of German social science scholarship and American scholarly work in comparable fields. As his own doctoral dissertation was concerned with the influence of German political thought upon the United States in the late nineteenth century, so has he helped to promote the flow of ideas from American political science to reinvigorate the study and teaching of politics in postwar West Germany. His eminent position in the contemporary German scholarly community was reaffirmed in 1965 by his election to the coveted position as corresponding member of the *Historische Kommission zu Berlin.*

His commitment to political theory and through it to the comparative analysis of political systems is, and has always been, the integrating theme in Charles Robson's professional life—his life as teacher, as department colleague and builder, and as practicing political scientist. He saw the "behavioral revolution" within political science as an opportunity to guide and inform the systematic gathering of data on empirical reality by the tests of relevance distilled from the insights of great theorists of the ages. In his patient and wise leadership as department head, he presided over—indeed managed—the transition of his faculty from traditionalist to modern political science, with genuine respect for all points of view, an encouragement to youthful ideas, and yet a healthy skepticism, disarming in its candor and refreshing in its freedom from doctrinaire rigidity or pedantic jargon. This eclectic spirit with regard to new ideas, new methods, new kinds of data was not lost on his students, nor on his faculty colleagues whether in Chapel Hill or in Berlin. Where Charles Robson is, there the oldest ideas and the newest techniques of analysis share open access to the scholar's market place. And out of the competition and the resulting mix, the minds of students and teacher alike are challenged. This is the heritage of Charles Baskervill Robson—this is what he means to us, to The University of North Carolina, and to political science.

FREDERIC N. CLEAVELAND

Charles Baskervill Robson

I. NORMATIVE DIMENSIONS

The Myth of Equality and the Actualities of Power

by Richard McCleery

THE DISTINCTION BETWEEN THE ELEMENTS

It is a strange and often unfortunate fact that men fail to distinguish between events in experience and concepts in analysis. On the discovery that such concepts as "sovereignty" or the "state" are useful in political inquiry, men jump to the conclusion that they are "true" and attempt to discover a substantive, empirical content for such terms. Hence, it should not be surprising —although it may be seriously misleading—that attempts are made to find substantive referents for the concept of "equality."

Equality is an ancient ideal in the heritage of Western man, though not so ancient as the problems of power that have driven him to political thought. It is a concept conceived in the world of creative imagination, woven of the fabric of dreams and wrapped in the tissue of poetry. In ages past the ideal of equality was part of the vision of kingdoms not of this world. Its relation to the affairs of human society is uncertain at best. Equality attains a precise meaning in the abstract realm of mathematics or the remote domain of metaphysics, but it tends to dissolve on contact with mundane experience. In the mind of man, it may be thought of as a seed stolen from the garden of the gods, a seed more suited to the soil of Eden than to the harsh and rocky realities of this world. In concrete experience, the fruits of that idea have as often been tyranny and terror as nourishment for the spirit of man. It is at one with liberty in the crimes committed in its name. The task of this essay is to consider the cultivation of equality in the present climate of the human condition, and its first step is to place that ideal in context with the facts of power in society.

Power is a matter of fact. A relatively stable pattern of authority and deference so characterizes the relations of man to man in organized society as to be a condition of society's existence. The idea of organization, in itself, implies the distribution of functions in a hierarchy. It is only with great difficulty that the co-operative relationships of individuals can be conceived except in terms implying superiority and subordination. A simple, pyramidal conception of power has framed the bulk of reflection on the subject, and the form of that conception has, in turn, dictated many of the conclusions reached by proponents or detractors of a particular social order. The quality of power as an immediate fact of experience has been formulated in such terms as an "iron law of oligarchy."

However, a visible diversity of power structures leads men to inquire into the nature and characteristics of society to which power is related, and to aspire to an order of power closer to the dictates of the heart. Thus, a structure of power is both fact and artifact. It has characteristics which are fixed by a given social order and its natural environment, but its characteristics are also shaped by the values and convictions—the character— of its participants. Analysis may distinguish the roles of social structure and ideology in shaping a system of power.

As a fact of social life central to experience, power has been an object of worship, of philosophical reflection, of aspiration and despair, and the subject of much empirical inquiry. Each of these approaches contributes something to the perspectives from which we view this aspect of human relations. Perhaps no perspective is adequate to plumb the depths of a relationship rooted deeper in the mind than consciousness can go. In that direction, it is enough to note evidence suggesting that all perception of power is colored by an image of the father, on the one hand, and of divinity on the other. The immediate experience of power is shrouded in a sense of awe and mystery to such a degree that some amount of half-calculated hocus-pocus attends its manipulation in any case from the installation of King Arthur to the inauguration of a president. Power fills psychological needs for its subjects as well as for those who execute it, and its functions in that respect are as controlling of its form as are the visible qualities of the situation in which it emerges.

Such psychic functions lead some to conceive of power as a nebulous, intangible quality—as a mystery of kings—and to further confuse the distinction between concepts and things. Power is variously understood, for each of its many facets offers a different dimension for analysis, a challenge to diverse approaches, and a risk that we mistake one aspect for the whole.

This essay is based on close observation of the workings of power in a society in microcosm—a custodial institution—and analytic reflection on it in a second.

POWER AND SOCIAL CONTROLS

The power relationships institutionalized in society constitute only the visible aspect of that complex system of social control internalized in individuals. In any human organization the greater part of the controls exerted on persons are deeply entrenched in habit and conditioned response. Indeed, the limits of human co-operation are more fixed by these internalized controls than by the structure of governmental arrangements or the logic of political philosophy. Hence, the study of comparative government may find that the institutional forms of monarchy, as in England, or of a people's democracy, as in Hungary, conceal effective structures of power quite unrelated to those forms. However, a more intensive, comparative study of politics discovers connections between the actualities of power and the constitutions of society or ideals toward which power is ordered.

To say that all government rests on consent, that it is consistent with values which underlie a given power structure, may only shift inquiry to the devices by which consent is rendered or induced. The political systems which grow out of anxiety and insecurity in the modern world have it within their power to intensify those conditions of their growth. But to say that the overt structure of power in society rests on some vast, basic, and mysterious forces in nature is to recapture a truth in the most primitive perception of the facts. Perhaps no force in nature is more powerful than that of habit, the tyranny exercised on the individual unconsciously by his membership in a group. An external structure of power mediates between the controls within the person and the forces in his natural environment, but the external structure grows as internal controls fail. Primitive man bowed in religious awe before the offices that symbolized power in his society because, while that power passed all understanding and engaged his deepest fears, it guaranteed his existence. Modern man reflects that heritage in the temple architecture of public buildings, and the sacrifices required by the modern state are no less demanding than those of ancient society.

A Special Case of Power

The actualities of power—dominance and submission, sanction and sacrifice—are given in all experience, but much of that experience is complex and defies analysis. An understanding of power involves, on one hand, analysis of the manner in which its overt structure is rationalized, and incorporated in a system of habit and belief, or mediated by sentiments of loyalty, affection, and faith. To distinguish these elements, it seems useful to add the examination of a deviant case to the literature of comparative politics—to consider a power system relatively unsupported by internalized social controls. Another approach to analysis is to consider the skeletal characteristics of organization, abstracted from a cultural context, and seek out the functions that emerge at the core of power relationships there. The simplest bureaucracy illustrates certain relationships which characterize the most complex societies and their structures of power.

A specialized type of bureaucracy, a prison system, fulfills in large degree the conditions for analysis. The prison demonstrates a situation of power in the extreme, which is relatively divorced from attitudes of loyalty or affection and the myths of legitimacy that complicate analysis as they make life more gracious elsewhere. Its population consists of persons subjected to physical constraints in proportion as their internalized controls have failed to regulate their behaviors within permitted limits of tolerance. The prison as a society in microcosm offers many opportunities for research. One may study the social backgrounds of its inmates and seek conditions related to the disability which subjects them to this system of power. One may study the formal system of power and discover the often unexpected limitations to which force is subject when authority is not acknowledged. It is also possible to examine the type of power structure that emerges in the inmate society under these conditions of confinement, and to explore the roles of force, of myth, and of ambition in the maintenance of that society. Finally, it is possible to examine the prison both as a special case of bureaucratic organization and as an example of a type of state, increasingly represented in the modern world, in which power is a quasi-monopoly of the ruling class.

Whether the prison is judged, on its external appearances, as the remnant of some ancient barbarism, or as a preview of some more complex barbarism of the future, the characteristics of its people and the culture that appears there provide instructive contrasts with a free society. It is commonplace to say that a convict gets what he deserves. But that observation comes close to being a law of gravity in political science, for all people tend toward a type of government consistent with their set of internal controls. The laws, as Montesquieu has shown, reflect the spirit that underlies them.

A closer look at the population of a state prison provides an insight into the spirit of those who, in modern times, inhabit and worship the prison state. The prison population is not a representative sample of the population at large, for it is disproportionately drawn from those elements of society most dislocated from traditional roles and alienated from the structure of society as a whole. It is drawn from elements of society that, elsewhere, have provided the foundation of authoritarian regimes. In origin, these men are isolates in modern communities, without group loyalties, marketable skills, regular employment, or permanent residence to attach them to objects of identification. They are alienated in proportion as they have lacked all sense of meaningful participation in the life of a community. The politics of the prison yard is a case in point for theories of the "politics of mass society."[1] Many inmates find an object of identification in the prison and a meaning for themselves in that society that they have lacked in the world outside. The personalities of such men have disintegrated largely because they themselves have not been incorporated into the complex and specialized societies from which they come.

There is a strange consensus which binds the ruler and the ruled within a prison. The principle on which its normally antagonistic factions agree is that "equality of treatment" is the only basis on which its system of absolute power can be either workable or tolerable. Inmate society rests on conditions as near to perfect equality as the wit of its custodians can devise. Common clothing, accommodations, duties, and food, and the prohibition of all evidence which would declare status or actions which

1. William Kornhauser, *The Politics of Mass Society* (Glencoe, Ill.: The Free Press, 1959), provided a number of concepts designed for the analysis of politics in general which prove especially useful for understanding the politics of alienation and authoritarian regimes in miniature.

would coerce deference, might be expected to produce the uniformities that philosophers once attributed to a state of nature. On the contrary, however, research on inmate society normally finds it to be ordered in a monolithic hierarchy of power, dominated by its own senior members and exacting a degree of conformity vastly more restrictive than official demands.[2] Removal of inmate leaders by official action regularly results in their replacement by others who do not seek the office. The responsibilities and hazards of leadership are thrust upon them.

The function of leadership in that situation seems to be the manipulation of psychologically satisfying myths which subdue anxiety and stabilize the relationship of the group to its environment of arbitrary power. Inmate leaders wield power by virtue of their capacity to define the situation to others in an arbitrary, power-dominated and anxiety-producing environment. Their informal definitions become the major premises in the logic of behavior of their fellows. This unsought authority of the inmate leader is without formal sanctions, legitimacy, or object, yet it is normally more controlling in the behavior of inmates than the power of the legitimate bureaucracy of the institution with its monopoly over the instruments of force. An inmate code denies the inmate access or appeal to formal power and, thus, gains a measure of independence from official government in proportion as men conform to the conventions of their own society.

The ruling class of the prison, with its command of force, law, and the distribution of goods, and with its militant structure of organization, would seem to fulfill all the conditions of absolutism and to be able to impose administratively-defined values on all aspects of behavior. However, research finds a paradox: a constant tendency to compromise the formal system of power. Only the most rigorous suppression of contact between official and inmate societies, a suppression enforced on both sides, limits the incorporation of values originating in inmate society into official decision. There are punitive, custodial institutions in which the inmates' boast of "running the joint" is valid. More often, the restriction on communication is reflected in a ponderous inflexibility of official commitments. For all their militant

2. Donald Cressey (ed.), *The Prison* (New York: Holt, Rinehart and Winston, 1960), digests a substantial body of research on institutional organization and change which is relevant to analysis of the prison as a political system. It provides the basis of generalizations here.

command of sanctions, prison bureaucracies are notoriously narrow in the scope of objects to which their power applies.

Such are the data and the paradoxical relationships on which analysis must work: the relationship of absolutism and equality, the limitations on a power which is based on every sanction but authority, the authority of positions based on nothing more than a capacity to define the terms of existence. Power in such circumstances cannot be understood as a quality of persons or as an object of will. It cannot be explained as an attribute conferred by law or as a consequence of command over instruments of force or the allocation of goods. That these characteristics are often associated with power may be taken as evidence of the ends for which power is employed rather than the conditions from which it rises. Extensive use of force in ordering the internal relationships of a prison or other society does not testify so much to the existence of a stable power structure as to its collapse. The manipulation of force or other symbols of authority may be adjuncts to its exercise, but a large part of the heart of the power relationship seems to lie elsewhere.

Power and Organizational Structure

The approach of the present inquiry is to seek a basis for the actualities of power by isolating elements of human relationships and projecting these through simple models of organization. Implications of these models can, in turn, be checked against the evidence of historical cases, or against power as experienced in society. In this fashion, it may be possible to identify a functional base of power apart from processes of its rationalization, exploitation, or abuse. Analysis distinguishes two generic types of organizational relationship: (a) that of the group to external objects or forces and (b) internal relationships among elements within the group itself. The thesis here is that *the basis of power within a group lies in a process of defining these internal and external relations in terms which serve as the premises of the behavior of members.* The act of definition and the knowledge by which it is informed emerge as central components of power.

In a major work on organization theory, Chester Bernard has defined authority as "the character of a communication by virtue of which it is accepted by a member as governing the action he contributes."[3] An alternative way of phrasing this might be, "In the beginning there was the word." If it is true that a definition of the situation governing group relationships lies at the core of power, however, the two types of relationship noted above should give rise to distinguishable types of power. These can be set forth in models for inquiry. (See Figures 1 and 2.)

An undifferentiated social system with multiple units performing similar functions should pose a minimum of problems with respect to ordering the internal relations among the units. Such a society might lack any device other than custom or ritual for adjusting its relations, but in the absence of such a device the society could not accommodate degrees of non-conformity or individualism. The active concerns of such a society would seem to turn on adjusting the relationship of all to the external forces to which the group must adapt. The power of definition might be expected to gravitate into the hands of those with the advantage of knowledge of the forces of the external world, and to be monopolized there in the absence of a vertical differentiation of roles to facilitate participation in the definitional process.

By contrast, a society differentiated in terms of specialized functions would find individuals less dependent on adjustment to the demands of external forces. Its problems, and devices for resolving them, might be expected to emerge in connection with the integration of internal diversities. The function of power would be the co-ordination of specialized activities. Given formal devices for that task, the group would be able to produce and tolerate a wider range of diversity in individuals. Given the logic of the model and what is known of organization, increase in the range of specialization would be marked by the elaboration of vertical gradations in the hierarchy, creating a class structure but permitting participation in the definition of internal relationships.

Is there evidence in history or experience to substantiate these elementary implications? They seem to correspond substantially to what is known of certain primitive political systems of the present and the past. Inquiry into these may elaborate the implications and, at the same time, refine the model with other variables as evidence requires.

3. Chester Bernard, *The Functions of the Executive* (Rev. ed.; Cambridge, Mass.: Harvard University Press, 1954), p. 163.

The ancient rural society was a closed community with a membership based on kinship and common property, and with a relatively simple caste system. It knew of no way to incorporate the alien except as a slave, or to greet the stranger except as an enemy. Where the institution of slavery existed, the status of the slave was not far different from that of dependent members of the family. In many of these societies, including those of Micronesia which have served romantics in our culture as the last abode of the "noble savage" ideal, the only device for dealing with wanderers or captives in battle was to kill them out of hand. The only alternative available for dealing with those too powerful to be killed was to worship them as gods—roles enjoyed briefly by adventurers such as Magellan and Cook in their meeting with such societies.

Very little subordination or deference marked the interpersonal relations of those who enjoyed the status of free men in the primitive rural society, but the life of the person was circumscribed by ritual to an extreme degree. Conformity to those rituals was a condition of every aspect of life. Extreme dependence on the forces of nature, which could only be perceived as arbitrary in that state of knowledge, generated the anxieties which were relieved by compulsive conformity. The priestly class in such a society enjoyed an unqualified position of dominance by virtue of some ability to predict (and thus, seemingly, to control) natural events. On the basis of that dominance it was able to exploit the anxieties which characterized such a society by the manipulation of myths, and the custody of those myths with their interwoven elements of explanatory science was a closely guarded monopoly of the priesthood.

General participation in the formulation of those definitions which governed group behavior was impossible, because the egalitarian structure of society lacked devices for the consolidation and vertical communication of opinion. Access to the elite function of defining the situation was limited by the absence of a hierarchy of positions leading to it, but exploitation of the power it conferred was also limited by the inability of the elite to alter interpersonal relations which were fixed in ritual and habit. It is noteworthy that the primitive, undifferentiated, rural society and its priesthood correspond closely to the characteristics and functions of the power structure of inmate society.

FIGURE 1. AN UNDIFFERENTIATED,
EGALITARIAN SYSTEM

External Forces of Nature
$$P = ke^*$$

---

m m m m m m m m m m m m m m m m '

---

s   s   s   s   s "

* Power equates with "knowledge of externals" and the capacity to define the circumstances with functional but reassuring myths in anxiety-producing situations. It is absolute in character but limited in the scope of its application.
' Membership rests on identity of function and conformity to rituals defining interpersonal relations in the community.
" The alien as a "beast," a "god," a "rat"—or a slave.

The undifferentiated, rural society earned a reputation for piety and resistance to tyrants, which it continues to enjoy. We still regard the yeoman farmer as the foundation of virtue and independence, and the high priests who presume to speak for agriculture manipulate considerable governmental power to perpetuate the rituals of the rustic state. Generations of Americans on the land have looked on the city with its political machinery as a sinful place, while their sons set off thence in hopes that the myth might be true. The celebration of rustic virtue is legitimate if it be remembered that independence is not individualism, that equality does not mean freedom, and that self-control is but partly conscious. The reputation of rural life is earned at the expense of immense anxiety, compulsive conformity, and an inability to adapt to changing social or economic conditions of power—as witnessed by rural resistance to social change in the South. It is something less than desirable to see the *status quo* as a direct expression of Providence.

Modern rural life is not identical with its ancient counterpart in either social structure or virtues. A thousand stories of traveling salesmen suggest that modern rural society has incorporated wider conceptions of community and some capacity to accommodate strangers. However, any egalitarian community retains some characteristics and potentialities of the model. Studying an intensely egalitarian America, one still dominated by a rural ideology, de Tocqueville asserted: "The principle of equality begets two tendencies . . . the one leads straight to independence and may suddenly drive them into anarchy; the other conducts

them by a longer, more secret, but more certain route to slavery."
De Tocqueville wrote as a friend, not an enemy, of democracy,
but he feared the tyranny of the majority as much as tyranny in
any form. He saw, in the undifferentiated, egalitarian society and
its compulsive conformities, the potentialities of the ancient,
priest-riden, slave empires of the past built on those foundations.
His prevision of the slave empires of the present may lend
authority to his insights for us.

Turning to the second diagram, the ancient urban society
corresponds to elements of the model when selected examples
are chosen. It is significant that the examples serve only in distinctive circumstances and periods of time. The city earned, in
antiquity, a reputation for moral waywardness which it still enjoys. More significant to our thesis of two types of power, it
tended to displace the dominance of a priestly class with another
order of power. One could explore endlessly the changes in the
human condition and the potentialities for man wrought by
urbanization. The ancient city and its modern counterpart
generate possibilities of degradation undreamed of in rural life,
but the ancient city gave its name to civilization.

At issue here are the organizational characteristics of a complex, specialized society and their consequences for the structure
of power in human relationships. The distinctive characteristics
of urban life are specialization and its inevitable associate, interdependence. One of the consequences of specialization for personality can be read in the works of ancients whose names are
long since forgotten: the fulfillment of the personality in creative
work, a realization of the "self" as a unique thing in the creation
of unique things, an expression of what we call *individualism.*
The great literature of the classical age elevated the problem of
man's relation to his society from the level of habit and custom
to that of rational inquiry. In Aeschylus and Plato, the issue of
justice replaced that of customary righteousness and the problem
of man's relation to the gods. More important, in their works we
see man himself emerging as a creature with the capacity to
govern his own behavior with principles of his own creation.
Common customs failed to govern differentiated individuals, and
the adjustment of internal relationships in society was one for
secular rather than priestly power.

FIGURE 2. A DIFFERENTIATED, HIERARCHICAL SYSTEM

$$P = ki *$$

$$n \qquad o$$

$$j \quad k \quad l \quad m'$$

(a) b c d e f g h i (a)''

(a)

* Power equates with "knowledge of internal relationships" and the capacity to define such relationships among specialized elements in ways which minimize conflict. Power of this type must rest on a flow of current information if the adjustments are to be functional.

' Each position which mediates between differentiated roles assumes the status and characteristics of an office as it shares in the process of defining relationships. The hierarchy of offices provides a structure for participation, making possible a representative democracy which elevates issues of human relations to a level of rational inquiry.

'' Vertical differentiation of status rests on a horizontal differentiation of roles, permitting toleration of individual differences but also the appearance of alienation (a) at various points around the hierarchy.

With the horizontal specialization of functions which is inherent in complex society, and with the problem of their integration, comes a vertical specialization of managerial roles. The role of co-ordinating diverse elements—defining the terms of their relation to one another—is a power role. In administrative jargon, the wider the effective span of control, the greater is the authority of a position. In a specialized system, this vertical differentiation of roles elaborates the complex structure, and the assertion of principles which govern inter-relationships is the core of executive power.

Experience of social organization seldom illustrates either of these power systems in a pure form. An agency may be nominally headed by a political official to relate its work to external forces, while an executive officer governs the internal affairs of the group. Some ancient societies had two monarchs, one for war and another for civil affairs. The relation of spiritual and political power is seldom better than an uneasy truce, and the subordination of military to civil power is uncertain at best. In practice, each type of power attempts to pre-empt the other to its own purposes, but social organizations tend to betray differences in the types of power distinguished by analysis.

The object of this analysis thus far has been to penetrate certain actualities of power. It has considered the relationships from which power emerges and the functions in which it inheres. To summarize this argument, it is possible to identify power as a consequence of social structure rather than a quality of persons—as a product of specialization rather than of will. This is not to say that the offices of power are not subject to exploitation and abuse; it is simply to counter the impression that they originate in exploitation and abuse! Behind the structure of power and its abuse in any complex society are a core of functions essential to social survival. They may be called the "functions of an elite" or the functions of organization, but they exist whether any class which might be called "elite" exists or not. President Nasser once described these functions as "a role in search of a hero."

THE EXPLOITATION AND ABUSE OF POWER

The necessity for roles which govern the relationship of diverse functions is clear, and the capacity of a class which monopolizes such roles to exploit these to its own advantage is obvious. However, study of the prison as an organization indicates that "centrality" with respect to information flows, rather than superiority of status, is the necessary condition of an ability to define relationships in a functional manner.[4] The profession of politics is as essential in an urban society as the profession of plumbing, and both these occupations seem to involve "dirty work" in terms of ancient cultural taboos. The urban society must acknowledge the importance of such functions, but it need not credit those who perform them with a status apart from ordinary men. Understanding the exploitation of power involves an identification of the conditions under which a class performing the definitional functions is able to constitute and maintain itself as an elite.

When society elevates control over internal relations to the level of consciousness, it makes power an object of ambition and a subject of calculated manipulation. The evolving organizational structures provide access to power apart from roles so restrained by ancient mores as to make power responsible in its execution. In Acton's phrase, "Power corrupts." Power unrestrained by internalized ideals is subject to abuses which have characterized its use and conditioned its perception through the ages. Carlyle

4. For a more detailed study of the relation of communication patterns to authority, see my *Policy Change in Prison Management* (East Lansing: Governmental Research Bureau, Michigan State University, 1957).

attributes the crucial roles of aristocracy and priesthood to "the very nature of man"—not to the structure of society. He sees a hero in every crucial role.

Exercise of the executive powers is so essential to a society that the existence of such powers may be plausibly regarded as providential. The powers are perceived as wonderful and mysterious in their intimate relation to internalized controls, and it is a simple, if illogical, step to address to the class that manipulates these powers the awe addressed to the powers themselves. Hence, the exercise of these powers by any element of a society can be advertised as the election of that element by Providence to fill its role. All that is needed to legitimize a ruling class is the assumption that power is inherent in the persons rather than in the functions performed. Three standard conditions of this misconception may be noted.

The first of these conditions is a consolidation of the two types of power identified. Such a consolidation can be achieved by art and sealed by the use of terror for political purposes, but it occurs most naturally in a military state. A condition of war requires the regulation of internal affairs with reference to external dangers on the basis of information narrowly distributed. Such a condition joins anxiety with the necessity for sacrifice (circumstances related to the execution of priestly functions) and the creation of militant agencies adaptable for purposes of internal coercion.

E. V. Waters notes a relationship among characteristics of a society which seems to hold as well in reverse: "Mass societies show a tendency to revert to a military form of social organization and thereby to adopt the social psychology of a specific stage of barbarism—that of a community in arms."[5] Reversed, this would say that the community in arms displays characteristics of a mass society, combining the arts of priestcraft with executive powers in a cult of the "god-king." The religion of the state and a deification of the ruler remain characteristic tendencies of the fully mobilized society.

A second condition for the exploitation of power by a self-constituted elite is the bureaucratization of those offices which participate in defining the terms of relationship in the society.

5. E. V. Waters, "Power, Civilization and the Psychology of Conscience," *The American Political Science Review*, LIII (Sept., 1959), 641.

Though the offices emerge by necessity, they may be conferred as a gift in ways which insure the bias of their exercise. The virtual monopoly of information which accrues to a ruling class through bureaucratic control over communication channels provides an effective guarantee of its power. The condition of a bureaucracy responsible to an oligarchy emerges with a failing will or the failing ability of the public to participate in the offices of power. When a bureaucratization of offices has insulated the exercise of power from popular participation, the power of definition may be employed with impunity and, as illustrated in the case of recent academic critics of our foreign policy, private objections may be discredited as subversive in intent or function.

A final condition for the exploitation of power follows so naturally from those above that it may be thought of as a perquisite rather than a prerequisite of absolutism. It is that the ruling class so monopolize the allocation of goods as to generate an impression that it creates such goods. That the goods are brought to certain elements of society by an act of political will suggests that they are brought into existence by an act of will. Those who have, through much of history, thought of themselves as walking on the "King's highway" were prone to imagine that a touch of the King's robe was a specific for scrofula.

POWER AND RESPONSIBILITY

In the evidence of history the secular, executive power has seemed to have a life of its own. It is different in basis and function from the priestly power. It has defied the efforts of previously constituted castes—priests, military leaders, landowners, or industrialists—to monopolize or contain it. As it defines relationships among increasingly diverse functions and new activities in society, it transcends the system of internalized values of a more primitive era and generates the eternal problem of how power may be held responsible. The problem of responsibility requires the discovery of some device to integrate the growing hierarchy of vertically differentiated roles.

There are some who see the presumptions of bureaucracy as an affront to God, and believe that Providence implants in every administrative Babel the seeds of its own destruction in a confusion of tongues. But as we wait for the elaboration of bureaucratic jargon to frustrate communication within the ruling class, the language of the tower grows ever more remote from that of the street, and the work of government remains undone.

Classical Approaches to Responsibility

The Greek city-states conceived various devices for the vertical integration of roles, with various degrees of temporary success. Plato's proposals involved, among other things, an effort to organize degrees of inequality into sharply defined classes and provide these with training relevant to their function in the whole community. His proposals were joined with limitations on the size of the community and the range of activities to be permitted, a reactionary recognition of the structural relationship between diversity and hierarchy central to this analysis. Another Greek device for the integration of roles was a primitive form of democracy, a widespread distribution of the functions of citizenship which Aristotle defined as "participating in the formulation and execution of laws." In classic times, democracy took the form of rotating the roles of juryman, judge and lawmaker among citizens in a manner which made impossible demands on leisure, communication, and motivation.

Although democracy failed in the primitive urban environment, it is noteworthy that it originated in that environment. It is not a product of the undifferentiated, egalitarian community, and it involves elements inherently foreign to that setting. Democracy arose in the type of institutional setting that made specialization, individualism, and a conception of self in relation to others possible. It emerged in a context of inequality and vertical differentiation of roles which provided a structure for participation. Those social conditions, if not essential for democracy, are closely related to its development in ancient and modern times. But those conditions alone are not sufficient for its effectiveness. In addition, some integrating principle for the relationship of roles is required if it is not to pursue its classic course into tyranny.

The notion of democracy received a poor verdict from the philosophers as a device for executing essential integrating functions in a diverse society. However, under the most favorable conditions, it was joined with the finest fruits of ancient civilization. Pericles was able to say of Athenean democracy, "While the law secures equal justice to all alike in their private disputes, the claims of excellence are also recognized." But that was a funereal remark, ironic in that it was addressed to the society that executed Socrates.

At some point ancient democracy failed, not just against some idealized criterion of justice but against the concrete criterion of survival. The power to define relationships will normally be exercised to the advantage of those who share in it. However, a natural limit on the exploitation of power is set by the necessity of not alienating or excluding from the system such specialized elements as are essential to its maintenance. The permanent alienation of workers, managers, guardians, or intellectuals is self-destructive in a system which has reached a certain point of complexity and interdependence.

At the risk of oversimplification, it is suggested that primitive democracy functioned while it retained the idea of community. In its transitional period, ancient urban society remained ordered in large part by rituals transmitted from its past through institutions which were religious in origin. The structure of social action and political participation, as reported in Aristotle's *Constitution of Athens*, continued to be based on the residues of kinship and tribal society, and the conception of a common community was transmitted by a religious heritage into an age of diversification. The sense of community, and internalized controls retained from an age when community was an objective fact, remained an integrating principle with which the problems of vertical differentiation and exploitation of power could be met. Primitive democracy failed when the principle of community failed.

Through much of history the essential functions of power have been exploited to make inequality the normal condition and oligarchy the standard principle of government. Amid the worst of that experience, men alienated from this world saw visions of another contrary to it in every major respect. The Stoic vision was one of a stable, ordered universe, a rule of law accessible to all through reason in place of the arbitrary rule of man. The Christian vision was one of a rule of love in place of a rule of fear, a Prince of Peace in place of the war lord, and a community of the spirit where each person was an object of inestimable value instead of dirt beneath the master's heel. That vision was rightly perceived as subversive by the authorities of the earth. There were seeds of anarchy in Paul's letter to the Galatians. "There is neither Jew nor Gentile, there is neither bond nor free, there is neither male nor female, for ye are all one in Jesus Christ." This was the most uncompromising doctrine of equality of all time, but it was a doctrine based on a vision—a vision designed to transform the facts of life—and not a matter of fact.

These visions so served to define the relation of man to the world around that their authority persisted in the Western heritage. While they seldom influenced the political order, and were often corrupted to the uses of power, they remained alive as ideals. Like grain from the tombs of Egypt, they take root where the climate of human relations is suited to their need.

The American Approach to Responsibility

A distinctive commitment of American political civilization has been to the principle of a limitation of power in society. Those who established this government believed that this was a "natural" and proper order and a model for the world of the future, and some who inherit their creation have accepted their assumption on faith. However, in the perspective of history, it becomes increasingly clear that American democracy with its limitations on power was a peculiar, if happy, accident of circumstances. Our democracy can now be seen as an almost unique outgrowth of a distinctive configuration of social conditions and convictions. Few men today can believe with the early constitutionalists that a Newtonian universe and all knowledge conspire toward this political result. Hence, they watch with concern the structure of institutions to which power is entrusted and the ideals by which it is restrained.

One of the significant conditions of the establishment of this political system was that the power structure of pre-revolutionary times was discredited and displaced without the substantial social revolution that has generated anarchy and tyranny elsewhere in our time. The nation emerged as a confederation of relatively self-contained communities, differentiated to a degree permitting a mature sense of individualism but not so specialized as to require elaborate control of the relationship among its elements.

It was a society in which some consensus existed on the set of social controls transmitted by religion rather than by the offices of government, but it lacked a religious bureaucracy as a center of power. In such a social setting, it was possible to incorporate the visionary ideals of the Western heritage as operating principles of a political system.

Crucial among those ideals was the concept of equality. It is an assumption of this tradition, an assumption made in an age of striking inequalities of wealth, status and accomplishment, that in some fundamental sense "All men are created equal and endowed by their Creator with certain inalienable rights." If this assertion of equality is taken as a denial of the most obvious evidence of experience, it must be dismissed as either idiocy or a transparent fraud. If the presumption of reasonableness is to be granted to its authors, it must be granted that they were not describing the crass evidence of material differences. The assertion must be read as saying that, behind superficial appearances, there is a more significant sense in which men are equal before nature and God.

The Stoic and Christian traditions were joined in the Age of Reason by the conception of nature as a complex, rational machine open to the inquiry of man. It is a vital but seldom noted fact that our traditional concepts of freedom and equality were based upon even more fundamental conceptions of nature and upon a community in which those conceptions constitute plausible principles of political behavior. They assume the type of universe in which men can and will order their own relationships around the necessities of the market and through open avenues of social and political participation.

Freedom and equality were concepts with which this society attempted to integrate the diverse roles and functions of a complex social system. Horizontal differentiations of function, the basis of individualism, were integrated by the impersonal compulsions of the market economy and by social necessities expressed in that form. Reliance on the dictates of economic necessity eliminated the need for an elaborate differentiation of vertical roles and offices to define relationships in society. Such vertical differentiation or power structure as did emerge of necessity was integrated on the principle of equality. This principle implied equal access to the process of defining social relationships, and equality of status before the laws which result from that process. As we have learned in examining certain concepts in physics and mathematics, concepts which work to solve particular problems can be taken as "absolute" only within the confines of a given universe of discourse. Freedom and equality, taken as absolutes, are ideas which work to solve problems only within a certain type of social and economic universe. David Thomson poses a problem for contemporary social thought by saying: "Political thinkers long ago abandoned the notion that liberty means absolute freedom to commit murder or theft, but they have not yet adjusted political theory to the notion that equality does not mean absolute similarity and uniformity. If attainable or even seriously attempted, absolute and abstract equality would, of course, spell the doom of culture and civilization."[6]

The American constitutional system has been one designed to restrain the exploitation of power while providing power adequate to the necessities of social organization. Its distrust and suspicion of power are expressed in the familiar principle of the separation of powers and a structure of official checks and balances. These institutional mechanisms of restraint are such that some modern scholars and reformers despair of our ability to muster a power to meet the crises of the present.[7] The principle of a separation of powers goes much deeper than the distinction among legislative, executive, and judicial functions in which it receives partial expression. More significant are the separation of church and state or of national and local governments. Perhaps most significant is the separation of the controls lodged in government from the realm of control reserved to the people. We hear much of democracy as majority rule and too little of democracy as self-government—as a system in which men have the responsibility of governing their own behavior as individuals.

The principle of the separation of powers applies to internalized ideals as much as to the institutional structure of power.

6. David Thomson, *Equality* (Cambridge: Macmillan, 1949), p. 9.

7. Complaint about the inadequacy of power has declined somewhat in the light of recent events in our foreign and domestic politics, but two thought-provoking analyses are: Arnold Rogow and Harold Lasswell, *Power, Corruption and Rectitude* (Englewood Cliffs, N. J.: Prentice-Hall, 1963), and James M. Burns, *The Deadlock of Democracy* (Englewood Cliffs, N. J.: Prentice-Hall, 1963).

Just as the institutional system is distinguished by its refusal to
assign dominance to a single agency, the character of American
citizenship is distinguished by a refusal to assign dominance to
a single ideal. In the realm of internalized controls, there are
checks and balances among the ideals of liberty, equality, and
community, between the role of conscience and the rule of law.
Within this structure of institutions and values, our society has
long maintained a climate of tolerance for individualism, structures for general participation in the process of defining relationships among its elements, and a functioning social order marked
by high levels of productivity. It has earned a considerable
measure of loyalty and affection for its work in solving problems
of the past. We may be concerned, however, with the adequacy
of these values and institutions for the problems of the present.

IMPLICATIONS FOR PRESENT POLITICS

The perspective developed here generates a number of implications for contemporary political movements and institutions.
The most important of these implications is an ability to see mass,
direct-action political movements as a symptom rather than
simply as a promise or a threat. These movements are a symptom of the failure of our structures of power to solve elementary
problems of social life for large classes of our people. They are a
symptom of widespread alienation—of large elements not incorporated in the political consensus or the structure of social action.
They are a symptom of a growing disharmony between the
formal institutions and the internalized values of social control
that presages a vast increase in governmental power.

Some are properly concerned with the relevance of traditional mechanisms of government for today's problems, but the
concern here is with the institutions of society and the constitution of ideas. The constitution of ideas is, at best, a relic of a
rural ideology in confrontation with the issues of a complex, urban
civilization. However, the larger system of social action and
control from which that ideology emerged and within which it
worked is rapidly dissipating.

The American civilization of the past was one in which a vast
majority of social controls were *social* and local. The pleasures of
citizenship and the actualities of power involved access to struc-

tures of action and decision which were more often in the living room than in the voting booth. Authoritative definitions of human relationship issued from those who were centrally located in structures of social communication rather than in formal offices of government. Over much of the nation, these structures of social and political participation in the local community have either defaulted to a national bureaucracy in the face of elementary problems or have exercised power in ways which have alienated and disfranchised masses of people. The incorporated middle class has abdicated or exploited the sovereignty which our institutional system placed in its hands. Now, it is faced with a politics of alienation and of mass movements, presenting reasonable demands with all the insistence of a vertical barbarian invasion. What will these alienated masses do, when they achieve "integration" with the middle class only to discover that the prerogatives of first-class citizenship have been dissipated there?

In the current preoccupation with freedom and equality, it is probable that we ignore the ideal of "community" which is the third member in the triumvirate of governing values in modern democracy. But therein lies the potential of the politics of direct action. The mass politics of alienated men becomes a revolution because the movement becomes an end in itself. The movement becomes the political community, an experience of participation in the exercise of freedom and power, for those excluded from all others. Just as, in the prison, many inmates find an object of identification and a sense of their own identity, members find themselves identified in the fraternity of the mass movement and prisoners of its momentum. They become captives of its concepts.[8]

The direct-action movements of the 1960's cannot be ignored, repressed, or dismissed as a passing fad. The exercise of force against them does not sustain authority; it testifies to its collapse. Their appearance indicates the failure of power to deal with the problems of modern life. These direct-action movements are armed with an energy and a sense of justice that the traditional political structures can ill afford to have diverted into

8. Hannah Arendt's *On Revolution* (New York: Viking Press, 1963) develops the relation between revolution and structures of participation in suggestive and frightening detail.

uncompromising opposition. If their vitality is not incorporated into a transformed structure of power and an enriched political civilization, they will overcome in ways and with consequences that are difficult to foresee. In either case, the structure of power will change, if not to adapt to the problems of our time, at least to reflect that inescapable relation of formal to internal controls that all organized society demands.

The challenge of our time, the role that requires a hero, is that of creating new meanings for the concepts of freedom, equality, and community, enlarged meanings which will enable these concepts to work on the problems of complex, modern society. We must abandon the notion that freedom, equality, and community are accomplished facts, for they are not facts at all. We must hope that those who have chosen the politics of the streets in preference to a structure of unresponsive institutions will abandon the notion that freedom and equality are things to be dispensed, or withheld, like food in a breadline for the poor.

The problems of alienation and conflict in American society are as pressing and real as those of food and shelter. Unless the concepts of this heritage are adapted to present necessities, they will be met with alien ideals; for the ideals of a politics of alienation are as foreign to our heritage as any imported from abroad. The mass politics of the streets is an extremely primitive politics marked by extremely primitive concepts, ideals no less primitive for being mouthed by religious leaders and chanted with religious fervor. The drive for equality in restaurants, in theaters, in housing, or in material possessions is in danger of being seriously misguided, for to accent such things is to ask men to trade their birthright for pottage. The essential thing that must be sought, and granted, if this political system is to survive, is equal access to the structures of social and political action by which men make themselves equal and free. The ideal of current mass movements seems to be that any difference in the material conditions of life creates some fundamental inequality in men. It is the antithesis of an antique ideal which held that, behind all superficial and material differences, men are equal because the base metal of their being is stamped with an image of the King of Kings.

For all the legitimacy of its complaints and the eloquence of its actions, the politics of direct action expresses concepts which bear bitter fruit. The appeal to conscience above law, for all its dignity, subverts the rule of law and the structures of political action by which law is made responsive to the needs of society at large. The politics of direct action breeds intolerance and a compulsive conformity akin to that of the garrison state or the prison yard, behavior which ill becomes free men. It makes for an unqualified absolutism about ideals that better serve the purposes of civil life in a balanced system of belief. It makes for an imposition of unilateral definitions on social relationships which is no less tyrannical for being right. Finally, for all their hopes of integration or renunciation of force, direct-action movements have a disintegrating effect which maximizes the necessity for and concentration of governmental power in society. Thus, they lay foundations for an unresponsive, bureaucratic militarism apt to divert domestic hostility into foreign adventures, and a structure of power raised ever farther beyond the reach of effective participation. Shall we place the blame upon the alienated or upon the bureaucrats? History may well lay responsibility at the door of those who waited until the politics of direct action became the last resort of desperate men—at the door of those who closed the door of social life upon their fellows.

There are some who fear that the "Syracuse" of modern democracy may lie as far away as Viet Nam. Unless we can muster the resources to solve the problems of our society, disaster may lie as near as Birmingham, Harlem, or Watts. Power is a necessity and an experienced fact of social organization which does not dissolve at the touch of ideals. At best, power may be tamed and civilized by man's ideals, turned into an instrument of achievement rather than oppression. But, in that hope, equality has the status of a means rather than an end. It is a concept, akin to that of infinity in mathematics, with which complex problems may be solved. A characteristic of a materialistic age in persons or societies is an elevation of the superficial to the level of fundamentals, a transformation of means into ends, and the construction of gods out of mud. In a time of confusion, it may be worth repeating lessons that civilization has learned in a primitive past and at elementary levels of organization. Power is a brute fact of nature. Equality is an ideal stolen, like fire, from the gods. The good society on earth must come from the inspired use of whatever materials lie at hand.

II. CONCEPTUAL
DIMENSIONS

The Ideological Orientation

by Alan P. Grimes

The purpose of this paper is to explore one aspect of research in political thought which may be contributory to the development of political science. That this task should need doing is indicative not only of the ferment which has continued in the political science profession after at least two decades of critical self-examination but also of the uncertainty which hangs over that area of the discipline traditionally known by the various names of political philosophy, political theory, or political thought, as this area has sought to offer a constructive function to the discipline of political science.

There is no need to remark here upon the considerable literature—and frequently repetitive arguments found therein—in which political theorists of various orientations have sought to salvage some function for what was traditionally thought to be the central area of the discipline.[1] It is enough to state the com-

1. See Arnold Brecht, *Political Theory* (Princeton: Princeton University Press, 1959); George Catlin, "Political Theory: What Is It?" *Political Science Quarterly*, LXXII (March, 1957), 1-29; Alfred Cobban, "The Decline of Political Theory," *Political Science Quarterly*, LXVIII (September, 1953), 321-38; Vernon Van Dyke, *Political Theory: A Philosophical Analysis* (Stanford: Stanford University Press, 1960), Ch. 9; David Easton, *The Political System* (New York: Alfred A. Knopf, 1953), Ch. 10, and *A Systems Analysis of Political Life* (New York: John Wiley & Sons, 1965), Chs. 1 and 2; Harry Eckstein, "Political Theory and the Study of Politics: A Report of a Conference," *American Political Science Review*, L (June, 1956), 457-88; Andrew Hacker, *Political Theory: Philosophy, Ideology, Science* (New York: The Macmillan Company, 1961), Ch. 1; Thomas P. Jenkin, *The Study of Political Theory* (Garden City: Doubleday & Co., 1955); Norton E. Long, "Aristotle and the Study of Local Government," *Social Research*, XXIV (Autumn, 1957), 287-310; David W. Minar, "Ideology and Political Behavior," *Midwest Journal of Political Science*, V (November, 1961), 317-32; Robert McCloskey, "American Political Thought and the Study of Politics," *American Political Science Review*, LI (March, 1957), 115-30; and Martin Diamond, "Comment on McCloskey" in *ibid.*; George Sabine, "What Is Political Theory?" *Journal of Politics*, I (February, 1939), 1-17; Leo Strauss, *What Is Political Philosophy* (Glencoe, Ill.: Free Press, 1960); Mulford Q. Sibley, "The Place of Classical Political Theory in the Study of Politics," and Frederick M. Watkins, "Political Theory as a Datum of Politics," in *Approaches to the Study of Politics*, ed. Roland Young (Evanston, Ill.: Northwestern University Press, 1958.)

monplace that the "givens" of the past are no longer in acceptance, and the net effect of this has been to place traditionally-
oriented political theorists upon the defensive in an age in which
political science has endeavored to become, in its organizing
concepts and in the nature of its evidence or proof, scientific.
Perhaps the most conspicuous recent evidence of this defensive
attitude on the part of political theorists is the presence in new
textbooks on the history of political thought of chapters which
seek to define such concepts as "political science" and "political
theory," to show that they really are compatible areas of interest
and that the theories of writers of the past do indeed merit study
by social scientists dealing with other kinds of data from the
present.[2] Again there is no need here to review the familiar lines
of the controversy between those loosely called "traditionalists"
and the "scientists." For what is important is that what is emerging, doubtless stimulated by the above conflict, is a different kind
of perspective in political thought which may be called here the
ideological orientation.

* * *

The ideological orientation represents but one aspect of functional analysis in contemporary social science. "The most dramatic development in sociological theory since World War II," it
has been stated recently, "has been the rise of functionalism to a
position of dominance."[3] The ideological orientation reflects in
large measure a convergence of sociological and political theoriz-
ing. It is natural, therefore, that where an older generation
turned to philosophers for the datum of political thought, a
younger generation has been informed by sociologists. In es-
sence, the distinction between the traditional approach of political thought and the ideological orientation may be seen by noting

2. See for example William T. Bluhm, *Theories of the Political System*
(Englewood Cliffs, N.J.: Prentice-Hall, 1965), Ch. I; Andrew Hacker, *Political
Theory*, Ch. 1; Lee Cameron McDonald, *Western Political Theory* (New York:
Harcourt, Brace & World, Inc., 1962), Ch. 20; David Minar, *Ideas and Politics*
(Homewood, Ill.: The Dorsey Press, 1964), Ch. 1; Frederick M. Watkins, *The
Age of Ideology—Political Thought, 1750 to the Present* (Englewood Cliffs,
N.J., Prentice-Hall, 1964).

3. Don Martindale, "Limits of and Alternatives to Functionalism in Sociology,"
in Martindale (ed.), *Functionalism In the Social Sciences* (Philadelphia: The
American Academy of Political and Social Science, 1965), p. 144. For a provoca-
tive critique of the functional approach see Charles B. Robson, "The Place of
Systems Analysis in Political Science—An Inquiry" (Mimeographed, Chapel Hill,
North Carolina, 1962).

that the former studied the thought of individuals (Plato, Aristotle—Mill, Marx), while the latter is concerned with the values and attitudes of collectivities (group, class, labor union, nation, etc.); the former stressed rationality and logical coherence, the latter accepts the unconscious response as well as the conscious formulation and is less concerned with the tests of logic than with the proofs of social or group acceptance. Where students of the traditional approach might ask of a philosophy Is it true?, students of ideology ask, Does it have a social or group existence? Such different lines of inquiry thus call for different kinds of proof. In the first instance logical coherence becomes of paramount importance, and philosophers from Plato to Marx are subjected to a close textual examination of their works to see if they have fallen into contradictory propositions, *non sequiturs*, or other logical traps. In the second instance logical incompatibilities and normative ambiguities are accepted as part of the factual data to be examined, not to see if these presentations are logical, but to see in what manner they are relevant to the political system. It is understandable, therefore, why many of the traditional textbooks on political thought terminated their discussions with nineteenth-century figures, with Karl Marx and his contemporaries; Marx presaged the newer line of inquiry, the ideological orientation with its implicit assumption that political thought, like other forms of political activity, performs a function in the political system.[4]

Prior to the nineteenth century it could be confidently assumed that the activity called thought had a standard of its own, independent of the social existence of the thinker. Objective truth was therefore discernible by reason, whose canons were at once universal and eternal, and whose subject was another universal and timeless entity, rational man. The introduction of the component "consciousness" as a qualifying adjunct to thought— with Hegel it was historical, with Marx socio-economic, with Freud psychological—undermined, however, the older tradition

4. For efforts of social theorists to reformulate the task of inquiry after Marx see W. G. Runciman, *Social Science and Political Theory* (Cambridge University Press, 1963); for the rise of ideology within the framework of a sociology of knowledge see Robert K. Merton, *Social Theory and Social Structure* (Glencoe, Ill.: The Free Press, 1957), Chs. 12 and 13; also see Reinhard Bendix, "The Age of Ideology: Persistent and Changing," in David E. Apter (ed.), *Ideology and Discontent* (New York: The Free Press of Glencoe, 1964), Ch. 8.

with its faith in the efficacy of reason, and its certainty of the existence of an objective truth. Thought transformed by consciousness became ideology.

Because there is both uncertainty and disagreement as to what meaning is conveyed by the term "ideology" there is, inevitably, disagreement as to when, where, and how ideology has existed. Henry D. Aiken titled his collection of selections from nineteenth-century philosophers *The Age of Ideology*. "My thesis, therefore," he wrote, "is not merely that the most salient and influential doctrines of the nineteenth-century philosophers are essentially ideological in character, but also that since Kant there has been an increasing awareness that the fundamental tasks of philosophical criticism belong not to 'science' in any ordinary sense of that term, but to something for which there is no other word but 'ideology.' "[5] Yet it would seem evident that not only since the nineteenth century, but wherever in previous societies there was a large degree of consensus as to what constituted the ingredients of reason, the subject matter of speculation, and the evidences called proof, there was present what is called ideology. Certainly "the heavenly city of the eighteenth-century philosophers" was an elaborately constructed ideological empire, a gothic edifice of thought, subsequently all but demolished by nineteenth-century criticism. And was the so-called "age of faith" any less ideological than the so-called "age of reason?" The ideological orientation, while itself a product of the historical development of philosophy and the social sciences, is not therefore historically bound to the contemporary age; it offers a different vantage point, a new mode of perception for viewing the social organism in the past as well as the present.

It must be evident that such an interpretation poses an enormous difficulty in the task of interpretation itself. For example, it may be stated: "Ours is an age of competing ideologies, an age which has been increasingly dominated by the sharp clash of differing political perspectives."[6] This position may then be illustrated by representative works on democracy, capitalism, socialism, communism, elitism, and nationalism; the writings of individual theorists are included because they significantly con-

5. Henry D. Aiken, *The Age of Ideology* (New York: The New American Library, 1956), p. x.

6. Alan P. Grimes and Robert H. Horwitz, *Modern Political Ideologies* (New York: Oxford University Press, 1959), p. xi.

tributed to the formulation of one of these major belief systems or ideologies. Political ideologies are accordingly defined as "those politically consequential belief systems which have determinate spokesmen and leaders and a politically consequential following."[7] Used in this sense and in this context there must be followers as well as spokesmen in order for the phenomenon called ideology to exist. Democracy is thus as much an ideology as is communism or fascism. In this view it is not the substance of the philosophical position that distinguishes political philosophy from political ideology, but the acceptance of the position by a significant believing public in a politically relevant way. Ideologists are thus not bad philosophers, but popular ones among some politically significant public. If we think of political ideology as a kind of civic religion, which attends to the substance of things hoped for and rests upon the evidence of things not seen, we may pursue the analogy by noting that not all who call upon the name of the Lord establish religious faiths, only those who acquire a religious following do so. Clearly, however, this contention is quite different from the imputation, if not outright assertion, that all that had heretofore been termed political philosophy was in reality ideology.

* * *

It is evident from the literature dealing with the ideological orientation that there is a clearer agreement about its derivation than about its definition. The great impetus to the study of thought as itself an aspect of ideology came from Karl Marx. "The mode of production in material life," he had stated, "determines the general character of the social, political and spiritual processes of life. It is not the consciousness of men that determines their existence but on the contrary, their social existence determines their consciousness."[8] The Cartesian proposition, "I think, therefore I am," was in effect turned around to read "I am, therefore I think the way I do." Whether or not one accepts the primacy in this relationship of Marx's obscure notion of the "mode of production," he must be credited with at least the seminal conception that there is some correspondence between social con-

7. *Ibid.*, p. xiii.
8. Karl Marx, *Introduction to the Critique of Political Economy* in *Capital and Other Writings by Karl Marx*, ed. Max Eastman (New York: The Modern Library, 1932), p. 11.

sciousness and social condition. Yet even with his insight that what the bourgeois had perceived as universal truth was nothing more than transitory class consciousness he failed to cope with the conundrum that has plagued students of ideology ever since: if consciousness is derivative from social existence (whether dominated or not by the mode of production), is it possible to apprehend transhistorical truth (including of course the first clause of the conundrum)?

The Marxian conception of ideology, for all its pejorative connotations of superstructure, false consciousness, masked thought, etc., became a useful point of departure for students concerned with political thought and the sociology of knowledge. In the twentieth century, Karl Mannheim, in *Ideology and Utopia*, a work of considerable significance and suggestiveness for students of ideology, noted not only the Marxian usage of the term as a device for unmasking the thought of adversaries—as Napoleon had done when he employed the term to belittle his critics—but also the dilemma which this approach held for Marxism itself. To call a system of thought ideology was initially intended to depreciate it. "What is depreciated," Mannheim observed, "is the validity of the adversary's thought because it is regarded as unrealistic. But if one asked further, unrealistic with reference to what?—the answer would be, unrealistic with reference to practice, unrealistic when contrasted with the affairs that transpire in the political arena."[9] It was thus presupposed that from the vantage point of reality one could view those victimized by false consciousness, those who were indeed both ignorant and innocent, like Plato's prisoners in the cave.

If erroneous knowledge was formerly checked by appeal to divine sanction, which unfailingly revealed the true and the real, or by pure contemplation, in which true ideas were supposedly derived, at present the criterion of reality is found primarily in an ontology derived from political experience. . . . Indeed we may say that for modern man pragmatism has, so to speak, become in some respects, the inevitable and appropriate outlook, and that philosophy in this case has simply appropriated this outlook and from it proceeded to its logical conclusion.[10]

9. Karl Mannheim, *Ideology and Utopia*, trans. Louis Wirth and Edward Shils (New York: Harcourt, Brace and Company, 1936), p. 72.
10. *Ibid.*, p. 73.

Where Marx had found ideology related to class interest, Mannheim found this notion far too inadequate and substituted the notion of situational orientation, there being as great a diversity in styles of thought as there is in styles of life. "The situational analysis is the natural mode of thinking in every form of experience which rises above the commonplace level."[11] Thought was not only related to but corresponded in some fashion with "real" life situations. "Thought is a process determined by actual social forces, continually questioning its findings and correcting its procedure."[12] Ideology as a useful conception of social and political analysis thus begins with an awareness of the diversities in ideological presentations, the complexity of relationships which reach beyond simple class consciousness. "But it is precisely this expansion and diffusion of the ideological approach which leads finally to a juncture at which it is no longer possible for one point of view and interpretation to assail all others as ideological without itself being placed in the position of having to meet that challenge. In this manner we arrive inadvertently at a new methodological stage in the analysis of thought in general."[13] What was once the exclusive possession of the Marxians had now become the instrument of all politically active groups in society, for each group could discredit its adversaries by claiming that what they believed to be thought congruent with reality was in fact only ideology. "As a result we are entering upon a new epoch in social and intellectual development."[14]

It was hoped by Mannheim—and by many others—that an ideologically-free social science, aware of the pitfalls of ideologically-bound thought, would arise, able to utilize ideological data for constructive research. But it is by no means clear that the concept of ideology has yet reached that stage of refinement, even in definition, at least in so far as a progressive accumulation of knowledge is concerned. The initial conundrum is still at hand. For example, is the concept of "social science" itself an ideological one, and as such situationally oriented?

It has been an accepted deficiency in Marx's thought that having unmasked bourgeois thought as ideology he considered

11. *Ibid.*, p. 107.
12. *Ibid.*, p. 105.
13. *Ibid.*, p. 74.
14. *Ibid.*, p. 75.

his approach to possess scientific detachment, and to be un-
tainted with ideology. Although he observed this deficiency in
Marx, Mannheim walked perilously close to the same pitfall
when he suggested, in effect, that only trained social scientists
could achieve the detachment necessary to see reality untinted
with the aura of ideology. One may ask, was not the so-called
detachment of the social scientist situationally determined?

The beclouded nature of contemporary discussions of ideology
may be seen in David Apter's perceptive essay entitled "Ideology
and Discontent."[15] Here, Apter finds that the United States is
becoming divided into

two mutually antagonistic and, in many ways, lonely groups. One is
composed of ideologues who devoutly defend unreason because they
are afraid that, in the face of reason, their orientation to the world
around them will fall apart and that in the process their world will
disappear. Ideology becomes a protection for people alienated from
their society—a protection against the final alienation. They therefore
stubbornly hang on to their ideologies in the hope that, by sheer
persistence, they will prevail against other ideologies or even against
reason itself. They represent the 'disestablishment.'

The second group is also alienated. Theirs is an alienation brought
about by 'superior wisdom,' that is, by the ability to penetrate the
ideologies of others and thereby to emancipate themselves. In this
group is the social scientist, who is the objective observer. He pene-
trates all the disguises created by the untrained mind or the ideological
mind and attaches himself to the image of the wise. He represents
the 'establishment.'[16]

But what appears to be a conflict between the social scientist and
the ideologist is revealed upon further discussion to be again a
conflict over ideologies, in which "science is a well defined
ideology possessing norms of empiricism, predictability, and
rationality as guides to conduct."[17] Thus, after a century of discourse on the nature of ideology, what was initially a murky conception has remained essentially obscure.

* * *

Not a little of the difficulty encountered by contemporary
students of ideology has been brought about by the multiplicity

15. Apter (ed.), *Ideology and Discontent*, Ch. 1.
16. *Ibid.*, pp. 37-38.
17. *Ibid.*, p. 40.

of roles in which the term occurs. It has upon occasion, for example, been used to comprehend those conceptualizations which were traditionally classified as philosophy, or religion, or sometimes science. In this sense ideology has been used as a substitute for the elusive yet suggestive Hegelian concept of the *geist*. In this broad sense, what has taken place in the Ecumenical Council in Rome has been a restructuring of Catholic ideology to bring it into line with some larger, more vague, yet more insistent ideological demands of today. In this broad view, the rise of a plethora of new nations and the concomitant collapse of colonialism are attributed to the impact of nationalism, as an ideology, in contemporary politics. At the opposite extreme, however, is the subjectivist's position that every man has his own ideology—the symbols, the language, the pictures he carries in his head to order and arrange reality for him. In part the difficulty with the term "ideology" lies in its relative newness as an instrument of social analysis, as well as in the complexity of the problems it attempts to deal with. The difficulties are inherent in the subject matter, and a language adequate to explicate the issue has thus far failed to develop. Students of ideology today are confronting somewhat the same problem as faced by nineteenth-century philosophers, about whom Henry D. Aiken has written:

In marked contrast to those of their eighteenth-century predecessors, their writings are usually difficult and frequently obscure. But a principal reason for this is that they were embarked upon an undertaking of which the latter had, as yet, only caught the barest glimpses. Now, it is easy to be clear and fluent, so long as one is content to use, without question, received concepts and methods that are already prescribed as 'rational' or 'valid.' But once one begins to question their eternal and universal necessity, and, accordingly to doubt whether objective standards and principles are inherent 'in the nature of things,' the whole task of philosophical analysis and criticism begins to appear in another light.[18]

While admitting the difficulties of the task, if the ideological orientation is to be useful some further discussion, definition, and clarification of its implications, at least, will be necessary. It may be helpful therefore to consider four very consequential propositions which usually lurk behind the use of the term ideology.

18. Aiken, *The Age of Ideology*, pp. 19-20.

1. There is no such thing as objective thought; only inter-subjectivity.
2. Conscience is a product of group consciousness.
3. Social consciousness is a function of social existence.
4. Significant thought affects social-political behavior.

In the first proposition the entire effort to arrive at objective thought is dismissed as a futile activity, a pursuit of illusions and ghosts. The belief that there is an objective standard, "out there" as it is sometimes stated, against which we may measure wisdom or truth or justice, is indeed only a belief. What is called thought has no life of its own nor agents at its disposal; the activity of thinking is a kind of activity undertaken by individuals; each individual thinker, in the final analysis, thinks subjectively. To the extent that the thinking of one individual is congruent with the thinking of another individual there is intersubjective agreement between the two, but it neither creates nor reveals an objective entity "out there." Since the activity of creating and defining concepts is ultimately a subjective one, what is thought by some to be objective truth, the argument runs, is only intersubjective agreement about the content of these concepts. No society, therefore, has some special touchstone to truth or justice or ultimate good; but an observable tendency exists for societies to believe they have such a touchstone when they only have intersubjective agreement. Believed social values may become factual ingredients for social and political analysis. Such values in one political system may be praised or deplored, but only to the extent that there is intersubjective agreement about them do they have any reality.

A difficulty is apparent in this first proposition, relating to the role of science. Is the law of gravitation no more than an intersubjective agreement? This issue, it would appear, may be handled in either of two ways. One may assert that Proposition One does not apply to science, which has its own system of cognition and validation. This approach then narrows the realm of the ideological orientation to that sphere of human activity involving the relationships among poeple that are not susceptible to the scientific canons of replicability and prediction. This results in a branching of knowledge into ideology and science, the modern counterpart of the fifteenth-century bifurcation into faith and reason. The law of gravitation is thus a different kind of knowledge from, let us say, a primitive Indian tribal belief that certain kinds of dances bring rain. The latter belief may be called ideology and the former, science.

The other alternative is to hold that all that is called knowledge is a product of intersubjective agreement, including the category called science. The law of gravitation and the Indian rain-dance law are equally ideological and arise out of intersubjective agreement. The intersubjective nature of thought allows for many variations in both authenticity and efficacy, which will of course vary with the stage of development of the culture. Modern societies demand different kinds of proof (another ideological concept) from primitive cultures before there can be intersubjective agreement about the validity of propositions.

The second proposition embedded in the ideological orientation is very similar to the first one; it is merely the other side of the coin. It derives initially from the Lockean conception of human understanding and is reinforced by the work of David Hume. In this discussion the conception of conscience has direct bearing on the problem of cognition of values. Where Proposition One denied the existence of objective standards "out there," Proposition Two denies the existence of objective standards "in here." The conscience of the individual, it is maintained, does not have some secret access to revealed truth, immutable standards of right and wrong, or any other certain standard for moral judgment. By rejecting the concept of innate moral perception, the ideological orientation emphasizes the role of group attitudes in shaping the moral standards of individuals. This follows of course from the intersubjective nature of knowledge itself; for knowledge is a social phenomenon. Thus, in attempting to understand social and political ideology, one must remember with caution that the normative standards he employs are the product of a group consciousness he has co-opted as his own. The tensions in American society over civil rights, for example, reveal how the conflict over moral standards has been related to differing kinds of group consciousness.

The third proposition, that social or group consciousness is a function of social or group existence, reasserts in general form a relationship that is categorically stated by Marx and elusively propounded by Mannheim. In its general statement it holds that there is some correspondence between the circumstances in which we find ourselves and our conception of the reality of which these circumstances constitute a part. Our apprehension of reality is thus affected by those conditions of reality which bear directly upon us. But more than this: condition or circumstances not only affect our consciousness of those conditions which bear directly upon us, but as we communicate with others similarly situated we construct conceptualizations of reality which we do not directly apprehend. In this fashion we gain an "understanding," so to speak, of what at first seems a chaos of events taking place outside our immediate experience. Members of the American Medical Association, for example, may directly apprehend that portion of reality conceptualized as the "doctor-patient relationship"; but to the extent that they interact with other A.M.A. members they tend to find that they share conceptualizations on a wider universe, transcending their personal experience—so that their enlarged conceptualized reality comprehends a kind of social welfare theory, economics, and moral philosophy as well. While it may be true that members of groups tend to accept the policy positions of their leadership, the policy of leaders must correspond in some fashion to the interest of the membership in order for these policies to be acceptable. If the intellectualization of reality known as group or social consciousness is thus largely derivative from group or social experiences, then an effective way to alter this consciousness is to alter the conditions of the group existence and thus their social experiences.

This raises the troublesome issue of the degree of determinism that social condition bears upon social consciousness. Obviously, the higher the degree of determinism in the system the greater will be the futility of argumentation as an instrument to alter the system. A totally deterministic system, in which thought or consciousness was merely and only a reflex response to situations, circumstances, or conditions, would not only render argumentation futile but would also remove ideology itself from its current role as a functional factor in the political system. On the other hand, if there is not significant correlation between ideological position, as an expression of social or group consciousness, and social condition or existence, then the study of ideology becomes equally absurd, and ideological victories would accomplish no substantive changes. The ideological orientation presupposes that existence is antecedent to consciousness up to, but short of, the point that this relationship becomes a rigidly deterministic one.[19]

Finally, the fourth proposition asserts that significant thought plays a part in the political system: it affects social-political behavior. It may precipitate political action or induce passivity and compliance, but the presence of significant thought is presumed to make a difference in behavioral response. More than this, however, is implied in the proposition; for it is presumed that the criterion of significance for thought is determined by the consequences it precipitates. Political philosophizing which fails to precipitate social consequences loses status, so to speak, among social scientists, to philosophizing which produces political effects. For it is political effects which give significance to the political act. Mussolini, Mao, Castro, and Khrushchev, for example, have taken on a significance for students of political thought once reserved for philosophers of the highest academic respectability, not because their thoughts were so profound but because their views were so publicly significant. Their hypothetical ordering of reality into an ideological format shaped the consciousness of millions of their followers. Significance is of course a value-laden term; but if, in above Propositions One and Two, extrinsic and intrinsic standards of judgment are removed, then it may be argued that this standard of significance is derived from the expressions of emphasis in contemporary social science literature. In this it would appear that what gives significance to political thought is its efficacy in producing consequences. To the extent that this observation is correct, political analysis has become thoroughly pragmatic.

* * *

If the above propositions constitute an adequate portrayal (or unmasking) of attitudes implicit in the ideological orientation, we may conclude by noting the relevance of this approach to a functional ordering of the political system. We may at once concur with the Aristotelian position that all polities aim at some

19. It was not an ideological conviction of religious liberty which brought about this phenomenon in America, but a pragmatic adjustment to opposing religions. The necessities of existence of religious pluralism anticipated the ideological formulation of these necessities into a doctrine of religious freedom. See Alan P. Grimes, *Equality in America* (New York: Oxford University Press, 1964), Ch. 1.

good, and find in political ideologies the authoritative articulation of the norms contained in this conception of the good. In this view political thought is not terminated with a study of nineteenth-century philosophers but continues as an ever-present part of our existence. Robert E. Lane aptly characterized this conception of political ideologies when he noted of them:

They are group beliefs that individuals borrow; most people acquire an ideology by identifying (or disidentifying) with a social group. They have a body of sacred documents (constitutions, bills of rights, manifestos, declarations), and heroes (founding fathers, seers and sages, originators and great interpreters).

And all ideologies, like all other beliefs, imply an empirical theory of cause and effect in the world, and a theory of the nature of man.[20]

The selection of the saints and sages to be revered in a political system constitutes a statement of ideological perspective in itself. The tendency toward ideological consensus in all viable political systems would seem to indicate that this conceptual ordering of statements and symbols portraying reality performs a vital function in the political community. David Apter has suggested that "ideology helps to perform two main functions: one directly social, binding the community together, and the other individual, organizing the role personalities of the maturing individual.

"These functions combine to legitimize authority. It is the relation to authority that gives ideology its political significance."[21]

The great difficulty with the ideological orientation has been the uncertainty as to what constitutes adequate referential data. The lines of research in this area have therefore remained fuzzy. Part of this difficulty is a definitional one, for different observers appear to look for different things under the rubric of ideology. This difficulty is to a considerable degree inherent in the concept itself, for the role of the observer is as much a matter of inquiry as that which is observed. It is not sufficient to state that the observer's role ought to be an impartial one; the crucial question is Can it be such? Thus the first question, What constitutes the datum of ideology both now and in the past?, is the first venture

20. Robert E. Lane, *Political Ideology: Why the American Common Man Believes What He Does* (New York: The Free Press of Glencoe, 1962), p. 15.
21. Apter, *Ideology and Discontent*, p. 18.

into a hall of mirrors, or, to change the metaphor, is to sight into a kind of intellectual kaleidoscope which reflects as much as it reveals. A further difficulty occurs in the effort to grasp the elusive and wispy substances called values (as opposed to the solid substances called facts) where the admitted position of reaching is from a value bias. Normative terms, while producing language equivalents, quite often signify different substantive relationships in different societies. While this makes analysis difficult it does not make it impossible; for normative statements ultimately refer to human relationships and conditions which may in fact be examined. And further, it is presumed in the ideological orientation that normative propositions originate from actual conditions of human relationships. Even the loftiest of values are rooted somewhere in human experience.

Having thus explored some of the meanings and difficulties of research in political ideologies, it is perhaps not out of place to offer an eclectic definition of what may be usefully meant by this concept. Political ideology provides a vocabulary for socially functional beliefs which: (a) gives identity to socio-political groups, (b) legitimatizes political action, and (c) affects a politically consequential following. Each of the ingredients, a, b, and c, appears to be present in some fashion in the contemporary literature dealing with ideology. The ideological orientation, by turning the focus of inquiry in political thought toward politically relevant data, thus offers a line of research quite compatible with a political science perspective which has become increasingly behavioral.

Beliefs: A Neglected Unit of Analysis in Comparative Politics

by Lester W. Milbrath

If one were to make a catalog of important unanswered questions in the field of comparative politics, the list probably would include the following: Why do governmental arrangements that work well in one nation or culture work poorly or fail in another? Why is government slowly evolving and stable in some nations and volatile and unstable in others? Why do nations which have similarities in their resource bases develop at radically different economic rates? Why do nations with goals that are amenable to one another still see events in different lights, have difficulties in negotiating and communicating with each other, and choose courses of action which bring them into conflict?

One explanation normally offered attributes these differences to differences in "culture." But, having said that, what has been explained? The thorough scholar would wish to know: What is different about the cultures? What aspects of a culture support governmental institutions? What kinds of cultural changes lead to what kinds of changes in institutions and procedures?

Considerable time must elapse before scholars will have answers to the questions posed above. It is my contention, however, that the quest for answers would be significantly aided if greater attention were paid to beliefs as a unit of analysis when comparing the characteristics of nations. Culture is expressed and is transmitted via beliefs. When parents teach their children the significant parts of their culture, they are essentially teaching them what to believe; and this is especially true when children are taught to react to and to approach the institutions of government. A child must learn a set of beliefs about what he is to do for the government and what the government should do for him. In this way a set of beliefs is inculcated in a child concerning appropriate times of obedience and disobedience to governmental authorities, and concerning government structure and the way government performs its functions.

Before proceeding further, a definition of "beliefs" would be appropriate, distinguishing this from related terms such as cognition, value, attitude, opinion, and ideology. Cognition incorporates the broadest range of phenomena because it is a component of that included in all the other concepts. One can cognize without either valuing or believing, whereas the reverse is not true. To a cognition may be attached two kinds of feeling, either separately or together. One kind of feeling is a valence; i.e., a person may be positively attracted toward or negatively repulsed from the object being cognized. Both values and attitudes are cognitions with attached valences.

We have no widely used generic term in the English language for the other kind of feeling that can attach to a cognition. It is a feeling that the object being cognized is credible (believable) or incredible (not believable), so that a belief is a cognition to which credulity is attached. This feeling varies in strength, being neither totally present nor totally absent, and in direction, since we disbelieve as well as believe. Both strength and direction are abstractly illustrated in Figure 1.

Figure 1
Range of Credulity

Strong Disbelief	Non-Belief	Unshakable Belief
100	0	100

It is important to note here that it is the feeling about the cognition which makes it believable or not; credulity is not inherent in the cognition itself. A cognition which is credible to some persons will be incredible to others, and some cognitions stimulate strong credulity while others stimulate such feelings very weakly. In one setting or at one time in one's life a cognition may prompt incredulity, but in another setting or at another time the same cognition may prompt credulity.

Another important point about these two kinds of feeling (valence and credulity) is that although they are distinctive analytically, they often attach simultaneously to the same cognition. The relationship between the two kinds of feelings is spatially illustrated in Figure 2. Cognitions with a valence only fall on the vertical axis. Those with a credulity only fall on the

Figure 2

Spatial Relationship of Credulity and Valence

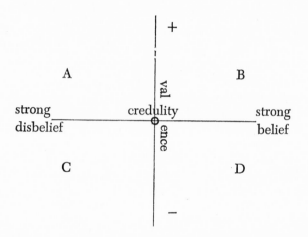

horizontal axis. If neither feeling is present the cognition will be located in the center of the diagram. If the cognition is believed and liked, it will fall in quadrant B; if believed and disliked, in quadrant D; if disbelieved and liked, in quadrant A; and if disbelieved and disliked, in quadrant C.

The two kinds of feeling also have interactive effects on each other. Research has shown repeatedly that we tend to believe what we like (many cognitions fall in quadrant B) and disbelieve what we dislike (quadrant C). This tendency is not always evident, however, for we believe many things we dislike (my enemy is stronger than I) and like many things we do not believe (I am flying like a bird). Neither is it always so that both feelings attach to a single cognition. We sometimes feel a valence without deciding whether or not we believe (listening to music or looking at a painting), and sometimes we believe without feeling a valence (two plus two equals four).

At times we have valences on two levels for a complex cognition, and sometimes these valences go in opposite directions. For instance, we have all experienced negative revulsion from the pain of an inoculation or a dentist's drill, yet, on another level and at the same time, we have a positive attraction to such temporary pain because we believe it will bring future pleasure (or at least avoid worse pain). Because we believe certain means-ends relationships to be true (inoculations prevent disease), we can readily choose to do painful things for the moment in anticipation of future benefits. Lacking the necessary means-ends beliefs, a child reacts only to the pain of the moment (runs from the shot). The superimposition of beliefs on valences enables us to choose mature courses of action.

The characteristics of these two kinds of feeling have some important research consequences. In everyday life both feelings often attach to cognitions and are often spoken of as a single feeling. Researchers writing items for survey studies must use everyday language and usually cannot communicate pure belief items or pure value items. The belief format can be used for both kinds of feelings, however, since most instances of valence toward an object can be restated as a belief. ("I like constitutional government" becomes "I believe that I like constitutional government," or "I hate Castro" becomes "I believe I hate Castro.")

Although the belief-value distinction is difficult to maintain for single items, it has some utility for directing the focus of categories of items. One can, for example, identify some items that focus on what a person actually does and then direct other items to discovering what a person thinks he ought to do. More importantly, the distinction alerts us to areas of inquiry that might be overlooked if we did not distinguish the two kinds of feeling. One's belief system generally is larger than one's value system, and by focusing only on statements with valences a research study might miss many things of importance. For example, a respondent's beliefs about how his government functions may be much more important for understanding his political behavior than knowing whether he likes or dislikes the way it functions. An impoverished understanding of what an individual can do vis-à-vis the government will not only be highly determinative of an individual's political behavior but may well shape his general attitude toward the government. If one focuses on a study of beliefs, he is likely to pick up both valences and beliefs, whereas an exclusive focus on values or attitudes increases the likelihood that important beliefs will be overlooked.

Conceptual distinctions can now be stated somewhat more

precisely. *Cognitions* are common to all the concepts considered here. They can exist separately from a valence or from a feeling of credulity (although that is unlikely). Credulity or incredulity attached to a cognition make it a *belief* or a disbelief. A valence attached to a cognition makes it an attitude or a value. *Attitudes* may be thought of as preferences, whereas *values* carry a normative component. If we value something we not only feel that the norm applies to us but that it applies to others as well (we all must value peace). Conversely we are not so distressed if others do not share our attitudes (I do not mind if others do not share my liking for ice cream).

Opinions are a somewhat larger structure than the simple feelings discussed above; they typically combine beliefs, attitudes, and values. Although an opinion may focus on a single object (e.g., I disapprove of Medicare), it usually is embedded in a larger structure of related beliefs, attitudes, and values. If this larger structure is elaborated and differentiated into a somewhat consistent hierarchy with application to a wide variety of specific objects, it may be called an *ideology*. Ideologies are important aids to making decisions, by having a hierarchy of values to be served and by containing a set of beliefs which suggest that certain institutional arrangements and patterns of action are most likely to realize those values. A proposed policy can be judged for its fit with ideological prescriptions and can then be readily accepted, or rejected, as the case may be.

Unfortunately, ideologies with a common name (e.g., Marxism) may be uniform in structure from person to person, and grave errors of interpretation and prediction can be made by assuming that from adherence to a common ideological label the same patterns of action will follow. Ideologies need to be broken down into component beliefs and values, as felt by specific adherents, before analysis and explanation can be very effective. Two important findings have come from some recent studies of these more specific beliefs: 1) few people have a logically consistent ideological structure, and 2) many people have such impoverished cognitions and beliefs about government and public affairs as to preclude their holding an ideology.[1] A person lack-

1. Angus Campbell, Phillip Converse, Warren Miller, and Donald Stokes, *The American Voter* (New York: Wiley, 1960), Ch. 9; Herbert McClosky, "Consensus and Ideology in American Politics," *American Political Science Review*, LVIII

ing beliefs about whether or not a policy will lead to the outcome he desires, or who has no ideas about what actions to take to try to get a policy adopted, is a person whose beliefs are insufficiently linked to form a hierarchical structure.

THE ACT OF BELIEVING

How does one decide if a cognition is credible or not? Fundamentally, we all depend on our five senses; and by sensing a cognition directly we are likely to believe that it is so. Things we have learned to believe from direct sensory experience form the center of our belief structure, and they tend to be firm and unshakable. More peripheral beliefs, which we have had to accept on the recommendation of others, are less firmly held but can sometimes be tested by our own sensory experience. There is a good chance that our beliefs will change about something we have cognized, but not sensed, when we finally get the opportunity to sense it (e.g., cognizing Eastern Europe via the public media produced a set of beliefs in myself quite different from those based on my direct experience while living there).

On reflection, it is striking how small a proportion of the totality of our beliefs is based on information picked up directly by our senses. For the most part we depend on information provided by others for the things we believe. But we cannot believe everything we are told; we have had to learn, sometimes bitterly, that we must question and doubt all new information. But how do we decide if the new information is credible or not? By far the most important factor is our *feeling* about the authoritativeness of the information. This tendency to accept as credible the information provided by authority figures is conditioned in children by their parents almost from the day of birth. The trend is continued by teachers, clergy, writers, scientists, and so forth throughout one's life. A second factor is the unanimity with which a belief is held by the people around us. Most of us are disinclined to doubt the veracity of something that everyone around us takes for granted as true. A third factor is our valence toward the cognition; if we want something to be true, we are

(June, 1964), 361-82; James W. Prothro and Charles M. Grigg, "Fundamental Principles of Democracy: Bases of Agreement and Disagreement," *Journal of Politics,* XXII (May, 1960), 276-94.

much more inclined to believe it than if we do not want it to be true.

We cannot directly sense those things that are the subject of most religious beliefs. Yet most religious people hold their beliefs very firmly, perhaps because all three of the above-mentioned factors pull in the same direction. Children are told that religious beliefs are true by the highest authorities (their parents, the clergy, and the very "word of God"), most of the people around them believe the same thing, and religious believers want desperately to believe. At the same time there is no evidence available to their senses which might challenge or contradict the belief so authoritatively handed to them. Furthermore, the authorities claim there is something virtuous about believing *in* something; i.e., one is fulfilled as a person by believing in a cause, and doubts or questions are inadmissible (or sinful).

When we speak of believing *in* something we suggest that extra emotional investment has been given to the belief. Usually this means that the belief has become a part of the security system of the believing individual. As such, it cannot be altered or abandoned without seriously disturbing that system. Because of this emotional dependence on the belief, a person will go to considerable lengths to defend a belief against assault, developing elaborate rationalizations to counter any possible challenging argument. It is the belief itself which is important, not a dispassionate test of its truth or falsity. This extra emotional investment characterizes not only religious beliefs, but many political, economic, and social beliefs as well. Most political ideologies, for example, are objects of just as strong a belief as are religious ones. It is as futile to use rational argument against one as against the other.

There are additional sources for the feeling of credulity which are especially necessary for those who are inclined to doubt beliefs handed down by tradition and authorities, and who are suspicious of the beliefs to which their own desires might lead them. Building on a base of central beliefs, many of which are confirmed by direct sensation, we all judge the credibility of new information by its "fit" with the existing structure of beliefs. Milton Rokeach tells of hearing on the radio one day that a camera had been invented that could take a picture of something that wasn't there. This did not fit with the pattern of already accepted beliefs which he used to judge new information, and he did not believe. Later he learned that it was an infrared camera, which was so sensitive that it could take pictures of the traces of heat left by an object even though the object had been moved before the picture was taken. This "new" information fit with Rokeach's belief structure, and it was now possible to believe that such a camera had been invented.[2]

Persons trained in positivism and the tenets of scientific method have a generally-accepted set of criteria for judging whether new information can be believed or not. If an investigator reports the procedures he has used to test the veracity of a finding, and if we accept those procedures as valid, we are inclined to believe what he has reported. If we can possibly repeat his experiment, and we then find the same thing he has found, we are much more inclined to believe, while still recognizing that a given individual can check only a minute proportion of the scientific findings reported. Despite this, we are inclined to believe most scientific findings because we have a general confidence in the scientific method.

There is a strong element of authority involved in the acceptance of scientific findings. Most people are insufficiently trained to be able to pass judgment on the procedures used in the many branches of science. They accept and believe such findings because of the authority and prestige of the scientists announcing them. In many respects scientists have become the new high priests of truth, with one important difference from religious high priests—i.e., scientists are willing to change their minds about truth when superior information is uncovered. Furthermore, scientifically verified truths are given additional support by their widespread acceptance in the population. Most people have had direct experience with the application of scientific findings to everyday personal problems and have found that the predicted facility does in fact "work" for them.

Persons trained in the positivistic approach to belief have learned to think probabilistically. This capacity helps to avoid emotional investment in a belief and the resistance to change that accompanies such investment. New information is accepted (believed) probabilistically with a certain level or degree of

2. Milton Rokeach, *The Open and Closed Mind* (New York: Basic Books, 1960), p. 48.

confidence. Should new information come along to challenge the former belief, one can easily change one's mind without disturbing one's security system. Whenever there is emotional investment in a belief it is likely that a myth will outlive the factual basis for its initial acceptance. Probabilistic acceptance of beliefs also softens the authority of science and helps to avoid some of the worst problems of blind following of that, or any, authority. Ironically, persons not trained in science and probability are more likely than scientists themselves to accept without qualification the findings of science.

One can extrapolate some characteristics of national belief-holding from this examination of the sources of beliefs. Because most beliefs are bestowed by authorities and are strongly supported by being widely shared, one tends to find a uniformity of belief in a given national culture. Because most nations or cultures have had somewhat unique historical experiences, they tend to develop a certain uniqueness in their national beliefs. If the nation has a unique language this uniqueness of beliefs tends to be enhanced, and national myths about the history and destiny of the nation can usually be found. Certain ways of deciding whether or not a problem exists and certain methods for problem solution come to be accepted as the only reliable methods. Certain patterns of relationship between the individual and the government come to be accepted as the only proper ones.

Students of comparative politics traditionally have tended to look at institutions, social functions, social structure, developmental rates and patterns, and ideologies as units of analysis. The major point of this paper is that the belief structure of a nation undergirds and partially explains all of these factors. Now that technical know-how enables us to study national beliefs systematically and thoroughly,[3] it is perhaps time to end their neglect as a unit of analysis. In the next section I shall suggest some analytical possibilities for cross-cultural research using beliefs as the primary focus of inquiry.

SOME ANALYSIS POSSIBILITIES

The suggestions which follow derive partly from my personal

3. A five-nation study conducted by Almond and Verba is an important first step in that direction. Gabriel Almond and Sidney Verba, *The Civic Culture* (Princeton: Princeton Univ. Press, 1963).

experience while living in Eastern Europe and in Scandinavia, and partly from a pretest which I conducted in the Chicago metropolitan area, during the summer of 1963, for a cross-cultural study of beliefs. The pretest sample was designed for wide variance, and it utilized random selection only within certain social strata. Half of the persons were chosen from the city of Chicago and half from Evanston. All ranges of socio-economic status were included; seventeen residents of Negro slums in Chicago were interviewed by a Negro interviewer. About twenty precinct captains, randomly chosen from the same neighborhoods as the other respondents, also were interviewed. The total size of the pretest sample was sixty-five. This sample is not representative of any territorially-defined population; it was designed primarily to test the workability of various methods. Yet some of the findings turned up by the pretest were so interesting that they are reported here to suggest possibilities for further analytical exploration. The reader is cautioned not to take them as representative of beliefs held by American citizens.

Sense of Boundaries on Rulers

Although they may have been taught certain things about a constitution, ordinary citizens seldom indicate much concern over constitutional matters. In fact, one could hypothesize that the better the constitution works, the less likely are the citizens who live under it to give it much thought. If one puts constitutional questions to them, as we did in the Chicago pretest, they are inclined to grope ineffectively for responses. (These were not questions about the fine points of constitutionalism, but simple questions about the rights and responsibilities citizens have under the Constitution.) For example: most could see no instance in which they might justifiably disobey a government order; most did not see the Constitution as a higher law, and would not disobey a law that violated the Constitution if they did; most disapproved of civil disobedience as a means of keeping rulers within bounds; most were unclear as to how a citizen can stand up to the government; and when confronted with hypothetical situations in which the government does something in violation of the Constitution, they could usually recognize the violation but were unable to imagine that it could occur or what they would do if it should occur.

Despite this inability readily to manifest their understanding of the need to keep rulers within bounds, some of the data suggest that a latent sense of boundary does exist. I would hypothesize that this sense of boundary is present in all nations or cultures, developed or underdeveloped, dictatorship or democracy. In oppressive regimes the leadership may prevent the sense of boundary from finding meaningful expression, but I would hypothesize that it is present nevertheless. In the Chicago pretest this sense was manifested by the ability of respondents to recognize instances of improper action by officials, even if they were unable to prescribe some means for boundary enforcement. Some small group experiments, conducted in conjunction with the survey interviews, suggest that group discussion sharpens this sense of boundary and enhances the probability that the group can decide on an effective course of action for attempting to enforce the boundary.

In these experiments, small discussion-groups (4-6 persons) were presented with a hypothetical situation in which some part of the government violates the Constitution (a clear-cut violation if judged by the tradition of Anglo-Saxon constitutional law). The group was asked first if the governmental action was proper or not and, if they decided it was improper, they were asked to choose a course of action to rectify the situation. (Although somewhat artificial, such group discussions are probably closer to a "real-life" situation than questions put to an individual respondent; most people, if confronted with a constitutional violation, would discuss it with their friends and neighbors and would choose a course of action in concert with them.) As the discussions proceeded, the participants found their conceptualization being sharpened; in addition, they almost always found themselves in eventual agreement about what is proper and improper. Although there was less unanimity about what should be done to counter the unconstitutional action, the group was usually able to select a common course. In one set of these discussions a short test of constitutional principles was administered both before and after the discussions; and the gain shown on the after tests suggests that the discussions were important learning occasions. Experimental controls, according to a complex Solomon design, were applied to make certain the gain was not just an artifact of the testing itself.

It would be useful to find out if this sense of boundaries is readily discoverable in other countries, especially in those which do not have a written constitution. I would hypothesize that such a sense exists and can be found. A reasonable expectation is that the position of the boundary varies from country to country; knowledge of this variance could be an important aid to understanding differences in the functioning of political systems. Probably a very important variation to be appreciated is the extent to which the people believe they can do something to hold their rulers in check should the boundaries be overstepped. The fact that in some nations the people believe they can do nothing because of an oppressive state apparatus does not mean that they have no sense of boundary. They may still believe that certain actions are improper, but are unwilling to pay the high cost of enforcing the boundary. Unfortunately, it is difficult to obtain data on what people would do to keep their rulers within bounds. In a stable constitutional system most persons have not confronted the situation and cannot effectively imagine what they would do. In a police state the authorities would be unlikely to allow researchers to go about asking people what they could do to check their rulers; and even if they did, one could not be confident of the respondents' candor.

Input and Demand Structure Linking the Individual to the State

Closely related to an individual's sense of boundaries are his beliefs about what he should do for the government and what the government should do for him. In the Chicago pretest we labeled these "inputs" and "outtakes"; they were called outtakes rather than outputs because we wanted to place emphasis on what the individual took from the government rather than on government performance. The pattern of these beliefs for a society shapes into what might be called its input and demand structure vis-à-vis government.

In the pretest individual input and outtake items were placed on small cards. In the first (or reality) sorting of the input cards, respondents were asked to sort them into three piles according to what they actually did: 1) those things they did regularly, 2) those things they did occasionally, and 3) those things they never did at all. In the second (or ideal) sorting of the same cards respondents were asked to sort them into three piles according to their sense of responsibility: "1) important responsibility to do, 2) medium responsibility to do, and 3) no responsibility at all." A similar "ideal" and "real" comparison was devised for the out-take items. An examination of the differences between the reality and ideal sorts discloses aspiration and rejections and carries a suggestion as to how well people believe their government is doing in specific programs.

Responses on the input and outtake items from the Chicago pretest were subjected to factor analysis. It may be interesting to look at some of the general findings even if the data cannot be taken as representative of American beliefs on these matters. As the individual factors and items are discussed an arithmetic mean will sometimes be reported, but this should be taken as characteristic of nothing more than this pretest sample. The cards were scored according to the numbers given above; thus, the lower the mean, the more regularly the activity was done or the more important it was believed to be. The input items shaped into four factors which were labeled: 1) keeping rulers within bounds, 2) political activity, 3) teaching children about government, and 4) citizen duties.

Most respondents reported that they seldom did (mean range 2.4-2.8) the things that fell in the first factor, keeping rulers within bounds. They acknowledged a medium responsibility to "protest vigorously and publicly if the government oversteps its boundaries" (1.88) and to "send messages of support or protest to party leaders between elections as well as at election time" (1.94). Still, they felt it was less important to "question the legitimacy of regulations issued by authorities before obeying them" (2.03), and rejected "join public demonstrations" (2.63) as well as "belong to a party or group trying to change the constitution" (2.54). These items show little support for vigorous defense of boundaries.

The general pattern on the second factor, political activity, was to acknowledge a somewhat stronger responsibility to be active in politics than was actually carried out. Especially strongly felt was the responsibility to "keep informed about politics" (1.215), and to "vote in elections" (1.00), both of which were so uniformly endorsed as to constitute a duty. Respondents also expressed a fairly strong responsibility to "engage in political discussion" (1.63), to "take an active part in a campaign" (1.66), and to "join a political party" (1.58), but in practice they fell a little short of this aspiration. Respondents felt little responsibility to "be a candidate for public office" (2.46) and it was hardly ever done (2.71).

On the third factor, teaching children about government, respondents said they had a strong responsibility to "teach my children the importance of give-and-take in the democratic way of life" (1.015) and to "personally see to it that my children understand and accept the responsibilities of citizenship" (1.015); they also reported doing these things fairly regularly (1.3). They reported only a medium responsibility to "teach my children to be active in politics" (1.69), and did it only occasionally (1.92).

Certain items were so uniformly considered important and so regularly done as to be considered duties. Voting and discussing have already been mentioned. Other items were: "pay all taxes," "have undivided loyalty and love for my country," and "perform military or national service."

The activities which individuals in this sample felt they had to do were fairly narrowly defined. Inputs are also a function of how potent or efficacious individuals believe their actions to be. To a considerable extent this sense of potency depends on an individual's beliefs about how the government functions. If he makes a demand, does the government respond? If he has been mistreated, does he receive justice? If he approaches bureaucracy, does he receive his rights without having to fight for them or curry favor? There are probably important differences in national beliefs about individual potency in these matters. Perhaps especially important to look for would be a belief that one can use one part of the government (e.g., one's representative) to get another part to take action. In the pretest, respondents were asked if their individual actions could affect the system. Somewhat over half felt some sense of efficacy, but only one-third felt a clear sense of individual efficacy, while nearly another third felt no sense of efficacy at all. On another question most respondents believed they would eventually receive justice even if some official treated them unfairly.

On the reality sort of the outtake cards, respondents were

again asked to sort into three piles: "1) those things the state does an efficient or active job of providing here, 2) those things the state does a moderately active job of providing, and 3) those things the state does ineffectively or not at all." On the ideal sort the instructions read: "1) those things the state has a strong or important responsibility to do for you, 2) those things you would like the state to provide but you don't feel quite as strongly about it, and 3) those things you believe the state should not attempt to provide at all." The outtake items shaped into five factors given the following names: 1) maintaining an open society, 2) economic opportunity, 3) efficiency & rectitude in government, 4) justice, and 5) less important outtakes.

Respondents generally appraised the items that fell in the first factor, maintaining an open society, as being moderately well done and being moderately to very important (range 1.33-1.73). The five items in this factor were "insuring equal opportunity for citizens to participate in making political decisions," "insuring adequate channels of expression for all citizens," "making available means or facilities to resolve conflict between private parties," "intervening to stop an individual or group from persecuting another individual or group," and "providing stability in society even if it means slowing down the rate of progress."

There was less uniformity in appraising the items that fell in the economic opportunity factor. "Providing a chance to make a good living" was judged as being moderately well done (1.692) and quite important (1.262). "Arranging things so it is easy for citizens to move from place to place, job to job, class to class" was judged as being a bit less well done (1.985) and moderately important (1.68). "Seeing to it that every man who wants a job can have a job" was considered not very well done (2.03) but quite important (1.31). "Providing welfare services" was perceived as reasonably well done (1.26) and somewhat less important (1.43). In other words, this sample felt the government could relax a little here, although the importance rating was still fairly high. "Providing free university education for all who can qualify" was perceived as not very well done (2.05) but moderately important (1.69). "Arranging things so that business is left alone" was perceived as not very well done (2.09) and moderately important (1.60). Generally, this sample said that they wished the government to provide jobs and university education, more effectively to leave a little more freedom to business, and to relax on providing welfare benefits.

The outtakes in the third factor, efficiency and rectitude in government, were all considered important (range 1.00-1.13), and most were believed to be well done: "taking actions that make one proud of his country" (1.49), "providing protection and security" (1.25), "providing public order" (1.20), and "providing strong leadership" (1.385). Two outtakes were believed to be only moderately well done, but still important: "being careful in using public money and trust" (1.72), and "competently handling foreign affairs" (1.72).

Only two items loaded heavily on the fourth factor, justice. "Securing civil rights and liberties for all" was believed to be only moderately well done (1.74) but important (1.11). "Providing justice for all" was thought of as somewhat better than moderately well done (1.57) and very important (1.00).

The outtakes considered least important fell in the fifth factor. "Trying to even out differences in wealth and prestige" was not only believed to be not well done (2.05), but also to be not very important (2.12). Rejection was even more pronounced for "adopting one official religion supported by the state" (2.63). "Providing celebrations, holidays, and parades" was believed to be reasonably well done (1.40) but not so important (1.80).

These findings suggest the kind of information that is available. Similar studies on adequate samples in several countries, carefully done, would produce some interesting comparisons and would provide partial answers to such questions as the following: How do the input and demand structures of societies with stable governments differ from those with unstable governments? How do the two structures differ for socialist and capitalist countries? How do the two structures differ for developed and under-developed countries? What minimal inputs are necessary to keep a government functioning adequately? What pattern of demands must minimally be met for a government to maintain support? When the minimal pattern of demands is better understood, what is the ratio of emotional to material outtakes among them? How do input and demand patterns differ across different strata of a society? Does the maintenance of constitutionalism (keeping rulers within bounds) require a minimal level of scrutiny and protest from the broad body politics, or is it satisfactory if this minimal level is provided only by the elite of the society? How does an individual's belief about his own potency (vis-à-vis the government) affect the pattern of his inputs and outtakes?

Popular Conceptions of Government, Politics, and the Constitution

A belief about a general concept may be a many-faceted complex of feelings. We attempted to measure some of this complexity in the Chicago area pretest by using Osgood's "semantic differential."[4] For each of three central concepts (government, politics, constitution) about 25 polar adjectives were presented; each pair of adjectives was separated by seven spaces allowing the respondent to judge which space best characterized the central concept (for example: giving — demanding, or dirty — clean). By checking one position between each of the 25 pairs a respondent displays a many-faceted semantic conceptualization. This over-all pattern also can show how positively or negatively he feels about the general concept. To avoid a set to respond either to the left or to the right side of the check sheet, and thus bias the over-all pattern, the presumably positive adjectives (clean, for example) were alternately placed on the right and the left side of the sheet.

Prior to systematic investigation, it was easy to suppose from many bits of evidence (letters to the editor, exposé-type newspaper stories, charges of corruption between antagonistic parties and candidates, etc.) that most Americans had negative feelings toward politics and government. The Almond and Verba five-nation study, however, showed that Americans generally had more positive feelings toward their government than did citizens from the other countries (England, Germany, Italy, and Mexico).[5] To see if feelings about politics differed from those toward government, respondents in the Chicago pretest were given the identical set of paired adjectives for the two concepts. The over-all results support the findings of the five-nation study: this sample had very positive feelings toward both politics and government. We hypothesized that they would have stronger positive feelings toward government than toward politics; this was true to a very

4. Charles E. Osgood, G. J. Suci, and P. H. Tannenbaum, *The Measurement of Meaning* (Urbana: Univ. of Illinois Press, 1957).
5. Almond & Verba, *The Civic Culture, passim.*

slight extent, but none of the differences between means was significant for this sample. This finding may be biased by the fact that about one-third of the sample were precinct captains. Obviously research on a much more adequate sample is needed.

The semantic picture can be presented simultaneously for the two concepts, politics and government. The adjectives seemed to cluster into four factors: evaluative, activity, potency, and essentiality. Under the evaluative factor respondents saw politics and government as largely honest, clean, attractive, honorable, open, straight, deep, good, creative, and leaning more toward happy than sad. Government was seen as a bit more unselfish than grasping, but the mean was equal between the poles for politics.

In the activity factor the respondents saw the two concepts as leaning toward friendly, many, giving, hot, uniting, exciting, and a shade noisier than quiet. Government was a bit more old than young, but the mean was equal between the poles for politics. In the potency factor the direction was very clear: they were seen as powerful, big, strong, and leaning more toward hard than soft. Under the essentiality factor they were seen as very necessary, serious, and everlasting.

A somewhat different set of paired adjectives was presented for the central concept of "constitution" than was administered for politics and government. This new set could be grouped into five factors: evaluation, majesty and essentiality, potency, activity, and flexibility. Respondents were highly positive in their evaluation of the constitution; they saw it as good, attractive, democratic, open, uniting, beautiful, and clean. The majestic-essentiality factor also showed highly positive connotations: majestic, deep, everlasting, necessary, fundamental, serious, and leaning toward long and old. Like politics and government, constitution was perceived as very potent: strong, powerful, leaning toward hard. On the activity factor it was seen as friendly, leaning toward quiet and giving, but equally slow and fast. No direction appeared for the flexibility factor; the constitution was perceived as equally rigid and flexible, equally innovative and traditional, and equally restraining and freeing.

Clearly displayed in all three of these semantic descriptions is great faith in the constitutional and political system of the United States. Possessing this kind of faith, it is understandable that this sample should feel little urgency to keep rulers within bounds. It also corresponds with the general vote of confidence given the government on the "reality outtake sort" where governmental performance on certain outtakes was judged. Possibly this positive feeling about political institutions, in this sample, stems from a greater than normal faith in the goodness of human nature. A semantic differential and an open-ended question used in the pretest both showed a very positive appraisal of the capacity of human nature to improve. Yet there was no correlation between this belief and seeing the political system as dirty or clean. Clearly missing from this analysis are comparable data from several other countries (as well as more complete data for the United States). With more complete data one could see if semantic conceptions affect patterns of inputs and outtakes, if they affect belief in the need to keep rulers within bounds, if they affect governmental stability, if they affect the pattern and rate of social change, and so forth.

Tolerance of Deviation and Change

It is inherent in the nature of believing to seek sustenance for our credulity by looking for the people around us to believe the same thing. So strong is this need for belief-support from others that there is a natural tendency in all societies to cast out those who believe differently from the dominant belief. Toleration of deviant beliefs does not come naturally, it must be learned—oftentimes only after bitter experience with the cost of intolerance. To become tolerant a person has to accept the possibility that his own beliefs may not be absolutely true. This is difficult for many persons because such doubts frequently constitute a serious threat to their systems of personal security. Frequently found supplementing this natural tendency in many countries of the world are government policies discouraging the expression of beliefs contrary to the officially accepted views of the government. Whatever the rationale (build national unity, create support for policies, protect the people from false doctrines, etc.), it is likely that the mass of people find some comfort in enforced belief uniformity.

In studying comparative politics one should not expect to find easy acceptance of deviation, but should look instead for ways in which a society tolerates deviation and accommodates itself to aberrations. It seems that deviants are more easily accepted when they are relatively few in number. Respondents in the Chicago pretest believed there were only a few extremists in the United States, and perceived little danger from them. Most respondents believed there was ample room for the expression of extreme opinions. Two-thirds of them believed minority rights should be protected even if the will of the majority should be frustrated, but two-thirds also said it would be proper for the government to outlaw an extremist group like the fascists or communists. The pattern of these answers suggests that this sample has very little concern about the problem of extremists and the protection of their rights, despite a profession of belief in minority rights. Other studies have shown high agreement on the principle of minority rights but little mass support for concrete applications to despised situations (e. g., allowing a communist to speak in your town).[6] The educated elite, however, is willing to protect both the right to deviate and its concrete applications. These studies suggest the hypothesis that in order for extremists and civil disobedience to be tolerated in a society, the right of peaceful expression must be stipulated in a basic law which the ruling elite believes it is important to protect.

The society's general level of tolerance probably affects its reaction to change as well as to deviation. Adherence to custom is a defense against the challenge of alien beliefs. I would hypothesize that strong adherence to custom and a low level of tolerance are positively correlated. It is possible, however, for societies to learn both to welcome change and to question customary ways. A nation's beliefs about change may be an important determinant of its ability to develop economically. Data on beliefs about change from countries at several stages of development would disclose whether a relationship exists between beliefs about change and rate of development.

The ability of a nation to tolerate alien beliefs may also affect its ability to get on well with its neighbors. A country that tolerates new beliefs is less likely to be defensive in contacts with foreigners, and it will be more likely to open its borders to commercial transactions and to tourist visits. It will look upon

6. Prothro & Grigg, *Journal of Politics*, XXII (May, 1960), 276-94; McClosky, *American Political Science Review*, LVIII (June, 1964), 361-82.

visitors from abroad more as persons to learn from than as possible spies. A country that feels it must defend its ideology from the intrusion of alien beliefs pays a high cost in greater friction with its neighbors and in losing a certain ability to learn.

Problem Definition and Modes for Problem Solution

In the sphere of activities in which government is involved, problems are socially defined and socially solved. Societies develop in their belief-structure typical ways of recognizing what constitutes a problem. A state of affairs that would be recognized as a problem in one culture may not be recognized as such in another culture. In Eastern Europe, for example, people are often required to stand in line to do certain things. The lines develop not so much because there is a shortage of goods or of personnel to wait on those in line, but because administrative concerns are not oriented to the reduction of lines. Lines simply are not recognized as a serious problem. In the USA, in contrast, thousands of people wasting thousands of hours standing in line would be considered a serious problem. It is not altogether clear why this situation is seen so differently in the two cultures, but a fair guess might be a different valuation placed on time and efficiency in each culture.

Even if a few individuals recognize a situation as a problem requiring solution, they are often stymied because the existence of the problem must be socially recognized. Lines in Eastern Europe are one example. Another example is the sacred cow in India; some Indians recognize the sacredness of the cow as a serious drain on the economy, a drain which must be removed before India can increase her standard of living. Yet their recognition that this is a problem is shared by only a small percentage of Indians and, until it receives widespread social recognition, little societal action to change the situation can be expected.

A society may not be able to define the nature of a problem even if it recognizes that a problematical situation exists. It is typical to escape from such a situation by declaring that it is impossible to solve the problem. (This is different from assigning low priority to a problem.) The impossibility, however, lies more with the inability to define the problem than with the inability to solve the problem once defined. Generally speaking, once a problem has been properly defined it can be solved. An emphasis on problem definition is itself a cultural belief. In many cultures people do not go about looking for problems to define and to solve. In the United States, by contrast, there is a national belief that nothing is so good that it cannot be improved, a perspective which seems relatively rare in the rest of the world.

Nations or cultures also have beliefs about preferred or "good" ways to arrive at social decisions. One such norm is, "The more persons involved in the decisional process, the better the decision." A contrasting norm emphasizes division of labor and allocates certain decisions to certain people (experts, for example), or to a leadership elite. Some norms emphasize time and efficiency at the cost of consensus: "Take a vote and let's get on with it." Others emphasize consensus: "We must discuss until we all agree." In some societies it is normal to have a smaller workgroup canvass the alternative solutions and lay these before the full decisional body; debate is often confined to these alternatives. In other societies the definition of alternatives is left unstructured prior to debate.

Modes for problem definition and solution probably affect the assignment of responsibility. A collective or consensual decision often leads to collective responsibility for its execution. Collective responsibility generally is more uncertain and erratic in execution than is individual assignment to a task for which the individual is then held responsible. Assignment and enforcement of individual responsibility is a culturally-learned behavioral norm which is much stronger in some cultures than in others.

Hopefully, the above examples are sufficient to suggest the importance of a comparative study of beliefs about problem definition and solution.

SUMMARY

The central argument of this paper has been that many important analytical possibilities are open to students of comparative politics if they will focus on differences and similarities in national beliefs as they compare national political systems. This comparison will also lead to greater understanding of the nature of beliefs and believing, and thus will lead to some understanding of the dynamics of belief change, which, in turn, is the central component of social change. National beliefs are now accessible to systematic study in many countries. Several specific suggestions were given for topics to include in a general study of beliefs: study of a sense of boundaries on rulers, study of the relationship between the individual and the state, study of popular conceptions of government, politics, and the constitution, study of tolerance of deviation and change, and study of modes of problem definition and solution. This list is meant to illustrate rather than to exhaust the analytical possibilities available from a focus on comparative beliefs. Other scholars and further study undoubtedly can suggest additions to the list.

Political Culture and the Idioms of Political Development

by Delos D. Hughes and Edward L. Pinney

The value of "political culture" as a concept is clearly indicated by the multiplying references to it in the literature of political science. Should one try to identify the contributions afforded by this concept and to assess their value, however, his conclusion might easily be that the results achieved by political scientists do not measure up to the promise with which they began. No apparent serious damage would be done to studies in which "political culture" appears prominently as an analytical device should references to the concept be eliminated; that is, we would not have learned less about political life.

Searching for some explanation for this curious situation, we are led to three conclusions: (1) Employing "political culture" fruitfully has been difficult because of the inclination of political scientists to rely on interpretations primarily intended as explications of the concept. Most of these interpretations are exercises in conceptualization, rather than efforts to operationalize the concept. (2) "Political culture" is a useful concept which could make a significant contribution to our knowledge of political life if it were understood and employed differently. (3) The problem which must be solved in order to exploit the usefulness of the concept is basically one of operationalization—specifically, "to discover and delineate the interrelationship between culture and behavior."[1]

The purpose of this essay is to present the considerations which lead to these conclusions and, with particular reference to the last of them, to suggest the possibilities and limitations in using the concept in comparative investigations of political systems. A twofold approach to the subject is employed, so that the

1. Charles B. Robson, "The Place of a Functional Approach to the Analysis of Political Systems in Political Science: An Inquiry," (Chapel Hill, N. C., April, 1962). This mimeographed paper is a revision of a paper delivered before the Southern Political Science Association convention at Gatlinburg, Tennessee, on November 2, 1962. It has been generally suggestive for our whole inquiry into political culture.

discussion moves from critical, analytical, and constructive considerations of "political culture" as a concept to a historical, empirical, and illustrative treatment of political culture as a phenomenon of our experience. To give the latter part of the analysis a sharper edge, specific attention is focused on political development—in this case, the example is India. In this aspect of modern political life, perhaps to a greater degree than in any other, the role of political culture is a leading one. We are afforded an ideal complement of theory and application, for, in Lucian Pye's words, "political development strikes at the roots of people's beliefs and sentiments about politics, and hence the process of development must be profoundly affected by the character of the political culture of a society."[2] Therefore, the initial concern of our essay is to delineate and develop the concept of political culture per se, and the further concern is to suggest briefly its utility in comparative analysis.

I

Gabriel Almond's popularization of the "political culture" concept marks the beginning of its extensive use in political science.[3] However, the initial formulation which Almond gave— "pattern of orientations to political action"[4]—left unanswered two basic questions: What is an orientation? And how is the orientation linked to behavior? These questions are not really answered by Parsons' and Shils' assertion that political orientations involve cognition, cathexis, and evaluation,[5] for the need is for some func-

2. Lucian W. Pye and Sidney Verba, *Political Culture and Political Development* (Princeton, N. J., 1965), p. 13. Robson has suggested, moreover, that an operational concept of political culture is of crucial importance for understanding "development" at all. Robson, "The Place of a Functional Approach," p. 13.

3. For a general review of this development, see Young C. Kim, "The Concept of Political Culture in Comparative Politics," *Journal of Politics*, XXVI (May, 1965), 313-36.

4. Gabriel A. Almond, "Comparative Political Systems," *Journal of Politics*, XVIII (August, 1956), 396. There is an unexplained discrepancy between Almond's usage—"orientations to political action"—and the usage in Parsons and Shils, *Toward a General Theory of Action*, which is cited as the source of the idea. The usage there is "orientation of action." See Talcott Parsons and Edward A. Shils (eds.), *Toward a General Theory of Action* (New York, 1962), p. 54 and also pp. 4, 5, 68. We have reduced the formulation "patterns of orientation to political action" to simply "orientation to political action." The same observations apply to either formulation.

5. Almond, *Journal of Politics*, VXIII, 396.

tional specification of "orientation." It is possible to understand that cognition, cathexis, and evaluation stand in some relationship to orientation and yet to be unable to understand what difference "orientation" makes in terms of behavior or environment.

The problem that initially arose with the introduction of Almond's discussion has not been substantially relieved by later discussions of political culture. Neither in Almond's studies with Coleman and Verba, nor in Samuel Beer's work, nor in the more specific treatments of the concept do we find answers to the two questions asked in the preceding paragraph.[6] An examination of the reasons for this weakness leads to some idea of how to remedy it. It is clear by now that political scientists have followed the lead of sociologists and anthropologists in developing their concept of "political culture." The rewards in such interdisciplinary borrowing can be very great, perhaps especially so when the concept of culture is involved. If politics is conceived as a specialized form of human social behavior, one would expect to find that the factors which bear on general behavior bear as well on the specialized behavior, in the appropriate specialized forms. Culture is a prominent category in the field of human behavior, so we reasonably expect an analogous category of "political culture" in the field of political behavior. As political behavior is a specialized form of, or perhaps part of, behavior generally, political culture is conceived to be a specialized form of, or perhaps part of, the general culture.

Judgments about the usefulness of the concept of culture in political science can be made without prejudice to the fruitfulness with which that concept has been used in other disciplines such as anthropology and sociology. A fundamental difference often exists in the treatment of culture by anthropologists and by political scientists. Anthropology has usually directed most effort toward description, in which culture is a dependent variable whose conceptualization will vary according to type of analysis.[7]

6. Gabriel A. Almond and James S. Coleman, *The Politics of the Developing Areas* (Princeton, 1960); Gabriel A. Almond and Sidney Verba, *The Civic Culture: Political Attitudes and Democracy in Five Nations* (Princeton, 1963); Samuel H. Beer and Adam B. Ulam, *Patterns of Government: The Major Political Systems of Europe* (New York, 1962).

7. See Jacques Barzun's very interesting discussion of the term "culture" and his account of the development of scientific interest in it. Jacques Barzun, *Science: The Glorious Entertainment* (New York, 1964), pp. 9 ff.

In political science the concept must be an independent variable, as suggested by Almond's supposition that a political system is "embedded in" political culture.[8] The political scientists' problem is to understand political system variation—to which end, we may suppose, political culture contributes.

There are two special problems which any self-conscious development of the "political culture" concept is likely to encounter. To begin with, the presuppositions underlying social science seem to render tautological such statements as "political culture=orientations of political action." Unless actions are random—in which case social science as presently understood is impossible—there must be some sort of orientation, probably in the form of certain predispositions or constant criteria for appropriate behavior in specific circumstances. Since random behavior *means* the absence of any orientation, then this factor is a necessary alternative to random-ness. Therefore, to say that "political culture-orientations of political action" is only to give a name to what has before been just an implicit assumption. The statement is analytic, but in no sense synthetic.[9] This being the case, the only apparent possible line of further investigation lies in refining the analytic statement rather than in operationalizing the original concept. The original conceptual strategy has limited the further results, and we could not realistically or fairly expect anything more.

In the second place, we may be tempted to direct more of our attention toward the concept of "political culture" itself than toward the empirical events to which it refers or which it might help to explain. Insufficient attention has up to now been given to operationalization of the concept, a failure that is apparent in several areas which we may summarize by way of illustration. Gabriel Almond's use of "political culture" depends heavily on Talcott Parsons' concept of "pattern variables."[10] The reference to and further application of Parsons' "traditional" and "modern" categories suggest to us that the political culture concept has in fact been operationalized, at least in a primitive way. It is not quite clear whether in Almond's view "pattern variables"="political culture" or whether the two categories are separate aspects

8. Almond, *Journal of Politics*, XVIII, 396.
9. See Arnold Brecht, *Political Theory: The Foundations of Twentieth-Century Political Thought* (Princeton, 1959), pp. 55 ff.
10. Almond and Coleman, *Politics of the Developing Areas*, p. 22.

of the same thing. In any case, the chief observation to be made is that the pattern variables as specified are still analytic. Several possible patterns of political behavior have been suggested and named, but we still remain in the realm of conceptualization rather than of operationalization. If behavior patterns are described as "diffuse" or "specific," "particular" or "universal," and these patterns are said to be articulated through "traditional" or "modern" cultures,[11] one can observe with an elementary logical analysis that no synthetic statement has been made.

Again, an overriding interest in conceptualization for its own sake may be suggested by the emphasis which is often placed on socialization in the transmission and perpetuation of culture.[12] It is difficult enough to understand how specific political opinions are transmitted in this way; to understand how orientations of political actions are transmitted without understanding what such an orientation is, is infinitely more difficult. Stating what is apparent—that socialization is a learning process and that culture is transmitted through socialization processes—tells us little about culture. As in the illustrations above, the assertion that patterns of behavior are learned implies that orientations of action are learned as well, that is, that culture is transmitted by socialization. Lamentably, however, we are no nearer an understanding of what culture is nor of the nature of its connection with behavior.[13]

11. *Ibid.*
12. In fact, in Almond and Coleman, *Politics of the Developing Areas,* the only index entry for "culture, political" is *"see* socialization, political." See p. 584.
13. The same characteristic interest in the concept of culture *qua* concept is evident in the attempts to identify its existential referents. Almond states that "political culture" is preferred over "public opinion" because the latter is "formal and rational in meaning" while the former conforms to the "behavioral approach." (Almond and Coleman, *Politics of the Developing Areas,* p. 4.) The position stated seems to be that "public opinion" and "political culture" are conceptualizations of the same referent but from different perspectives. We commonly assume that public opinion can be read from certain objective indicators, but "orientation of action" cannot—unless one falls back on the action itself as an indicator, in which case the propositions are again tautological or analytic. The immediate cause of this difficulty seems to be the ambivalence of such approaches to the nature of the culture concept with regard to its subjective-objective character. It is not clear whether culture comprehends that which can be experienced through the senses, as the popular usage of the term to refer to the arts and other manifestations of man's civilization suggests. Even the refinements of Parsons and Shils do not clear up the ambiguity about culture as an objective phenomenon. They speak of "objects" of orientation and develop an elaborate typology of such objects—social, non-social, physical, and cultural (!)—to which actors are

We have examined these points in order to show that an interest in "culture" may easily lead to conceptual elaboration but not necessarily to synthetic results. In borrowing the concept for political science, we may, and indeed we probably have, incurred, unintentionally, a rigidity as well—a rigidity due to a somewhat uncritical cross-disciplinary borrowing. The remedy for this disability, which is suggested by our critical examination, lies simply in conceptualizing "political culture" in terms of a general, operational framework—the most obvious being "political system." This is, of course, just what Almond has proposed.[14] But his analysis, by asserting that the political system is "embedded in" political culture, does not integrate culture into the system concept. As we cannot think of political system except in terms of political actors (or, more precisely, political roles), our efforts must focus on the *functional* import of "orientations of political actions" of actors within political systems. The focus, in other words, should be on what a political orientation *is* or *does* in terms of actors, and thus, in aggregate, in terms of political systems.

Before proceeding further, let us be clear about the difference between what Almond has already done and what has just been suggested. Almond's propositions are that people act, in ways that can be variously categorized, *because* they have internalized certain orientations of action; that the components of such orientations are cognitive, cathectic, and evaluative; that these orientations are patterned to correspond with the various behavioral categories; and that these orientations are transmitted through socialization processes, which is to say that cognitive, cathectic, and evaluative patterns are learned. Our analysis suggests that the explanatory value of all of this is not unlike that of the familiar reference to the dormitive potency of opium. As an alternative, we need to develop the concept of political culture as a way of explaining why political systems evolve as they do and why they differ. But initially we must understand the functional significance of culture, how it influences the behavioral responses

oriented. But the student is always faced with elaborations of this sort rather than with applications in the world of his experience. Such applications, as we have suggested, are precluded by the very nature of the approach taken in anthropology and sociology.

14. Almond and Coleman, *Politics of the Developing Areas*, pp. 5-58.

of a political actor and how it is translated through socialization into aggregate political behavior.

II

The presumption that political culture is a useful concept rests upon the reconstruction of our understanding of it. This reconstruction begins with the assumption that any two basically similar political systems may respond to similar stimuli differently, and that if the stimuli are repeated the response in each system will be the same as in the previous instance. Moreover, exposure of the same two systems to a different stimulus will produce responses the difference between which corresponds to the difference between the two systems.[15] The difference in the responses of the two systems to the same stimulus is due to cultural difference. Political culture, therefore, is a useful concept because we have identified it as the critical explanatory factor by a process of definition. In its barest form: *"Political culture is that which accounts for the inter-systemic differences in responses of political systems to identical stimuli when all other variables have been accounted for."* There are four essential points to be made about this formulation: (1) it refers to a situation of complete knowledge; (2) it is "functional"; (3) it is comparative; (4) it is "residual." Some further development of these points should make the definition clearer.

(1) The formulation we are using is subject to qualification because it is difficult to take into account *all* possible variables bearing on any political situation or phenomenon. It is difficult, perhaps impossible, to know what all the relevant variables are. All physical and social sciences face this problem, but it does not make scientific investigation useless, nor does it destroy the utility of the present formulation. The conclusions of this type of research are always tentative, always subject to revision upon discovery of new relevant variables. In our specific case, political

15. An interesting variation is the case of identical stimuli to one system at different points in time. One would expect, for instance, that a political system would respond in one way to its first experience with an economic depression and respond differently to subsequent depressions. Our model accommodates this case by assuming that *different* systems are being examined at the various points in time. At the initial point (t_1) we examine system S_1; at the next point (t_2) the system is described as $S_1 + $ *experience at* t_1 or S_2; at t_3 the system is $S_2 + $ *experience at* t_2 or S_3; etc.

culture is a rather inclusive concept including a whole category of phenomena, which to a considerable degree can be differentiated from other categories.[16]

(2) That this description of culture is "functional" is very nearly self-evident. In contrast with anthropology we are not interested in specifying what culture *is*, except in terms of what it *does*—that is to say what function it performs in political systems. The problem may be compared, for illustration, to an attempt to understand the difference between a respiring and a non-respiring organism. In that case it is helpful to understand what lungs *are*, in a structural sense, in order to understand what they *do*, in a functional sense. But it seems clear that the function of lungs can be described with some specificity and value without any direct observation or measurement of the organs themselves. When the object of investigation is non-physical, this stage of description is the first step, and there are good reasons to believe that any further description is simply unnecessary, and probably confusing, reification.[17]

(3) We have formulated "political culture" specifically as an analytic tool for *comparative* analysis. It has too often been overlooked that except in comparative analysis culture has no meaning and thus no utility. It is not strictly correct to speak of culture with respect to a political system *in vacuo*, but only when there is a comparison with another system, or at least an implicit comparison. Culture implies a *difference* in behavior. To say something about the culture of one political system is to say something about other political systems, at least negatively if in no other way. Therefore, we have incorporated this aspect of the concept into its definition explicitly.

(4) These several features just discussed are summed up in the last—that political culture is a "residual" concept. It is perhaps easiest to explain this idea with a parallel from physical science. Culture is very much like the "constant" used in mathematical formulations of physical relationships, such as "π" in

16. Variables which bear only a mechanical relationship to behavior, for instance, are not included in the cultural category—for example, variables in the realm of physical environment or physical limitations of actors. With further examination, we might be able to narrow down the non-mechanical category as well.

17. See Vernon Van Dyke, *Political Science: A Philosophical Analysis* (Stanford, 1960), pp. 63-64.

geometrical relationships of circles, or Planck's constant, "h," in the quantum theory of thermodynamics. Clearly one must be very careful in using this device, for this "constant" is to be used as a "variable" where inter-system comparative analysis is involved. Culture is a "constant" *intra*-systemically. This means that when every other variable has been taken into account, that which is required to explain the difference between behavioral responses from one political system to another is culture. If we could assign to culture a quantitative value (which we cannot), the application of that same value to comparisons of any other situations would give results corresponding to actual behavioral responses.[18]

Thus:[19]

$$\text{Stimulus}_1 \rightarrow (\text{System } [\text{Culture}_1]) \rightarrow \text{Response M}$$
$$\text{Stimulus}_1 \rightarrow (\text{System } [\text{Culture}_2]) \rightarrow \text{Response N}$$

And:

$$\text{Stimulus}_2 \rightarrow (\text{System } [\text{Culture}_1]) \rightarrow \text{Response X}$$
$$\text{Stimulus}_2 \rightarrow (\text{System } [\text{Culture}_2]) \rightarrow \text{Response Y}$$

So that:

$$M : N : : X : Y : : \text{Culture}_1 : \text{Culture}_2$$

Again, to take stock of the development of our argument: We propose that so far as political scientists are concerned, it does not really matter what culture *is* in the sense of its objective, structural existence. The problem of this essay is to develop a definition of culture that is productive, easy to use, and not contradicted by experience. Political culture is originally defined or discovered as a "constant." We are aware of certain influences on political behavior characteristic of political systems or subsystems for which we cannot account. We name this "culture," and then try to specify what sort of entity fulfills the functional requirements set by our analysis. The investigator does not look at some structural "culture" and then attempt to describe and understand it. Rather, he notices missing elements in behavior

18. Although we have not been able to explore the matter fully here, the suggestion has been made that the residue should be considered as composed both of "culture" and of "randomness." It does seem reasonable that system responses may incorporate a random factor which could be included in the formulation here, so that the "constant" — randomness = culture. We are indebted to William Buchanan for this suggestion.

19. Note that the systems are identical by virtue of all other variables having been taken into account.

theory and then attempts to figure out what would be needed to supply the explanation required. Taking single similar organisms in a standard stimulus-response situation, it is obvious that responses to identical stimuli may vary. Therefore, we postulate that something about the organism itself explains the difference. If it is not physical, then we postulate a psyche. In comparisons of political systems the same analytical process applies, although the problem is much more complex. Having identified several factors which help to explain the variations of response, we are still left with an unexplained residue. This we call political culture. Like the human psyche, political culture is a construct.

Although it may not matter, this is probably how the concept of culture was developed in the first place. It does matter, however, that this is probably the view of the concept which is most likely to produce results in comparative behavioral analysis. This view makes clear the *functional* nature of the category. It should be abundantly clear that culture is an analytical device rather than being existentially real. Whether in fact there may be an existentially real thing to which our analytical device corresponds is another matter which is raised again briefly below. We are at particular pains to state the special view of "culture" proposed here. Only by being clear and rigorous about the nature of the device can we avoid the circular reasoning that characterizes many treatments of culture and find ways to apply the concept fruitfully in political analysis. These are the applications to be investigated in the following discussion.

III

Functional analysis in social science developed as a mode of analysis based on an inherent tendency of the data—the tendency of the subject to maintain itself, to persist. This tendency is, in fact, the distinguishing characteristic of the form in which the data are observed—the *system*. It is a tendency which may be contrasted with the accomplishment of some end external to the system, or with the perfection of the system itself in terms of some normative standard. Functional analysis—in the strict sense—thus represents both a new emphasis and a new observation.

If we examine the data of political analysis, viewed as systems, it appears that there are other inherent tendencies present, in addition to the tendency of systems to maintain themselves.[20] In every system, or even in every organism, there is an interpretive tendency, or perhaps more precisely, an interpretive necessity. That is, in any system, and particularly in biological and social systems, some procedure must exist for internalizing stimuli. The procedure may be mechanical, as it is wholly in all non-biological and non-social systems, and as it is partially in all other types of system. And the procedure may be non-mechanical, as it always is when the stimulus is non-physical, and as it may partially be when the stimulus is physical, in the case of conscious biological and social systems.

It seems clear that whether we speak of "orientations" or of "culture," the previous considerations necessitate our considering political culture to be a characteristic of the system, that is, internal to it, rather than part of the environment.[21] The relationships explained in Part II indicated that this was the factor accounting for differences in the responses from similar systems to similar stimuli. Therefore, our hypothesis is that *the interpretation of stimuli is the critical point in the process and thus the point of cultural influence.* The argument is neither novel nor startling, although it appears to diverge from some current ideas about the role played by culture. In some conceptions culture does not function as a selecting device or transforming medium through which stimuli pass in being received by the system, but rather as an effective limitation on the capacities or abilities for response. It appears much more reasonable, however, to assume that any response is theoretically possible but that some are inappropriate for the stimuli as interpreted in the system, than to assume that some responses are not possible but that any stimulus is internalized by every system in the same way. This view has a considerably greater potentiality for explaining change in responses (e.g., political development), particularly rapid change.

When we suppose that orientations of political actions in some way involve cognition, cathexis, and evaluation, we must also suppose some object to which these processes are directed.

20. These other tendencies do not seem to be *necessarily* related to the persistence drive, but rather independent of it. Although not directly relevant to our present concern, it is interesting to speculate whether these other tendencies might themselves provide bases for new research modes.

21. As we have noted, the use of the phrase "embedded in" to describe the relationship of culture and system is ambiguous. *Supra*, p. 70.

Almond's suggestions do not include any specification of these objects, and thus there is no indication as to whether Almond is referring to the interpretation aspect of systemic functions or to the other end of the process, the translation of stimuli into behavior. However, his references to Parsons' and Shils' "cognition," "cathexis," and "evaluation" are useful and can be made to apply.[22] The major problem is to discover the object(s) cognized, cathected, and evaluated.

It is basic to our approach to this problem that *culture must be viewed as an internal (subjective) rather than an external (objective) factor*. The political culture of a system is analogous to the psyche in human actors.[23] If we substitute "political system" for "actor," we may substitute "political culture" for the psyche (or "social system" and "general culture," respectively). This analogy is more than simply casual, for the cultural component is in a sense the cumulative psychic component for the population included in a system with respect to certain types of stimulus and response. This is not to say that culture is merely the aggregate psychological characteristics of a population, for that would imply that it may be a resultant from or an average of a number of discrete and not necessarily similar psyches. Whereas it is clear that the cultural characteristics of a population are characteristics of all, or most, or at least the greater part of its members. That is, the "residues" are widely shared.

With this view of the "cultural" component in political behavior in mind—a sort of "cumulative psychic filter" or transforming medium through which stimuli to the system are internalized —the analytical problem is to describe this component so as to make it useful in understanding the stimulus-response relationships (and perhaps ultimately to predict response, where stimulus is given). Again, it must be clear that the description is not of something existentially real, but of that which is necessary in order for us to understand response when stimulus is known and the system is known.

We propose that political culture is to be viewed as a picture of the political system, a picture composed of cognitive, cathectic, and evaluative components. This proposal can be identified as an

22. Almond, *Journal of Politics*, XVIII, 396.
23. See *supra*, p. 76.

"as-if" type of construction.[24] Political culture functions for a political system and for the actors whose roles compose that system *as if* it were a picture of the political system. It may be that there is no such existential picture and/or that some other formulation would be as useful as this one. Basically, however, culture *must be* functionally equivalent to this view, and thinking of culture in this way has considerable operational utility, which can be seen as we examine further some characteristics of the cognitive, cathectic, and evaluative processes.

The response of a political system to any stimulus will first be conditioned by the conception of that system held by the actors whose roles compose it. More precisely, rather than a view of what politics is, we may think of this conception as a view of what is political and what is non-political. This cognitive component of political culture is conditioned by at least three kinds of influence upon the actors in the political system—custom, need, and imposition (force). It is customary to think of some aspects of life as political, some as non-political, and some as either political or non-political depending on their contexts. Men have thought in such ways for long periods of time and their children learn from them to think in these same ways.

It is further apparent that the needs which actors have, perceived or unperceived, influence their distinction of the political from the non-political. If, for example, controlling the reproduction of a population or supplying it with food cannot be managed satisfactorily by the customary non-political agencies, then this management might well be transferred from the non-political category to the political category. This seems to be what is happening in India today.

Finally, the population may be *forced* to recognize some aspects of life as political or as non-political. This type of influence poses special problems for the analyst, for it is not clear whether or not the forced categorization is really internalized. It may be that behavior is a response to the act of forcing itself rather than to the cognition of something as "political."[25] In any event, systems are forced in some sense to accept certain cogni-

24. See R. B. Braithwaite, *Scientific Explanation: A Study of the Function of Theory, Probability and Law in Science* (New York, 1960), pp. 88-93.

25. Alternatively, we might interpret the response as explained by the alteration of cognition due to some special kind of need, to preserve one's life in the face of a threat to it, for instance.

tions of the political or of the non-political. This force must, of course, originate outside the system, for it is not logically possible for a system to force itself. (It may be true that one political sub-system is forced by another sub-system within the context of a broader, inclusive system, but strictly speaking this too is a forcing from an external source.)

The second component of the view of the political system is cathectic. Cathexis refers to the affective relationship of actors to the system—again noting that we are speaking in an "as-if" mode. In positing this type of relationship we rely on the assumption that man reacts positively or negatively, that he likes or dislikes that which is cognized.[26] Whether or not this is a *necessary* concomitant of cognition is moot. But cathecting the political system is a necessary precondition for participating in it, for playing a role. At the very least we can say that role-players, in the aggregate, cathect the political system.

The relationship in this case is influenced by two factors. Custom is an influence on cathexis, as it is on cognition. The view that the political system is "a good thing" may become customary and be transmitted through socialization. Another influence is the effect upon actors of the outputs of the political system. If perceived interests are affected adversely by system outputs, one is likely to cathect the system negatively; if they are favorably affected, a positive reaction is likely. These reactions, however, are uncertain, because the possibility exists that the character of system outputs may change, affecting interests differently in the future. And these reactions are further uncertain because the customary, learned cathectic relationship may dominate the cathectic facility, rather than the relationship occasioned by immediate experience of system outputs.

Finally, we must consider the evaluative component of the view of the political system. Any political actor, and thus any group of actors, may be forced to select among a group of objects, for purposes of allocating resources to them or because possibilities for action are limited to mutually exclusive alternatives. The political system itself may be the object of this sort of evaluation. A clear instance is in the selection of a political career over some other type of career—an evaluation of politics is implicit and perhaps explicit. Actors may choose to go fishing rather than to

26. See Parsons and Shils, *Toward a General Theory of Action*, pp. 10-11.

vote, not because they reject politics—not because they react (cathect) negatively to the political—but rather because in relation to fishing politics is less valuable according to a value-standard held. It was a frequent comment of observers on the scene in South Vietnam during the early stages of large-scale American military involvement there that the Vietnamese themselves attended to the conflict very desultorily, as an activity which could be, and was, suspended upon the approach of certain holidays. (The characteristic was, incidentally, frequently described as "cultural.") This inclination, if it has been accurately reported, shows the evaluative relationship with respect to the political system very clearly, along with the resulting outputs of the system.[27]

Quite the same influences bear on the formation of evaluations of this sort as bear on the formation of cathexes, the only difference being that the context is comparative. The influences of custom-socialization and of experience with the political system in relation to experience with other structures will account for the evaluative component of any view of that political system. We can add, however, that this component has both a specific and a general aspect. That is, a general scheme of values may be learned or developed by experience, a value scheme to which particular objects, events, or relationships may be connected. On the other hand, an order of preference among specific objects, events, or relationships may also be learned or developed by experience.

Before concluding this explanation of what a view of the political system comprises, we should make a final observation which is critical for explaining the connection between culture—that is, the view of the system—and behavior. In a sense, a political system represents potential behavior, available energy, future response. Although it is true that any stimulus to a system *necessitates* a response if the stimulus is mechanical and the system is physical, it is not nearly so clear why a non-physical system responds or why systems respond to non-mechanical stimuli. The answer lies in the tendency with which we began the discussion, the tendency (or necessity) to interpret. It appears

27. If the assumption is correct that this situation in Vietnam has changed—that the option of the people is for political activity to a great degree today—then we have some interesting comparative data at hand from which to estimate the nature and degree of cultural influence on behavior.

that cognition alone may not necessitate any response, but that cathexis and evaluation do. Cathexis and evaluation are, in a sense, energy releasing. They clearly necessitate some behavior and, unless we stretch the meaning of that word, this means overt, observable behavior. The cathexis or evaluation is completed and given meaning only when there is a behavioral expression. So far as the behavioral scientist is concerned, cathexis and evaluation exist only when behavior expresses them.

We have reached a point in these considerations at which some major theoretical problems have been explored. The argument is not a complete one. In developing a concept of political culture and in explaining the relationship between political culture and behavior we have not attempted to be comprehensive but to be heuristic. In the remainder of this essay, in which our attention turns to operational explorations, the intention again is to be heuristic rather than comprehensive. The data to be presented are drawn chiefly from the Indian situation, which is a particularly useful one for pursuing the analytical problems of political culture in a comparative context, for here within a single political system one finds multiple political cultures—that is, different views of the political system. In the discussion which follows, we will examine the Indian political culture(s) in the context of the problems of political development in the post-independence period.

IV

It is customary in contemporary political science to look upon the political order of the new states as dichotomous—as having a modern, secular, urban political elite on the one hand, and traditional, predominantly agrarian masses making up most of the society's population on the other. Political scientists have therefore come to think of "modernization" in terms of the imposition or spontaneous emergence of increasingly effective and legitimate "modern" values in a traditional population, with an eye among the elites toward encouraging greater popular participation according to a rational Plan. As primitively stated, this understanding contains some demonstrable truth. It should be small wonder that the indigenous elites, in emulation of the West, are suspicious of the persistent parochial residues that reflect centuries-old values, habits, and outlooks; or that they deny the validity of any political motivation other than that of modernization and development.

The problem of "political development" as an urgently felt need in India has a conceptual counterpart as a problem in the literature of political science. Political development as such became a focal point of concern only as recently as the early 1950's, and among scholars of comparative politics there is very little agreement as to its meaning. In a recent study, Lucian Pye identified at least seven "meanings" of political development, each of which has one or more sites of appropriate application.[28] The meanings overlap a great deal, of course. Most of them represent variations on a common theme of administrative cohesion, maximum resource exploitation, and the rise of democratic values. Still, there is a problem for the non-area specialist in using a concept with so many localized meanings. This problem is aggravated to some extent by a tendency in Western social science to think of development in terms of the diffusion of a "world culture," described by Lucian Pye as "based on advanced technology and the spirit of science, on a rational view of life, a secular approach to social relations, a feeling for justice in public affairs, and above all else, on the acceptance in the political realm of the belief that the prime unit of the polity should be the nation state."[29]

It is evident that the language of "political development" is expressed in several different idioms, each chosen no doubt because it is believed appropriate to the problems of any single culture.[30] It may be, for example, that the particular idiom of development in one new country draws upon an explicit and perhaps traditional tie between political-administrative elites on the one hand and a single, ethnic sub-culture on the other, as apparently is the case in Ethiopia, where for centuries the Emperors have been selected from the ranks of the Amhara.[31] In such a

28. Pye and Verba, *Political Culture and Political Development*, pp. 11-12.

29. Lucian W. Pye, "The Political Context of National Development," in Irving Swerdlow (ed.), *Development Administration: Concepts and Problems* (Syracuse, N. Y., 1963), p. 26.

30. The idea of idiomatic politics and its consequences, in India, for modernization and development, is given careful attention by W. H. Morris-Jones in "India's Political Idioms," in C. H. Phillips (ed.), *Politics and Society in India* (New York, 1962), pp. 133-55.

31. Donald N. Levine, "Ethiopia: Identity, Authority, and Realism," in Pye and Verba, *Political Culture and Political Development*, pp. 247-50 *et passim*.

case, where an ethnic minority achieves elite status and thus becomes the custodian and standard-bearer of the "national culture," political development and change must probably be achieved in large part by modifications in the relevant beliefs and sentiments of the dominant sub-culture.[32]

In India the idiom of development must be different. Apart from the traditionally superior Brahmins—who are often removed by religious or economic necessity from deep political involvement—there is no single ethnic group with an India-wide claim to "custodial status." The situation seems to be approximately the reverse. Indeed, students of Indian politics are prone to introduce their subject with a discussion of its difficulty and by pointing to the wide range of ethnic and lingual units and of conflicting idioms in the articulation of basic values and sentiments, including those sentiments most directly involving politics. In what idiom, then, might one state the Indian problem of development? And what behavioral referents could be adduced to illustrate convergence, accommodation, and change in the "political culture" of the Indian Union?

Not unlike that in most other new states, political life in India has only recently been characterized by intensive mass participation. Heretofore, it was commonly assumed, the only thing that held together the sprawling and diverse cultures of the Indian sub-continent was the "steel frame" of the Indian Colonial Service. Prior to independence, most of the energy invested in politics by Indians was on behalf of the national Movement against the British *Raj*. After 1947, there arose a predominantly urban, Western-oriented elite committed to establishing a democratic, secular regime; devoted to rural uplift and dramatic advances in social justice for the masses; and determined to reconstruct Indian society along modern lines by ultimately eliminating the caste, lingual, tribal, and communal bases of loyalty among India's population. The short-range result was an abrupt shift of power to the urban sources of political parties, rational long-range planning, and national administrative controls.

We do not mean to give the impression here that the first post-independence Indian leaders made a deliberate or disruptive break with the traditions of a half-million villages, where 85% of the population lives. Asian civilizations, in contrast with the

32. *Ibid.*

West, have usually grown from rural foundations.[33] These village underpinnings in Indian society were not to be jettisoned in the urban dash for modernization. But being relatively new as centers of power and control free from external (i.e., British) coercion, the cities in India were the logical and appropriate nerve centers for the initiation of political change.[34] The cities and larger towns enjoyed the initial advantages of having no strong traditionalist fabric to unravel, and of being the inheritors of the two basic Indian unities in 1947: the unity of the higher administrative service (IAS) and the unity of the Congress Party. When Indian leaders referred to "the unity of India" it was usually this urban-inspired and elite-dominated culture to which they made reference.

There was, however, another cultural base, much broader and much less amenable to—indeed, barely aware of—the need for unity, much less for political development. Stated in terms of this paper's analytical framework, the first Indian centers of political energy, of reform and development, manifested patterns of cognition and cathectic and evaluative responses to those cognitions that were light-years distant from the cognitions and responses of the vast majority of the country's population. The disabling features of this gap were to become poignantly clear in the early years of development planning.

The central objective of official planning in India was defined in the First Five Year Plan, begun in April, 1951: "to initiate a process of development which will raise living standards and open out to the people new opportunities for a richer and more varied life."[35] Although the first Plan took explicit notice of the "broader social environment" which would have to serve as the springboard for all development plans, the basic drive was for economic growth and there clearly was no time to instruct the village millions in the need for national economic advancement. The National Planning Commission and the various state planning agencies, equipped with the language of political modernity,

33. The significance of the difference in this respect between Asia and the West is discussed in some detail in Maurice Zinkin, *Asia and the West* (London, 1951).

34. Myron Weiner, *Party Politics in India: The Development of a Multi-Party System* (Princeton, 1957), pp. 11-12.

35. *The First Five Year Plan*, Planning Commission, Government of India, April, 1951.

were therefore sensitive to the manifest need for political and economic development. They set about to induce the Indian farmer, for example, to adopt more scientific techniques of cultivation. (India's crop yields annually are among the world's lowest.) In the process the Development Officers, agents of the higher administrative service, often failed to find a common psycho-cultural meeting ground with the cultivating villagers. It is frequently easier to construct a million-ton steel industry than to effect important changes in farmers' thinking about water irrigation or the use of agricultural fertilizers and contraceptives. The perception of need by the development planners and their field Development Officers was not usually matched by a similar perception among farmers in the villages of Gujerat, Bihar, or Maharashtra.

One particularly revealing account of the reactions among India's rural folk to the introduction of technological changes tells of utterly "inappropriate" responses.[36] Even in areas where some material improvements were achieved, these improvements were not usually reflected in a rise in domestic living standards, but in an emerging pattern of hard-working wives and increasingly leisured husbands. In the light of these and other evidences, one may reason that the occasional nature of the first Plan's successes was prompted by insufficient attention to the primary target of the rural uplift program: the farmer, his personality and motivations, and the real conditions of his life.

It is a recurring and significant fact that the most productive farmers in India are not necessarily those working the richest soil or nearest the irrigation canals, nor those with the best natural environment for agricultural production; but rather those who are agriculturalists by caste, such as the *Sadgops* in West Bengal, the *Jats* in the Punjab, and the *Patidars* in Gujerat. These latter work under no caste or saintly prescription against working on the land. Hence they are usually found to be better cultivators, whether they own land or not, than the land-owning, higher

36. For instance, the desire in Kerala for an aerodrome when there were barely the resources to build dry-weather roads that would handle bullock carts; the refusal (or inability) of Harijans (Untouchables) in Kabistalam village (Madras) to consider owning more than five acres of land, which would have quadrupled their crop yields. ("After all, we have been growing our crops like this with only rain water for thousands of years.") Kusum Nair, *Blossoms in the Dust: The Human Factor in Indian Development* (New York, 1963).

castes such as the *Rajputs* or *Banias*. Kusum Nair concluded from her traveling experience in 1958 and 1959 that the major assumption of development planning in the 1950's was faulty— the assumption that there is a widely shared wish for self-improvement and for a corresponding rise in consumption levels. The indications, in fact, are not that there is a floor below which no one wishes to fall, but rather that there is a ceiling beyond which no one is willing to venture. In a situation of limited and static aspirations, plans for development must fail when they rest upon a conscious wish for self-improvement among Indian villagers. More often than not, if an Indian farmer looks to the stars, "it is only to worship them, not to pluck them."[37]

The problem of varying perceptions of development in India has been further complicated by the fact that basic values still vary drastically from one village to another, even within the same district and even when other considerations are constant. Given, then, different patterns of cognition generally, and in the absence of uniform evaluations, it would be naive to expect a uniform response to common incentives and stimuli. It would appear therefore that the Community (Village) Development Program could never become a self-generating process with its own momentum unless the social structure of the community and the value system that informs it were to determine (rationally or otherwise) that Community Development is plausible and desirable. Government programs, such as Community Development and land reform, must accommodate these basic and enduring differences in local and caste values and then construct formulas that draw upon, rather than fly in the face of, traditional cognitions and evaluations. It was not enough to introduce model institutions, such as *panchayats* (village councils) and farming cooperatives. These institutions could not break up the existing caste basis of power, influence, property, and status. Although since 1947 India has probably enacted more land reform measures than any country in the world, it is clear that these measures have met with visible success only where the impetus to reform was conjoined with existing, indigenous values and with the traditional structure of articulation and ambition.

It was in a context of growing dissatisfaction that the Government of India inaugurated a series of studies of all Community

37. *Ibid.*, p. 193.

Projects, the best known being the Report issued in 1957 under
the chairmanship of Balvantray G. Mehta.[38] This Report urged
abandonment of the strongly centralized controls of planning and
development, and reinvestment of *panchayats* and regional and
district units with local development functions. Beginning in
Andhra and Rajasthan states in 1959, the "decentralists" gained
the upper hand and began to institute the now nation-wide trend
toward *Panchayati Raj*. Whether this movement is a loyal reflection of the Gandhian image of India as a federation of village
republics, or simply a result of the efforts by local Congress
politicians to advance their own power with the local administration, the consequences are approximately the same. The past
several years have seen a marked dispersion of power and the
growing influence of local officeholders, along with an intensified
struggle for the local, district, and state offices newly endowed
with power. Into the bargain has gone considerable disenchant-
ment, if not alienation, among members of the earlier elites, who
look upon the reversion to local standards as a return to parochialism and who look with poorly disguised disapproval on the new
scramble for power in the State Legislative Assemblies.[39] The
question remains: are there indications of reconciliation between
locally ambitious politicians and the central planners, in common
acknowledgment of political and economic priorities? And, in
any case, has the redistribution of power in India helped to
clarify the meaning of political development for Indians by
reducing the number of cultural norms and imperatives?

v

In the past ten years the evidence has been gathering to sustain the argument that the multiplicity of cultural directions, supported by caste and language in the traditional sphere and by
cosmopolitan aloofness and an ethic of service in the modern
sphere, are being given a new and quite different direction by the
independent pressures of politics. To some extent the new

38. The Balvantray Report is summarized and subjected to critical, but
friendly, commentary in Hugh Tinker, "Autonomy and Community in Village
India," *Pacific Affairs*, XXXII, No. 4 (December, 1959), 354-76.

39. The early dissatisfactions among intellectuals in the new states are
described as characteristic and, in some respects, unavoidable, in E. A. Shils,
"The Intellectuals in the Political Development of the New States," *World Politics*,
XII (April, 1960), 329-68.

rewards of politics have induced outward changes in social relations and in approaches to authority. The dispersion of power to the *panchayats*, the *Zila Parishads*, and the State Legislative Assemblies; a marked expansion in government activities; the growing intimacy of contact between Indians and government agencies; and the further democratization of society by the substantial breakup of rural economic and political power concentrations have all contributed to what Myron Weiner has aptly called an "emerging mass political culture."[40] Whereas the elite culture in Indian political life has been sustained by its own built-in socialization process, the mass culture is only beginning to construct such a process out of the many particularistic cognitions and evaluations. This emerging pattern of political socialization in the Indian mass culture is basically traditional in tone and style; still, it has come to inculcate among state and local political actors an appreciation for the allures of power and for the patronage and status that power brings with it.

From this we suggest that the idiom of political development in India, if not in all the new non-Western states, is *national development*, that is, development toward a more homogeneous set of cognitions, cathexes, and evaluations, and toward universal acceptance of a common primary allegiance. To the extent that the Community Development Programs, the later dispersion of power, and the resulting stimulus to political participation yield greater homogeneity and a more secular framework for conflict resolution and policy making, to that extent some measurable "political development" has taken place in India. It is, of course, quite another matter to establish that this tendency toward the secularization of multiple cultural norms leads to a closing of the psychic gap between the elites and the mass, or that the present generation of Indian leaders can reinforce the present direction of secularization with other "modern" elements. On this question must hang the outcome of national (i.e., political) development in the Indian Union.

The potential for secularization of the major traditional props in India deserves some further comment, for there are no more important aspects of political life in Hindu society than the maintenance of caste and the veneration of the *Brahmin*. In some

40. Myron Weiner, "India: Two Political Cultures," in Pye and Verba, *Political Culture and Political Development*, pp. 199 ff.

recent instances, however, the perception of a shared political or economic interest in a particular section of India has been the occasion for widening the older basis of caste contact to include a number of related endogamous castes. Added to this are the improved transportation standards through extensive road-building programs, whereby the technical means for inter-caste contact has been further facilitated.[41] This does not mean a reduction in the political significance of caste, but probably the reverse: the extension of caste identity into ever broader reaches and encompassing a large number of allied caste groups.

One recent study boldly asserts that no dichotomy exists in India between traditional society and modern polity, but rather that the modern institutions of politics (parties, civil service, etc.) "establish their hegemony precisely by taking into their confidence the pluralities of the antecedent culture." According to this study, caste has provided a crucial and enduring medium for articulation of traditional and changing values in a manner commensurate with the symbols and processes of the modern political system.[42] The basic lesson learned from one caste federation, the *Gujerat Kshatriya Sabha,* is that whenever necessary, castes will make common cause with adjacent caste groups, even traditionally rival ones, for the furtherance of shared political goals; so that networks of personal influence follow, which cut through caste rigidities and tend to widen the basis of loyalty. In this sense, caste has considerable "secular potential" for aggregating inter-caste political interests in an interactional framework, producing a new form of caste organization based on similar interests and shared status aspirations.

Although to some extent the urge among lower castes to ally with higher ones is traditional (sanskritization), this would not explain the increasingly secular outlook of the upper castes—the need to function effectively in a modernizing and ever more competitive polity. Indeed, in the case of Gujerat the initiative came from the well-to-do *Rajputs;* and the motivation behind it

41. Lloyd R. Rudolph, "The Political Role of India's Caste Association," *Pacific Affairs,* XXXIII (1960), 1-22. See also M. N. Srinivas, *Caste in Modern India* (Bombay, 1964), pp. 15-41.

42. Rajni Kothari and Rushikesh Maru, "Caste and Secularism in India: Case Study of a Caste Federation," *Journal of Asian Studies,* XXV (November, 1965), 33. This case study was of a caste federation in Baroda and Kaira districts of Gujerat, and more specifically of the *Gujerat Kshatriya Sabha.*

points to an important shift in emphasis, "from the preservation of caste traditions and customs to their transformation through political power."[43]

With regard to the increase in political activity among the Indian villages and districts, and with regard to the consequences this could have for secular national development, there is considerable agreement as well as some similarity in thinking among students of Indian politics. The "gap-closers" of W. H. Morris-Jones' "modern and traditional idioms," the change described by Myron Weiner from a "punitive" to an "instrumental" image of government, and the "fusion of parochial and cosmopolitan outlooks" depicted by Lucian Pye are all references to roughly the same two things.[44] They are describing, first, the hard data drawn from Indian politics that point unmistakably toward an increasingly participant orientation across the length and breadth of the land; and second, they are voicing the hope that changing functional needs in India will somehow force to the surface the structural roles that will fit the pieces into place.

The idea that a new, synthetic Indian political culture is emerging, neither modern nor traditional but a composite of both, and drawing upon the older institutions and ways, has fairly clear parallels in other contexts. In his treatment of political culture and the modernization of Japan, for example, Robert E. Ward has suggested that traditional and modern cultures are "neither mutually exclusive nor polar opposites," and that the old, pre-Restoration political culture in Japan had a high developmental potential and was therefore readily adapted to a modern political life-style, mainly through the control devices of traditional society.[45] In short, Japan's unique record of modernization and development is explained in large part by the fact that modern Japan was only a short step, if a careful one, from traditional

43. *Ibid.*, p. 40.
44. Morris-Jones, "India's Political Idioms," p. 150; Weiner, "India: Two Political Cultures," p. 220; Pye, "The Political Context of National Development," p. 21. See also the observation of Richard L. Park that "Given time and responsive leadership, it is likely that the traditional and the rapidly modernizing elites would blend their values in pursuit of national goals. . . ." Richard L. Park, "Local Government and Political Development," (Paper delivered at the American Political Science Association convention, Washington, D. C., September, 1965), p. 4.
45. Robert E. Ward, "Japan: The Continuity of Modernization," in Pye and Verba, *Political Culture and Political Development*, especially pp. 78-82.

Japan. Japan, therefore, reflects today "a sort of mutually supportive or 'reinforcing dualism' in which the relationship between the two sectors has often been symbiotic rather than antagonistic."[46]

In a similar way successful efforts in India to plant the modern institutions of political order have been most conspicuous where they are reinforced by, not in conflict with, traditional ways. For example, local *panchayats* apparently work most effectively when their local leadership rests upon a traditional mystique. In the village of Dosma in Bihar state the village leader chosen was a woman, not because she was a woman, but because she was the widow of the ex-*Zamindar* of the area.[47]

The politicization of caste and village in India has not occurred in quite the way the urban and administrative elites would have had it. In many cases the rising ambitions of local politicians, combined with the generally low level of local administrative performance, have resulted in an elaborate system of corruption and bribery, usually in the form of a direct payment (*Bakshish*) from an interested person or group to a government official in order to expedite some administrative action.[48] These payments tend to be regularized by rates which vary according to the official's rank and other considerations. They also appear to have a functional relationship to the development process. In this respect, the functionality of the system-wide tendency toward corruption in Indian administration resembles similar tendencies in other modernizing contexts.[49]

In spite of all this, or perhaps because of it, members of the elite culture continue to view with some alarm the convergence of India's multiple political cultures into an increasingly homogeneous mass culture. Elites tend to react to competition and *Bakshish* with a growing despondency and a tendency to move

46. *Ibid.*, p. 80.
47. Most women in Bihar still practice *purdah* and are very backward educationally. See Nair, *Blossoms in the Dust*, pp. 94-95.
48. Weiner describes this sometimes elaborate practice in "India: Two Political Cultures," pp. 221-23. See also the comment on various responses to "corruption" in India, *ibid.*, pp. 142-44.
49. Martin Needler, "Political Development of Mexico," *American Political Science Review*, LV (June, 1961), especially 310-11. See also Edward L. Pinney and James E. Conley, "On Political Modernity in Mexico: Consensus and Recruitment," *The Southwestern Social Science Quarterly* (December, 1963), pp. 225-36.

farther away from rather than closer to the politics of the Indian countryside. Animated by principle and endowed with a sophisticated outlook, the national elites give very little indication of tolerating, much less encouraging, the political scrambles and patronage networks at the State Legislative Assemblies. To the extent that this distrust and suspicion are widely diffused throughout the elite-dominated structures, the pace of change and national development will be slow, halting, and perhaps disruptive. It is possible, on the other hand, that the intensification of massive political involvement will ultimately breed a greater capacity for acceptance and trust. In any event, it seems apparent that an understanding of the live trends and directions in India must depend upon a careful appreciation of the relevance of political culture in determining the peculiar idiom of political development.

VI

Appropriate formulation of the concept of political culture is characterized in various ways which are noted above.[50] A specific operational criterion is its usefulness in explaining why political systems develop as they do. The developmental patterns of post-independence India could be attributed to either or both of two types of influence: the directed efforts to bring about specified changes in Indian life, and the undirected "independent pressures of politics" which have introduced changes not formally part of a development "plan." The success of the former influences has been mixed in terms of the ends pursued. The latter influences have produced a fairly clear tendency in the system to develop according to some common analytical criteria for understanding the direction of political change.

On the basis of the argument presented in the early part of the paper, political culture as we construct the concept can offer helpful understanding of the behavior of the Indian system. The chief factual consideration is the presence within the Indian Union of several political cultures, variously coextensive with caste, language group, and state. Although a different focus in analysis would produce other dimensions of difference among cultures, our focus produces a unidimensional continuum defined by a "modern"-"traditional" axis. It is not simply as a matter of

50. *Supra*, p. 75, for example.

definition that we equate "modern" with certain cognitive, cathectic, and evaluative patterns, and "traditional" with others. There is empirical confirmation that among castes, etc., which instinctively tend to maintain customary patterns, the political system itself is cognized, cathected, and evaluated in appropriate, stable terms. In the groups that favor change in the directions perceived to be modern, our data show that the political system is cognized as inclusive and participatory as to membership and expanding as to scope of its activities; it is cathected positively for reasons of its instrumental value for nationalistic and economic goals; and it is evaluated preferentially over all other "traditional props" of the society such as village, caste, linguistic group, tribe, state, or religious sect. This description, of course, refers to the limit of the "modern" end of the continuum. It would be more exact to think of three separate continua, to wit:

TRADITIONAL				MODERN
exclusive			inclusive	
non-participatory			participatory	
static	(cognitive)		expanding	
negative			positive	
(obstructive)	(cathectic)		(instrumental)	
national political			national political	
system is prefer-			system is prefer-	
red to no other	(evaluative)		red to all other	
structures			structures	

This schema emphasizes the variety which we find in India. The variety of political cultures stems from the relative positions possible on the continua, and also from the fact that relative position of a population on one continuum is not necessarily coordinate with its relative positions on the other continua, nor is change in position even from one to the others.

To clarify this schema somewhat more we can return to one of the previous considerations: Is there any existential picture of the political system which corresponds to our constructed one? For the Indian situation, at least, the answer seems to be that the existential picture is only partial, the degree of its completeness varying among cultural groups. Whereas the Indian modernist can be very explicit about the inclusiveness of the political system, the Indian traditionalist may have almost no conception of

a "political" category at all. His expression of cathexis and evaluation may be traditional, his explicit rejection of the political
instinctive. Yet at the same time his behavior may fit into the
modern sector of these three continua. The village Indian may
profess distinctly traditional views, yet increasingly he *acts* "as
if" he held a different view of the political system. This sort of
anomaly perhaps helps to explain the cultural dualism which
several observers have noted. In order to bridge the gap between
"modern" behavior and "traditional" profession and belief, some
sort of satisfactory marriage of the two is required, to insure the
orderly and successful management of the development of the
nation and to preclude the alienation of the population.

The plans forwarded by the participants in the modern political culture—the members of the predominantly urban, Western-
oriented group structured primarily by the unity of the IAS and
the national leadership of the Congress Party—were directed
toward certain objective projects which were considered modernizing, and also toward the transformation of the other cultural
perspectives which threatened achievement of these goals. As we
have suggested, success was mixed, for the elite viewed the
problem from its own cultural perspective. The assumption is almost automatic in a modern political culture that increased productivity is a good thing from any point of view and that its
promotion as an output of the political system is appropriate.
The earlier reference to Kusum Nair's observations indicated
how unrealistic the assumption was in the Indian experiment. In
a cultural context in which concern for agricultural productivity
is not recognized as a political responsibility, in which political
officials are viewed with distaste and mistrust in any case, and in
which the religious remedy (prayer or the "ascetic option"), or
village alternative (borrowing), is preferred to application to the
state, then the sheer increase in productivity no longer appears as
simply a good thing. It is overlaid with a network of cognitive,
cathectic, and evaluative considerations which are difficult to appreciate from outside the cultural context. One cannot, in fact,
appreciate them, because every perception is colored by one's
own cultural point of view.[51]

51. This, of course, raises some question about the enterprise of social science
itself, although the reference here is to cross-cultural perceptions by political
actors. Some considerations of the problems of the sociology of knowledge are

On the other hand, the political system does seem to be evolving toward modernity under the "independent pressures of politics." Our model of political culture accommodates this situation too. An increased participation in the political system requires on the part of the participants a view of the political system in which this activity is proper. The politicization of some part of the society will tend in itself to modify all views of the political system in the direction of greater scope and degree of participation, especially when such politicization alters traditional relationships with other groups. The reason obviously is that some reorientation is necessary following such a rupture. A reorientation *through* the political is the only appropriate, and sometimes the only possible, way to accomplish it. The redistribution of power in the society represents just such adjustments, the affected cultural patterns tending to be more homogeneous as a result. The only response possible is some degree of modernization—for to respond at all is to respond politically. It is not surprising, then, that observers should begin to notice an emerging "mass culture" that is, in this case, an increasingly modern political culture. Mass culture in the political realm is modern, for it represents a view of the political system which is inclusive and participatory, expanding in scope, instrumental in pursuit of traditional-individual and innovative-social goals, and primary among the alternative personal and social agencies for achieving them.

Observations of changes in the mass are therefore simply observations of changes in cognition, cathexis, and evaluation, changes that reflect (or constitute) basic shifts in the cultural determinants of response to the stimuli of the political system. Whether or not such perceived changes are real and enduring, an operational concept of political culture will bring real benefits in helping to untangle the intellectual knots that appear in approaching the problem of political development. To the extent that political culture has been made operational as a concept for traversing a wide range of styles and changes in style, to that extent can we rely on its usefulness for probing the mysteries of political life in a limitless variety of cultures.

available in Karl Mannheim, *Ideology and Utopia* (New York, n.d.) and in Jacques J. P. Maquet, *The Sociology of Knowledge* (Boston, 1951).

III. INSTITUTIONAL DIMENSIONS

New Dimensions of West German Federalism

by Taylor Cole

I

For many years, West Germany has proved to be an attractive laboratory for students of federalism. The Empire and the Weimar Republic, and, more currently, the Federal Republic following the Nazi period, have been analyzed by a never-ending procession of competent critics. New terminology has come into use, and controversies no longer rage between the students of an earlier day over the differences between *Bundesstaat* and *Staatenbund*,[1] but between those who view the West German state as a decentralized unitary one,[2] or a unitary one with a "quasi-federal constitution,"[3] or a "unitary federal state";[4] and the federal system as being "executive-legislative federalism,"[5] "administrative federalism,"[6] or "co-operative federalism."[7] All of these points of view have able exponents, and all of them throw some light on certain aspects of the West German political system. However, they leave room for a new incursion, presented from still another point of departure and with special emphasis on the period since the national election of 1961. These changes have

1. Rupert Emerson, *State and Sovereignty in Modern Germany* (New Haven, 1948), Ch. 3.

2. Werner Weber, *Spannungen und Kraefte im westdeutschen Verfassungssystem* (2nd ed.; Stuttgart, 1958), pp. 18-19; Olle Nyman, *Der westdeutsche Foederalismus* (Stockholm, 1960), pp. 181 ff.

3. K. C. Wheare, "Some Theoretical Questions About Federalism," mimeographed IPSA paper (Oxford, Sept. 19-24, 1963), p. 5; *Federal Government* (3d ed.; London, 1953), p. 26.

4. Konrad Hesse, *Der unitarische Bundesstaat* (Karlsruhe, 1962).

5. Peter H. Merkl, "Executive-Legislative Federalism in West Germany," *American Political Science Review*, LIII (Sept., 1959), 732-41.

6. G. Sawer, "Federalism in West Germany," *Public Law*, VI (Spring, 1961), pp. 26-44; Herbert Jacob, *German Administration since Bismarck: Central Authority versus Local Autonomy* (New Haven, 1963), pp. 178 ff., 206 ff.

7. Peter Lerche, "Foederalismus als nationales Ordnungsprinzip," in *Veroeffentlichungen der Vereinigung der deutschen Staatsrechtslehrer*, Heft 21 (Berlin, 1964), pp. 70-71, esp. literature cited in fn. 18; Paul G. Kauper, "The Constitution of West Germany and the United States: a Comparative Study," *Michigan Law Review*, LVIII (June, 1960), 1152, 1157; Roger H. Wells, *The States in West German Federalism* (New York, 1961), pp. 81, 93-98.

seen the end of the Adenauer era, an end heralded by the national election of 1961 and embodied in the results of the election of September 19, 1965. This last election strengthened the position of Chancellor Erhard in his relationship with the Adenauer faction of the Christian Democratic Union, a relationship sometimes referred to as the "two-chancellor" system.

The point of departure for this paper will be the conception of federalism as a process for reaching a continuing adjustment or a dynamic equilibrium between the centripetal and centrifugal, the unifying and the disunifying, forces in a society. In political context, it is the process by which, under the impact of centrifugal and centripetal pressures, a continuing adjustment is made in the relationships between the central government and the governments of the constituent units of a political system.[8] Put in the phraseology of C. J. Friedrich, federalism

is *either* the process by which a number of separate political organizations, be they states or any other kind of association, enter into arrangements for working out solutions together, that is to say adopting joint policies and making joint decisions on common problems, *or* the process through which a hitherto unitarily organized political community, as it becomes differentiated into a number of separate and distinct political sub-communities, achieves a new order in which the differentiated communities, now separately organized, become capable of making out separately and on their own those solutions they no longer have in common.[9]

I will start with the assumption that there is still a wide, if tacit, acceptance in Germany of the concept of the nation-state, with Hegelian undertones, as being the ultimate source of morality and law.[10] The state in Germany, to quote Leonard Krieger, became "both the actual organization and the ideal symbol for the compatible integration of . . . areas of individual freedom into the established order of political government and social hierarchy."[11] Consistent with this view, the forces which were

8. William S. Livingston, *Federalism and Constitutional Change* (London, 1956), p. 4; Robert O. Tilman and Taylor Cole (eds.), *The Nigerian Political Scene* (Durham, N. C., 1962), p. 62.

9. "New Tendencies in Federal Theory and Practice," mimeographed IPSA paper (Geneva, Sept. 21-25, 1964), p. 3.

10. Ralph Dahrendorf, "Conflict and Liberty: Some Remarks on the Social Structure of German Politics," *British Journal of Sociology*, XIV (Sept., 1963), 197 ff.

11. *The German Idea of Freedom* (Boston, 1957), p. 469.

operative in varying degrees during the period of the Empire were centralistic and integrative, and operated to minimize group diversity and the autonomy of constituent units. The decay of federalism during the Weimar Republic culminated in the end of federalism during the Third Reich. More immediately, the facts of economic life have led to a decline in intra-state federalism in western Europe and have been particularly operative in Western Germany. The façade of a revived but artificial federalism in the Bonn Republic must be interpreted on a background of "industrial combines, mail order houses, opinion factories, labor unions, communication and transportation system, run on a unified basis and under a common law."[12] Contributing to make the federal features more of a façade have been the "pulls" toward the center generated by the growing significance of foreign relations, defense, and emergency considerations, which are handled in Bonn, and the decline in importance of the limited number of powers reserved to the states. An aggressive federal bureaucracy has allegedly contributed to these "pulls." The governmental and party leadership during the Adenauer era meant national leadership, which effectively converted the Christian Democratic Union from its earlier leanings in 1948-49 into a centralist instrument.

It is also maintained that the artificiality of the constituent units, the German states (*Laender*), provides little basis for sound counterdevelopments. Only Bavaria and the Hansa cities of Hamburg and Bremen can be said to have a genuine historical continuity, land tradition, regional patriotism, and community consciousness; the others to varying degrees are the results of post-World War II fiat, and the creation of some of them was coupled with the dismemberment of Prussia. Early public opinion polls showed little popular understanding of the activities, or acquaintance with the officials, of the states, and little interest in the continued existence of the states.[13] Despite the

12. Otto Kirchheimer, "German Democracy in the 1950's," *World Politics*, XIII (Jan., 1961), 259, and "The Decline of Intra-State Federalism in Western Europe," *ibid.*, III (April, 1951), 293-97. See also the papers by Heinz Kreutzer, Ossip K. Flechtheim, and Gert von Eynern in Ossip K. Flechtheim (ed.), *Bund und Laender* (Berlin, 1959).

13. In 1953, some 60 per cent of a random sample of Germans indicated that they would favor the outright abolition of the *Laender* in favor of a "centralized national government in Bonn." Erich P. Neumann and Elizabeth Noelle,

effervescence of interest groups in Germany, there are many which are both centrally-located and -oriented and few which are committed to "states' rights." The voters in Germany, it is claimed, are also "nationally-oriented." In short, both long- and short-range considerations have contributed to minimize the significance of Munich, Duesseldorf, and Hamburg, and have pointed to Bonn where the center for decision-making on all major issues is to be found.

Despite considerable validity in this analysis, which results in presenting a composite straw man, the contention here is that it fails to take adequately into account the role of the "federalizers" in the German political system, to borrow an expression from Professor Dolf Sternberger. The federalizers during a period of integration may well be the institutions and groups of a particular state, such as those in Prussia in the German Empire during the second half of the nineteenth century; during a period of disintegration or separation, they may include such institutions and groups as the nationalist parties, as in the case of independent African states formerly in the British Empire and now in the Commonwealth. In the Federal Republic, I shall consider the chief federalizers to be those institutions which are mobilizing effectively the legal forces and group pressures in order to limit the centralization and centrally imposed unifying trends, to maintain a continuing partnership between Federation (*Bund*) and states, and to support the dynamic role of the constituent units in the West German political system. The institutions which are playing the key part in reflecting the outlook, in preserving the autonomy, and in guaranteeing the effective and co-operative involvement of the states in the German political system are the Bundesrat, the Federal Constitutional Court, the major political parties, and certain of the institutions of the states. It will be the objective of this paper to examine each briefly, and to assay its part in the swing of the pendulum of federalism toward a new equilibrium in the post-Adenauer period.

II

First mention may be made of the Bundesrat. Article 50 of the Basic Law provides that "the *Laender* shall participate

Antworten: Politik in Kraftfeld der oeffentlichen Meinung (Allensbach am Bodensee, 1954); Jacob, *German Administration*, p. 210.

through the Bundesrat in the legislation and administration of the Federation." The Bundesrat is composed of a total of 41 members, of whom from 3 to 5 members, depending on population, are selected by the Governments of each of the *Laender*. Each delegation votes as a bloc. The Bundesrat was originally viewed as a "continuous Congress of *Land* Ministers" and it has maintained this character to the present. Much of its work is in fact done in its committees, which are composed of members from the state administrations.

Since the Bundesrat has been carefully studied in the recent period by a number of thoughtful scholars,[14] I shall limit myself to two general observations. The first is that its functions have assumed added importance with the passage of the years and are more significant today than could have been anticipated by the framers of the Basic Law. Legislation of specified types, affecting, for example, the physical structure of the federal government, the rights and competences of the states, the administration of much federal legislation, certain fiscal measures, etc., requires the approval of the Bundesrat. The extent of the sharp and unanticipated growth in the volume of this type of legislation can be seen in the fact that during the four legislative periods between 1949-1965 some 1,178 out of 1,934 bills acted upon by the Bundesrat fell in the prescribed categories (as defined by the Bundesrat). Though the use of the Mediation Committee between the two houses involved only 181 bills during the first three parliamentary periods, and though the Bundesrat imposed its initial veto on "second passage" in only 17 instances,[15]

14. Edward L. Pinney, *Federalism, Bureaucracy, and Party Politics in Western Germany* (Chapel Hill, 1963); Jacob, *German Administration*, Chs. 6-7; Karlheinz Neunreither, "Politics and Bureaucracy in the West German Bundesrat," *American Political Science Review*, LIII (Sept., 1959), 713-31, and "Federalism and West German Bureaucracy," *Political Studies*, VII (1959), 233-45. Neunreither's studies are based on his larger work, *Der Bundesrat zwischen Politik und Verwaltung* (Heidelberg, 1959).

15. Minister President Georg Kiesinger in *Ueber die bundesstaatliche Ordnung der Bundesrepublik: Beitraege zu Fragen des deutschen Foederalismus* (Bonn, 1962), p. 10. During the fourth parliamentary period, which ended in July, 1965, there were 39 calls involving 37 bills (*Gesetze*) for reference to the Mediation Committee, composed of members from the two houses of Parliament. Of these requests, 35 came from the Bundesrat, 1 from the Bundestag, and 3 from the Government. This number of bills referred to the Mediation Committee may be compared with 71 for the first, 61 for the second, and 49 for the third parliamentary period. *Bundesanzeiger*, Jan. 17, 1962, p. 4, and information furnished by officials of the Bundesrat.

there is reason to believe that the anticipated reactions by the Bundesrat may have influenced the Government and the Bundestag in the initial framing and handling of a great amount of the legislative product.

Second, despite some tendency to duplicate "Bonn politics" in the *Laender*, and in certain important cases to become an "agency for the subordination of *Land* to federal policy,"[16] there is compelling evidence that the Bundesrat as a legislative body acts as an effective agent of state interests. "The Bundesrat does in fact act specifically to protect governmental integrity and freedom of action at the *Land* level," contends Edward L. Pinney, "and does in fact maintain a sensitive and protective attitude within the Federal Parliament toward *Land* governmental interests."[17] The clearest instances are those where the Bundesrat has taken its position in response to importunings from the state governments in the face of contrary positions taken by the Federal Government and by the Bundestag. Three recent illustrations may be cited. The Bundesrat in 1963 refused to approve the increase in the percentage distribution of revenues from the income and corporation taxes accepted by the Government and the Bundestag, and the final adjustment which secured Bundesrat approval resulted in a much smaller allocation to the Federation than had been demanded and expected.[18] The original position of the Bundesrat found its rationale in the vigorous criticism by Minister President Franz Meyers of North Rhine Westphalia, and his colleagues, of the use of fiscal powers by the Federation to subvert the division of powers in the Basic Law, and his appeal to the Bundesrat to check this trend by the use of

16. Pinney, *Federalism*, p. 137.

17. *Ibid.*, p. 173.

18. The Cabinet of Adenauer had argued that the percentage allocation to the Federal Government should be increased from 35% to 40.5% for 1963 and to 41.5% thereafter. The final agreement reached, after acrimonious discussion and legislative actions which brought the position of the Bundesrat into square conflict with that of the Government and the Bundestag, was that the Federation would receive 38% in 1963 and 39% in 1964-66. See *Bundesgesetzblatt* (*BGBL.*), 1964, Part I, p. 137, and documents in James K. Pollock and John C. Lane, *Source Materials on the Government and Politics of Germany* (Ann Arbor, 1964), pp. 304-5. Approximately one-fourth of the expenditures of the Federation comes from its percentage of these taxes. Each percentage point increase is estimated to yield 0.5 billion DM. Peter Scholz, *Die Deutsche Demokratie* (Munich, 1964), p. 151.

its veto powers under Article 106(4).[19] To take a different type of recent illustration, the Bundesrat in 1964 rejected on "second reading," for the first time in its history, the ratification law for a treaty between the Federal Republic and Spain which had been approved in the Bundestag by a decisive majority.[20] In the late summer of 1965, the Bundesrat also rejected the controversial *Wasserhaushaltsgesetz*, one of the several measures passed by the Fourth Bundestag toward the end of its session in 1965.[21]

By and large, the Bundesrat, where electoral considerations have entered, has followed the Bundestag in approving measures involving appropriations from federal funds.[22] A major exception was its action, in 1965, in securing a heavy reduction in the appropriations voted by the politically conscious Bundestag in the 18th amendment to the Equalization of Burdens Law.[23] At the same time, the Bundesrat during the most recent period has shown determination and rigidity in asserting its powers in instances where either the financial position or resources of the states are adversely affected or where there are threatened restrictions on their administrative competences. Its early reservations to two of the laws finally enacted in 1965 to deal with emergency situations, after amendments had been added, are in point.[24]

The role of the Bundesrat in providing a meeting ground for federal and state bureaucracies will be separately discussed.

19. *Klare Aufgabenenteilung zwischen Bund und Laendern* (Duesseldorf, 1963). Note also the later reactions of Minister President Zinn of Hesse in *Frankfurter Allgemeine Zeitung*, July 9, 1965.

20. *Ibid.*, Dec. 19, 1964. The ratification law of the treaty, which provided certain social security benefits to former members of the Spanish "Blue Division" active on the German side during World War II, was ultimately approved by the Bundesrat after consideration by the Mediation Committee. *BGBL.*, 1965, Part II, pp. 273 ff.

21. *Frankfurter Allgemeine Zeitung*, July 10, 1965; *ibid.*, July 23, 1965.

22. Thomas Ellwein, *Das Regierungssystem der Bundesrepublik Deutschland* (Cologne, 1963), p. 181.

23. One favorable newspaper comment on this action by the Bundesrat might be quoted:

"Den braven Maennern im Bundesrat muss ein Loblied gesungen werden.... Indem sie von ihrem verfassungsmaessigen Recht Gebrauch machten, erreichen sie die Streichung von vierundeinerhalben Milliarde DM aus einem Gesetz, das der bewilligungsfreudige Bundestag im Schlussgalopp von den Wahlen beschlossen hatte."

From *Berliner Tagesspiegel*, reprinted in *Frankfurter Allgemeine Zeitung*, July 27, 1965.

24. The *Schutzbau-* and *Selbstschutzgesetze*.

Here one need only say that the Bundesrat does provide a forum for the effective presentation of the positions and points of view of the state bureaucracies in its committees, and especially where procedural matters are involved.

In the view of Karlheinz Neunreither, the Bundesrat has strengthened the position of the states vis-à-vis the Federal Government, has served as an effective check on legislation which had with Cabinet encouragement been passed by the Bundestag, and has provided the *Land* bureaucracies with "means for checking federal legislative and administrative activities."[25] These conclusions have been widely accepted in the years since publication of his study in 1959.[26]

III

The position of the Federal Constitutional Court as the guarantor of the Constitution and as the umpire of the federal system has been analyzed on a number of occasions.[27] The legal position and powers of the states have been carefully interpreted by the Court in a number of decisions beginning with the first major case in 1951, the Southwest Case.[28] In sum, the Court has placed heavy stress upon the division of powers in the Basic Law and has given careful recognition to the reserved powers, including those in the cultural sphere, which fall within the "exclusive competence" of the *Laender*, as well as to the equal rights of the

25. Neunreither, *American Political Science Review*, LIII (Sept., 1959), 729.

26. Ellwein, *Das Regierungssystem*, pp. 172-82; Hans-Josef Vonderbeck, *Der Bundesrat—Ein Teil des Parlaments der Bundesrepublik Deutschland* (Meisenheim am Glam, 1964), pp. 88-89; and Peter Hahl, *Die Bundesaufsicht durch den Bundesrat* (Munich, 1964), pp. 89-102.

27. See literature cited in Taylor Cole, "The West German Constitutional Court: An Appraisal After Six Years," *Journal of Politics*, XX (May, 1958), 278-307, and "Three Constitutional Courts," *American Political Science Review*, LIII (Dec., 1959), 963-84; and a recent appraisal by a former member of the Court, Ernst Friesenhahn, "Aufgabe und Funktion des Bundesverfassungsgerichts," *Beilage zum wochen Zeitung Das Parlament*, B 6/65, Feb. 10, 1965, pp. 3-20.

28. 1 BVerfGE 14. A summary of the main "constitutional principles," or interpretations, to be derived from these cases has been prepared annually for official purposes by Georg Diller, and published as a *Beilage zum Bundesanzeiger*. See, in particular, the "Rechtsprechung," under Part II of the Basic Law ("The Federation and the States"), Part VII ("The Legislation of the Federation"), and Part X ("Financial Affairs"). The issues since 1962 are No. 42 of March 1, 1962; No. 67 of April 5, 1963; No. 84 of May 6, 1964; and No. 85 of May 7, 1965.

Laender under the Constitution.[29] During its decade and a half of activity, the Court moved slowly and carefully at first to consolidate its position, to acquire a high *esprit de corps* among the members of its two Senates, now composed of eight members each, and to issue a sophisticated collection of decisions involving constitutional questions. From the beginning, the Court has consistently and sympathetically concerned itself with the federal developments in Germany, though its attitude "toward the constitutional position of the *Land* governments" was not marked as much during the early days as it was later by its concern to enhance their position in the federal system.[30]

The evolution of the role of the Court from one of early restraint to one of "judicial activism,"[31] insofar as the decisions affecting federal relationships are concerned, can be best traced through the decisions in which the Court's interpretation of "federal comity " (*Bundestreue*), based on the general provisions of the Basic Law governing federal relationships, has been unfolded. The Court, through its Second Senate, explicitly discussed federal comity in the Housing Funds case from Bavaria in 1952,[32] and then proceeded to develop this concept in a series of subsequent decisions. In one of them, involving the constitutionality of North Rhine Westphalia classification and salary scales, the Court, while recognizing that the scales *could* affect improperly those of the Federation and of other *Laender*, upheld them as falling within the state's province and as "giving their civil service a particular countenance."

In the Concordat and Atomic Weapons Referendum cases in 1957 and 1958, the Court broadened its interpretation of the substantive content of federal comity. In the Concordat Case,[33] the Court, in simultaneously recognizing the continuing validity of

29. Guenter Zehner, "Die Rechtsprechung des Bundesverfassungsgerichts zum Aufbau des Staates," in *Das Bundesverfassungsgericht* (Karlsruhe, 1963), pp. 199 ff.

30. Gerard Braunthal, "Federalism in Germany: The Broadcasting Controversy," *Journal of Politics*, XXIV (Aug., 1962), 559-61; Donald R. Reich, "Court, Comity, and Federalism in West Germany," *Midwest Journal of Political Science*, VII (Aug., 1963), 206.

31. This characterization is questioned in a thoughtful article by a member of the Court, Hans Kutscher, "Staat und Wirtschaft in der Rechtsprechung des Bundesverfassungsgerichts," *Schriftenreihe der Hochschule Speyer*, XXII, 239 ff.

32. 1 BVerfGE 299 (1952); Reich, *Midwest Journal of Political Science*, VII (Aug., 1963), 208-9.

33. 6 BVerfGE 309 (1957).

the Concordat of 1933, and the constitutionality of allegedly conflicting school legislation of Lower Saxony, as falling under the reserved powers of the state, again took an opportunity to discuss federal comity. In the Atomic Weapons Referendum Case,[34] the Court felt that the *Land,* Hesse, had violated its obligations under federal comity in failing to take action to prevent certain municipalities from holding referenda on atomic rearmament. Comity here had been violated not by *positive* action of the *Land* but by its *failure* to act.

These cases were a prelude for the Television decision of Feb. 28, 1961,[35] where the Court gave strong evidence of its un-written concern over the dangers of uncontrolled centralization.[36] In this case, the Court held that a series of actions of the Federal Government leading ultimately to the creation of a new television corporation under federal control had resulted in a violation of the freedoms guaranteed under Art. 5 of the Basic Law. The Court consequently granted the relief requested by the four plaintiff state governments which had charged an infringement on their reserved powers in cultural matters and a lack of "respect for the federal order." In so deciding, the Court also stated in sharp and no uncertain terms that the Federal Government by the style of its action had gone beyond the bounds of acceptable procedure. The entire "constitutional relationships between the nation and its constituent members, as well as the relationships among the constituent members" are governed by the obligations of federal comity, said the Court. These relationships require the use of proper procedure, which in turn assumes the equal treatment of all states and the avoidance of improper pressures to secure state acquiescence in federal wishes.[37]

34. 8 BVerfGE 123 (1958).

35. 12 BVerfGE 205 (1961). An English translation of the pertinent selections from this decision may be found in Pollock and Lane, *Source Materials,* pp. 138-39.

36. Edward McWhinney, *Constitutionalism in Germany and the Federal Constitutional Court* (Leyden, 1962), p. 60.

37. Note the summary in Georg Diller, "Die Rechtsprechung des Bundes-verfassungsgerichts im Jahre 1961," *Beilage zum Bundesanzeiger,* No. 42 of March 1, 1962, pp. 11-12. There has been no major case since the Television decision in which the Court has had occasion to discuss federal comity. For sub-sequent references by the Court, which have neither added to, nor, contrary to some claims, subtracted from the breadth of its interpretation in the Television decision. See 13 BVerfGE 54 (1961), pp. 75 ff., and 14 BVerfGE 197 (1962), p. 215.

"Where the development of Bonn federalism is concerned we are in the realm of judicial supremacy," commented one competent observer, "and the principal instrument the Court has evolved for exercising its oversight is its doctrine of federal comity."[38] Without question, the Court, in giving application to its own premises regarding federalism and federal comity, threw down the gauntlet to the Adenauer Government, which had made a political issue of the television matter. If the Court has thus become in a special sense the supreme arbiter of the federal system, then the danger in failing to exercise adequate judicial self-restraint in the period ahead, as Gerhard Leibholz, a professor and distinguished member of the Court, has observed,[39] is an obvious one.[40]

In short, the work of the Court has been marked by the assumption of broad discretionary power, particularly through its interpretations of federal comity, in its decisions involving federal relationships. The Court's position has been buttressed by the respect for a judicial interpretation of a written constitution and by the prestige which the Court has deservedly acquired in West Germany. This confidence in the Court has been reflected in the provisions of projected constitutional amendments and legislation to deal with emergency situations, in which the position and normal functioning of the Court are carefully safeguarded. But there are storm signals, as illustrated in the summer of 1963 when unhappy members of Parliament successfully opposed the re-election of one of the judges.

Whatever the pitfalls which may be faced by it in the future, the Court has in the meantime given effective judicial recognition of the importance of the states in the federal system. For this reason, the Court joins the Bundesrat in the ranks of the major federalizers, indeed, as the most important one.

38. Reich, *Midwest Journal of Political Science*, VII (Aug., 1963), 223.
39. In a preface to McWhinney, *Constitutionalism*, p. 16.
40. Thoughtful and sympathetic explanations and interpretations of *Bundestreue* by members of the Court may be found in Willi Geiger, "Die wechselseitige Treuepflicht von Bund und Laendern," in *Foederalistische Ordnung* (Koblenz, 1961), pp. 113-28; Hans G. Rupp, "Zum Problem der Bundestreue im Bundesstaat," *Festgabe fuer Carlo Schmid* (Tuebingen, 1962), pp. 141-52, esp. p. 152; and (President) Gebhard Mueller, "Bundestreue im Bundesstaat," *Festschrift fuer Ministerpraesident Kurt Georg Kiesinger* (Stuttgart, 1964), pp. 213-34.

IV

The political parties, which have a special recognition in Art. 21 of the Basic Law, are also among the important institutions participating in the collective efforts of the federalizers. Much has been written on the shift in the positions on federalism of the CDU, the party in power, and the SPD, the party out of power, during the past 16 years. Certainly, the traditionally "centralist" SPD became during the Adenauer period a defender of state and local autonomy. Nearly 50,000 *Parteibuchbeamte* at the state and local level had come in 1965 to provide the backbone of the party, which had increasingly entrenched itself in the governments of a large percentage of the urban areas as well as of certain of the states. The SPD's advocacy before the Federal Constitutional Court has been mentioned, and this ground need not be covered again. A brief reference to internal organization, methods of nomination, finance, electoral trends, and other developments would be in order, however.

In terms of organization, the Social Democratic Party (SPD), with the largest dues-paying membership, is the most centralistically organized of the parties. With a far smaller number of dues-paying members, with more limited economic enterprises and on-going activities, and with fewer party agents, the Christian Democratic Union (CDU) is, at least in theory, a more loosely organized party.[41] The Free Democratic Party (FDP) has had a tradition of "maximum decentralization of structure and diffusion of power," and the semi-autonomous state parties provide much of the strength of the Party as a whole. The confederated character of the Party means that the composition and decisions of the leadership at the top frequently represent compromises of the state party chieftains.[42] Certainly, the FDP, if we exclude the Christian Social Union (CSU), is *organizationally* the least centralized and most *Land*-oriented of the major parties.[43]

41. Arnold J. Heidenheimer, *The Government of Germany* (New York, 1961), p. 71. But on the complexities of the internal party structure, considered from a sociological point of view, see Ulrich Lohmar, *Innerparteiliche Demokratie* (Stuttgart, 1963), Part I. Lohmar is an active SPD member.

42. Ellwein, *Das Regierungssystem*, pp. 78, 81; Gerard Braunthal, "The Free Democratic Party in West German Politics," *Western Political Quarterly*, XIII (June, 1960), 334-35.

43. No attempt has been made to compare the programs of the major parties

The nomination procedure of party candidates for the Bundestag is regulated by national law.[44] Speaking generally, the selection of constituency candidates rests with the constituency party organizations or membership, in accordance with the election laws which have sought to decentralize and democratize the procedures. The party lists for selection by proportional representation are filled at the state level, with nominations usually being made by the *Land* executive committee but with formal approval by party conventions required. It is difficult to generalize about the influence of the central party leadership, which is certainly present in varying degrees in these selections. However, it is clear that local considerations are usually more important than are any conflicting preferences of the central leadership in the choice of constituency candidates.[45] While the central party leadership plays a more direct and effective part in the final preparation of the state lists, here again *Land* considerations and influences are quite important.[46]

Public information on party finance, which has been quite limited in the past, was considerably broadened by the factual disclosures in the oral hearings in June 23-24, 1965, of the case brought before the Federal Constitutional Court by the Allied German Party (DP/BHE) and the Bavarian Party (BP), questioning the constitutionality of federal appropriations through the Ministry of the Interior for party purposes in 1962 and 1964.[47] The *Land* Hesse joined in the proceedings as an interested party and attacked the constitutionality of *any direct* federal appropriation to political parties.[48]

---

as they were presented during the Bundestag election of 1965. However, it may be mentioned that the FDP is the only one of these parties which favored the establishment of a national ministry of culture during that election campaign.

44. The Law of May 7, 1956, as amended through Feb. 14, 1964. *BGBL.*, 1964, Part I, pp. 61 ff. See especially Part IV of the present Law.

45. Ellwein, *Das Regierungssystem*, pp. 82-83.

46. Lohmar, *Demokratie*, pp. 70-73. Cf. Alfred Juettner, *Wahl und Waehlen* (Munich, n.d.), pp. 68 ff., a study distributed in 1965 by the CDU/CSU parties. On the role of the *Land* committees in the selection of the *Land* lists of the SPD, CDU, and FDP parties in Hesse and Lower Saxony in the 1965 Bundestag election, see *Frankfurter Allgemeine Zeitung*, June 25, 1965.

47. The decision of the Court was to be rendered in November, 1965, after the parliamentary election but was postponed until some later date.

48. The oral hearings are not published and the author is relying upon notes taken by him during the public depositions by the Treasurers of the political parties represented in the Bundestag. The best summaries of these hearings may

The following facts are pertinent for the moment. First, as a sequel to the decision of the Federal Constitutional Court in 1958 declaring unconstitutional those provisions of the federal income-tax laws permitting deduction of party contributions for income-tax purposes,[49] the Federal Government began in 1959 to make appropriations to political parties. By 1962, the amount of the appropriations had increased to 20 million DM, 5 million being allocated for political educational purposes and 15 million for general party purposes, and by 1964 to 38 million DM, all of which was allocated for general party purposes. Second, the approximate percentage of the total expenditures of the national parties derived from public funds at the national level between 1962 and 1964 had grown from 41% to 55% in the case of the CDU (out of total expenditures in 1964 of 32.4 million DM), from 32.6% to 39.6% in the case of the SPD (out of total expenditures in 1964, not including any funds from its economic enterprises, of 44.8 million DM), and from 32.2% to 52.8% in the case of the FDP (out of total expenditures in 1964 of 13.7 million DM, of which nearly 6 million came from state sources).[50] The amount derived in 1964 by the CDU from membership dues was 3.2 million, and by the SPD was 15.1 million DM. In sum, the percentage of *publicly reported* expenditures of the two coalition parties derived from public sources in the *non-election year* of 1964 had

be found in the *Frankfurter Allgemeine Zeitung*, June 23, 1965, and June 24, 1965, and the *Stuttgarter Zeitung*, June 23, 1965. The most complete survey of the literature is to be found in Wilhelm Kewenig, "Die Problematik der unmittelbaren staatlichen Parteifinanzierung," *Die Oeffentliche Verwaltung*, XVII (Dec., 1964), 829-40. Particular mention is there made of Ulrich Duebber, *Parteifinanzierung in Deutschland* (Cologne, 1962) and Theodor Eschenburg, *Probleme der modernen Parteifinanzierung* (Tuebingen, 1961), and other writings by these two authors. Useful data may also be found in U. W. Kitzinger, *German Electoral Politics* (Oxford, 1960); Ulrich Duebber and Gerard Braunthal, "West Germany," *Journal of Politics*, XXV (Nov., 1963), 774-89; and Nevil Johnson, "State Finance for Political Parties in Western Germany," *Parliamentary Affairs*, XVIII (Fall, 1965), 279-92, esp. pp. 287-90, where drafts of Government and SPD bills to deal with public financing of political parties are compared.

49. 8 BVerfGE 51.

50. Some rough comparisons can be made with the year 1963, that is with the year before the augmented appropriations of 1964 were available, by reference to "Pressemitteilungen und Informationen SPD," No. 109/64, of March 17, 1964. Note comments on these figures in Hans Friedrich and Winfried Zehetmeier, *Parteien* (Munich, 1964), pp. 116-17, a study distributed by the CDU during the 1965 election campaign.

increased to well over one-half of their total reported outlays.[51] Third, the growth in the amount of direct public subsidies to the parties, distributed in accordance with the discretion of the central leadership of the parties, has apparently served to strengthen the control of the central party organizations and to reduce their dependence upon private, as well as state, sources of support which might have more regional and even local orientation. Fourth, the allocation of direct federal subsidies was limited to those four parties represented in the Bundestag in 1964 namely the CDU, CSU, SPD, and FDP. Minor parties, including at least one of the plaintiff parties dependent upon particular state support, claimed with substantial justification that they had been deprived of "equal chances" under Art. 3 of the Basic Law in the appropriations made for party purposes in 1962 and 1964.

The revelations before the Court in the "Party Finance" case suggest that this type of public party financing, whatever its merits, had the effect both of increasing the authority of the central leadership of the major parties and of restricting the competitive chances of minor parties[52] which were state-based and locally oriented. It was also revealed that there were varying but important responsibilities of the state organizations working at state levels, and subject to particular state influences, which affected the federal relationship within the parties. However that may be, the decision of the Court will affect vitally the internal federal relationships of the major parties as well as the "equal chances" of minor parties.

Those features of party organization and development in the matter of party finance which stress the aspects of state or local influence or control can, if uncritically viewed, give a misleading picture. The changes in the electoral laws from 1949 through the

51. Kewenig estimated that approximately 60% of the major party expenditures in 1964 came from public (federal *and* state) sources. *Die Oeffentliche Verwaltung*, XVIII (Dec., 1964), 840. The difficulties in procuring reliable statistics on *all* expenditures for *all* purposes for political parties, however the limits be defined, are obvious. See Duebber and Braunthal, *Journal of Politics*, XXV (Nov., 1963), 776-81.

52. Heidenheimer observed in 1957 (two years before the policy of *direct* public financing at the national level had been instituted) that, in the case of the CDU "in contrast to the theory underlying its federal organization," campaign funds flowed not from the *Laender* to Bonn but from "the national to the local level." "German Party Finance: The C.D.U.," *American Political Science Review*, LI (June, 1957), 385. Cf. Duebber and Braunthal, *Journal of Politics*, XXV (Nov., 1963), 774-89.

third law of 1957, as amended in 1964, resulted in the creation of a National Boundaries Commission, the stiffening of the minor party quotas (so that a party must now secure either three constituency seats or five per cent of the popular vote before being entitled to seats under the proportional distribution arrangement), and the elimination of the states in actual practice from any effective participation in the distribution of the seats under the combined *Land* tests for the application of the D'Hondt system of proportionality. These changes all seem to stress the national and unified aspects of the electoral system.[53] Indeed, U. W. Kitzinger has charged that "the evolution of the electoral system in fact clearly reveals on the one hand a progressive abandonment of States' Rights and the progressive adoption of a rather more federal basis of calculation, and on the other hand an increasing severity in the application of the 5 per cent clause against small parties."[54]

How much these electoral law changes have affected the voter appeal is an open question, but the results have clearly indicated a progressive increase in the percentage of popular votes for the three major parties, the SPD, CDU/CSU, and FDP, at both the national and state levels. The percentage for the three parties in national elections has grown from 72.1% of the total in 1949 to 96.4% in 1965 (86.9% of the 1965 percentage for the SPD and CDU/CSU, and 9.5% for the FDP).

Despite some currency of local issues and the fact that *Land* elections are held at times different from those for national elections, the voting pattern in the state elections through 1961 was not far different from that in the national elections. In these *Land* elections, beginning with those for the period 1950-1953, the FDP and the minor parties have progressively declined in the average popular vote received and in the number and percentage of Landtag seats held.[55] Nevertheless, the FDP, in the light of

53. The significance here of the surprising fact that constituency members of the CDU have shown less deviancy in their voting in the Bundestag than the party list members is not clear. See G. L. Rueckart and W. Crane, "CDU Deviancy in the German Bundestag," *Journal of Politics*, XXIV (Aug., 1962), 479.

54. "West German Electoral Law," *Parliamentary Affairs*, XI (Spring, 1958), 222.

55. See the electoral data in Egon Klepsch, Guenther Mueller, and Rudolf Wildenmann, *Die Bundestagswahl 1965* (Munich, 1965), pp. 148-50.

some gains in the national election of 1961[56] and the results of state elections after that date, was in 1964 represented in the coalition government at the national level, held in 1964 some 23 out of 96 cabinet posts in the *Laender* (including Berlin), and was included in nine out of eleven of the state party governing coalitions (six with CDU/CSU minister presidents and five with SPD minister presidents or equivalent).[57] Minor parties were represented by one cabinet member (GDP) in Hesse and by one (BP) in Bavaria. This FDP cabinet representation in 1964 was a substantial growth in number of portfolios over 1962 when the party held only thirteen. These figures evidence a broadening of the national base of the FDP, although its leadership and support are still heavily concentrated in two or three *Land* centers. They also evidence the fact, significant for a study of federalism, of the continued decline in the strength of minor parties which are *Land* and regionally based.

There are a number of explanations which can be offered for these party developments: the economic prosperity, the electoral law, and others. But all of them must also take account of the role of Chancellor Adenauer as the "broker" and "master integrator" of the CDU.[58] The Chancellor helped in narrowing the voters' alternatives, in the end, to pro- and anti-Adenauer choices. As a consequence, the impact of the party system not only in the states but also on the Bundesrat and the Federal Constitutional Court necessarily reflected the experience of the Adenauer era. During this era the Bundesrat exhibited a hesitancy to clash with either the Government or the Bundestag where strong partisan

56. The FDP secured 12.8% of the votes cast in this election, although the FDP's 1961 gains did not include a single constituency seat.

57. See compilation in Pollock and Lane, *Source Materials*, p. 175. As of the end of 1964, the SPD held 850, the CDU/CSU 811, the FDP 182, and other parties 26 out of the 1869 seats in the Bundestag and Landtage. *Frankfurter Allgemeine Zeitung*, Nov. 24, 1964. The FDP lost three of its seven Landtag seats, but is still represented in the CDU-FDP coalition government following the *Land* election in the Saar on June 27, 1965. *New York Times* (int. ed.), June 28, 1965. There was in July, 1965, only one instance of a governing coalition of CDU/SPD members, typical in the *Laender* in 1950. The FDP continues to form part of the governing coalition following the national election in 1965.

58. Peter H. Merkl, "Equilibrium, Structure of Interests and Leadership: Adenauer's Survival as Chancellor," *American Political Science Review*, LVI (Sept., 1962), 638 ff; Samuel H. Barnes, *et al.*,"The German Party System and the 1961 Federal Election," *ibid.*, LVI (Dec., 1962), 911.

issues were involved.[59] A growing recognition of the significant position of the Bundesrat in the political scene had encouraged the national political party leadership to participate more actively than earlier in state elections. Indeed, it has been argued that state elections have tended to become "indirect Bundesrat elections" and that *Land* political activity has become a "partisan instrument of the Federation and therefore has contributed to centralism generally."[60] While this situation may well have obtained during some of the years of the Adenauer era, when the Chancellor and his party certainly involved themselves intimately in state elections and state cabinet changes, it is doubtful that the Bundesrat has been the central concern of the national parties in state elections since 1963.[61]

As previously mentioned, party considerations have involved another constitutional organ, the Federal Constitutional Court. Events in 1963, possibly in a reaction to the Television decision, for the first time brought into play conspicuous partisanship in the case of legislation affecting the Court and the re-election of judges. A weakening of the independence of the Court through various forms of parliamentary action, particularly in the election of partisan or incompetent judges as political rewards, would certainly have unpredictable effects on the federal system in the years ahead. At least, there has been no instance of failure to re-elect any of those judges who are known to be, in German parlance, "federally" oriented.

In sum, the major political parties have served to an important degree, but certainly not exclusively, as agencies for centralization and the diminution of the place of the *Laender* in the political process. The institutional role of the parties as federalizers has probably been unduly minimized and must be carefully reappraised in the light of electoral developments, legislative change, and judicial decision during the post-Adenauer period.

59. Arnold H. Heidenheimer, "Federalism and the Party System: The Case of West Germany," *ibid.*, LII (Sept., 1958), 824-26; Pinney, *Federalism*, pp. 90 ff.

60. *Ibid.*, pp. 92-93; cf. Fritz René Alleman, *Bonn ist nicht Weimar* (Cologne, 1956), p. 353, and Theodor Eschenburg, *Staat und Gesellschaft in Deutschland* (Stuttgart, 1956), pp. 627-32.

61. Note the supporting comments of Friedrich Karl Fromme, "Eine Zumutung an den Bundesrat," *Frankfurter Allgemeine Zeitung*, July 13, 1965.

V

The institutions of the German states, however recent their creation, obviously play a key role in the federalizing process in West Germany. According to certain polls, there was a marked growth in the popular acceptance of the states during the period between 1952 and 1960, and the large percentage in 1953 of persons favoring the "dissolution" of the states has shown a sharp decline.[62] There appears to be an increasing awareness of certain of their functions.[63] Some experimentation in the states has attracted attention.[64] It is also possible that the alleged artificiality and lack of internal community of the states have been over-stressed.[65]

Under the division of powers in the Basic Law, the list of eleven powers granted exclusively to the Federation is heavily supplemented by the list of twenty-three concurrent powers which can be exercised by the states only in the absence of prior national action. In fact, the Federation has largely preempted the field of concurrent powers. In addition, the Federation is empowered to enact "framework laws" which affect other matters. The reserved powers of the states are few in number and are largely limited to cultural affairs, education, religious affairs, local government, police, and some aspects of agricultural regulation. In general, it is customary to speak loosely of the *Bund* as being responsible for legislation and the *Laender* for administration in Germany.

The enumeration of these powers may suggest misleading interpretations. It fails, for one thing, to take account of the

62. *Jahrbuch der oeffentlichen Meinung, 1958-1964* (Bonn, 1965), pp. 458-59. Cf. fn. 13 above.

63. This is indicated particularly for cultural and police matters in data collected by the Institute of Applied Social Science (IFAS) of Bad Godesberg in 1963-1964. At the same time, the popular awareness of the activities of the Federation and the communities (*Gemeinde*) was considerably higher than that of the states. Data collected on inter-system relationships by co-operating political science and social science institutes at the University of Cologne for the years 1961-1962 also indicate a comparatively low "salience" for the *Land* North Rhine Westphalia, as compared to its communities and the Federation.

64. Steps in 1965 in North Rhine Westphalia to provide retirement pay for members of the *Landtag* can be cited. See also the author's article, "Functional Representation in the German Federal Republic," *Midwest Journal of Political Science,* II (Aug., 1958), 256-77.

65. Cf. Klaus Obermayer, "Krise und Bewaehrung des Foederalismus," *Die neue Ordnung,* XIX (Feb., 1965), 19 ff., esp. 30.

trends in governmental expenditures. The percentage of tax income of the Federation in 1963 (estimated, however, for 1963
on the basis of a 35% and not a 38% return to the Federal Government on the income and corporation taxes) increased by 102%
over 1955 and by 71% over 1958; that of the states and communities, in 1963, by 164% over 1955 and by 91% over 1958. In budgeted
expenditures, those of the Federal Government approximately
equaled those of the states and urban communities of over
10,000 population combined.[66] Over 60% of these national expenditures in 1963, and an equally high percentage in 1964, went
for social welfare and defense purposes. Competent authorities
have estimated that approximately one-third of the personnel
and nearly one-fourth of the budgets of the states (excluding the
Saar) in 1959-60 were allocated for educational and cultural purposes.[67] These figures may not be any more significant than a
mere enumeration of the "powers" which are reserved to the
states, but they do point up the increasing percentage of total
tax revenues received by the states under the complex arrangement for their allocation, and the expenditure of important parts
of this revenue in the exercise of their reserved powers.[68]

The administrative role of the states must be viewed in the
light of the several types of federal and state administration in
Germany.[69] Particular weight may be placed here upon the state
administrative execution of federal laws and the delegated
administration to the states by the Federation. Three points may
be made regarding the role of the states, in their various adminis-

66. Bund Ministry of Finance, *Finanzbericht, 1963*, pp. 42-43; *Kulturpolitik
der Laender, 1963-1964* (Bonn, 1965), esp. pp. 40-42 for the text of the administrative agreement of June 4, 1964, between the Federation and the states, dealing
with the joint encouragement and financing of scientific research.

67. Wells, *States*, p. 95; Merkl, *American Political Science Review*, LIII (Sept.,
1959), 738. The Permanent Conference of Ministers for Education and Cultural
Affairs of the States in the Federal Republic of Germany have compiled data
indicating that in the fiscal year 1962 the Federation, states, and communities of
over 10,000 inhabitants had, in round figures, total expenditures of 50.0 billion
DM, 35.3 billion DM, and 18.2 billion DM respectively, of which expenditures
for educational and cultural affairs represented 2.3%, 20.7%, and 18.3% at the
respective levels. Staendige Konferenz, *Zur Information* (Bonn, 1965), Sec. 14.

68. Peter H. Merkl made an interesting analysis of expenditures for costs of
services at the national and state levels and found that more than one-half of
the average state budget in 1953 went for "independent functions of the
Laender." See table in *American Political Science Review*, LIII (Sept., 1959),
738.

69. Basic Law, Part VIII; Eschenburg, *Staat und Gesellschaft*, pp. 764-65.

trative capacities, during the recent period. The first is that much of the administrative activity of the states, even in the execution of federal legislation, involves a substantial amount of discretion over funds, agencies, and personnel, and, in view of the necessary adaptation to the peculiar circumstances and traditions of the states, "the execution of federal laws by the Laender is not at all a mechanical subordinate process."[70] At the same time, a number of factors, including the nature of the civil service staff, the legalistic outlook of the administrators, and various types of external controls, which can range from federal regulations (requiring Bundesrat approval) to direct federal intervention, provide responsiveness of the state agents for the execution of federal decisions.[71] Second, the state bureaucracies find ample opportunity for a reflection of their own positions in the Bundesrat, especially in the important work of the committees. Indeed, one of the major services of the Bundesrat is to provide the base for an exchange of varying points of view and for a continuing dialogue and working arrangements between the bureaucracies of the Federation and of the states.[72] The result is widely referred to as "administrative federalism." Third, the interest groups frequently present their cases to the bureaucracy at the state level and, through it, hope to see their interests represented by the state administrative officials in the work of the Bundesrat. Despite the considerable attention which has been given to interest groups in West Germany in recent years,[73] the extent and nature of the reliance upon contacts at the *Land* level to influence not only state but also national decision-making has not been adequately studied. But it is believed that interest-group activity at the state level has increased substantially during the past four years.

The co-operative aspects of West German federalism are evidenced increasingly by a growing number of co-operative federal-

70. Merkl, *American Political Science Review*, LIII (Sept., 1959), 734, 740. On German attitudes toward the administrative activities and confidence in the administrative competence of the government, see Gabriel A. Almond and Sidney Verba, *The Civic Culture* (Princeton, 1963), pp. 428-29.

71. Jacob, *German Administration*, pp. 198-212.

72. Pinney, *Federalism*, pp. 174 ff., esp. pp. 203-8.

73. See the analysis and literature cited in Wolfgang Hirsch-Weber, "Some Remarks on Interest Groups in the German Federal Republic," in Henry W. Ehrmann (ed.), *Interest Groups on Four Continents* (Pittsburgh, 1958), pp. 96 ff.

state arrangements (as in certain police matters), federal-state-local arrangements (as in housing), inter-state arrangements (through treaties, *Staatsvertraege*), and administrative agreements (*Abkommen*) among the states (especially in radio, education, cultural fields).[74] Over 339 such treaties and agreements were concluded between 1949-1960; over 500 agreements of the permanent Conference of Ministers of Education and Cultural Affairs alone were implemented during the same period. The number of treaties and administrative agreements has been growing with great rapidity in the 1960's.[75] These various types of agreements point toward the growing horizontal aspects of cooperative federalism in Germany and suggest that future discussions of German federalism must take them more and more into account.

In the future, German federalism will certainly witness important developments involving the position of the communities in the system. Constitutionally speaking, the area of local government falls under the jurisdiction of the states. As a rule, federal legislation which affects local authorities requires both the approval of the Bundesrat and the prior action of the state legislatures before application. At the same time, Art. 28 of the Basic Law provides that "communities must be guaranteed the right to regulate, under their own responsibility and within the limits of the laws, all the affairs of the local community."

These communities, within their constitutional and legal confines, are accordingly involved in a complex series of intergovernmental relations. Some are vertical, involving various types of relationships between the units themselves through special functional authorities and associations to further the common purposes of the local authorities.[76] The growing demands upon the

74. Hesse, *Bundesstaat*, pp. 19 ff; see also comments of Minister President Georg-August Zinn in *Ueber die bundesstaatliche Ordnung der Bundesrepublik*, p. 20. It is estimated that over 80 *Land* organizations are co-ordinating *Bund* and state activities and functions.

75. A recent example of an important agreement is the one between the Federation and the states for the creation of a Development Commission (*Bildungsrat*). The membership of this Commission, which is composed of representatives from the Federation, states, and communities, is modeled on that of the Research Council (*Wissenschaftsrat*). Text in *Bulletin des Presse und Informationamtes der Bundesregierung*, No. 122/S. 981, July 16, 1965. For a reference to this as a "Dokument des foederativen Prinzips" by the Burgermeister of Hamburg, see *Die Welt*, July 16, 1965.

76. See Wells, *States*, pp. 75-82. *The Deutscher Staedtetag* (cities), *Deutscher*

local authorities for greater services, coupled with the lack of adequate resources to meet the demands, have led to increasing insistence that the communities be viewed as fiscal, if not constitutional, partners with the *Bund* and the states in a "three-layered" German federal system.[77] Some tax yields were specifically earmarked for the communities by constitutional amendments in 1955 and 1956.[78] In addition, increasing steps have been taken to encourage regional planning and to deal with the problems of metropolitan areas in general.[79]

The German political parties gave much attention in the election campaign of 1965 to the status and needs of the communities and to their constitutional and legal rights. One can predict for the future closer relationships among the Federation, states, and communities, on the one hand, and among the various local authorities themselves on the other. Within the rigid constitutional confines, the trend is increasingly toward the "co-operative" aspects of the federal process.

VI

In this paper, I have limited myself to an apprasial of new dimensions of German federalism. The argument has been that there exists in West Germany a set of institutions which have collectively functioned as the federalizers—that is, they have served to limit, or at least to moderate, the impact of the long- and short-range forces which have been pressing for greater centralization, and centrally-imposed unity and integration in the Federal Republic. The institutions selected for study have been

Staedtebund (cities of middle size), *Deutscher Gemeindetag* (villages), and the *Deutscher Landkreistag* (*Kreise*), the chief local government associations, are united in a Federal Union of Community Central Associations.

77. Heinz Laufer, "Das demokratische Regime der Bundesrepublik," *Beilage zur Wochen Zeitung das Parlament*, B 30/65, July 28, 1965, pp. 22-24. For a discussion of financial reform involving the communities as one of the "three pillars of the state" by federal, state, and community spokesmen, see "Das Forum der Welt," *Die Welt*, July 10, 1965, Sec. VII. It is to be noted that the Federal Constitutional Court has on several occasions denied the constitutional possibility of *any* third component, to be added to the Federation and states, in the federal system. 13 BVerfGE 77 (1961); Ulrich Scheuner," Struktur und Aufgabe des Bundesstaates in der Gegenwart," *Die Oeffentliche Verwaltung*, XV (Sept., 1962), 647-48.

78. BGBl., 1955, Part I, pp. 817 ff.; *ibid.*, 1956, Part I, pp. 1077 ff.

79. An increasing number of surveys of metropolitan areas is appearing. An illustration is the IFAS survey of Munich in *City Muenchen* (Bremen, 1963).

the Bundesrat, the Federal Constitutional Court, the major political parties, and certain institutions of the states. These institutions are serving effectively, though in varying degrees, to provide a balanced equilibrium in Germany and, during the period from 1961 and 1965, their weight has been increasingly felt.

The end of the Adenauer era and the national election of 1965 provide a new setting for the future operation of these federalizing institutions. One observable trend, that toward co-operative federalism, is seen in an increasing variety of functional inter-relationships and in a number of shared functions at all levels of government from the community to the Federation. This development is marked not only by the number of vertical interrelationships but also by the horizontal ones as well, especially at the state level. It is consequently my view that the federal process and the resulting dynamic equilibrium in Germany are being marked not by a lesser, but by a greater recognition of the diversifying forces and centripetal pressures in Germany.

The Integration of Latin America

by Federico G. Gil and John D. Martz

Motivated like other underdeveloped countries by the desire to liberate themselves from dependence on raw-material exports while raising their living standards, the Latin-American republics have taken impressive strides along the road toward economic growth. Both leaders and governments became convinced not long ago that industrialization was the magical panacea to cure all economic ills, concomitantly leading to the wealth and eminence they seek. This zeal grew into a virtual obsession with many technicians and political leaders. Although advances in industrialization brought profound changes in social and political patterns, they did not automatically and infallibly remedy Latin America's ailments. The Latin-American nations in recent years have been faced with a serious slackening in the rate of industrialization. Frequently lacking the requisite natural resources as well as the techniques demanded for the development of heavy industries, they have further suffered from inadequate financial means and a continuing dependence upon foreign sources of capital. Those countries which made impressive progress toward a developed economy shortly after the conclusion of World War II, such as Argentina, Chile, and Uruguay, are precisely those which are now plagued by the most oppressive economic stagnation.

The gradual but mounting disillusionment with the early postwar drive for industrialization has begun to recede, with a new formula taking its place. During the last decade, technicians and economists have been advocating the idea of regional integration as the most efficacious, indeed, the *only* viable instrument for enabling individual Latin-American countries to realize their aspirations toward development. Over a period of time political leaders first grew receptive to and then enthusiastic about the technicians' viewpoint. Integration has consequently been a recurrent theme of interest and concern to the councils of political parties, organized labor, industrialists and businessmen, intellectual leaders, and other segments of Latin-American public opinion. Outside observers have generally been inclined to dismiss this new current as a contemporary manifestation of the century-old romantic vision of a united Latin America once entertained by the liberators of the emancipation era. This would seem to represent an underestimation of the strength and dynamism of what has become almost a hemisphere-wide movement. Those who maintain the view that regional integration is an inescapable necessity are constantly increasing in number.

Advocates of the contention that integration is the answer to modernization point to several factors which characterize the complexities of Latin-American economy. To begin with, regional growth has been slow and inadequate. The rate of increase for gross product is well below that of the developed nations, and this has been accentuated by the truly spectacular population explosion. The latter has meant that production gains have been absorbed disproportionately in feeding more mouths. The process of industrialization has stagnated as a consequence of inherent limitations of domestic markets and an inability to compete in the world market. Industrialization can scarcely expand beyond a rudimentary stage as long as national economies are based on raw-material exports, which fail to produce income sufficient to pay for the capital goods required by industry. For many, the solution to present difficulties lies in the expansion of markets to a regional basis, thereby meeting the cost of new basic industries. Evidence of a strong trend toward regionalization of socio-political relations in other parts of the world is cited by "integrationists" as further support of their position.

A series of factors is enumerated as facilitating acceptance of the notions of interdependence and the need for a concerted regional approach to economic development in Latin America. These include the following: the supporting attitudes of newly-emerging political forces; the impatience of a burgeoning middle class which demands opportunity for progress and access to higher economic achievement; the desire of an emerging bourgeoisie for enlarged markets; the now-frustrated dreams of development based exclusively on commercial relations with foreign nations; the scourge of inflation; the impact of the wealth-producing capacity of science and technology as demonstrated in the more developed areas; and the growth of both an industrial proletariat and an awakening mass of rural workers. The attitudinal and psychological impact of these forces has contributed to a "revolution of expectations," which has also been mobilized by the champions of the integration movement. Such factors have strongly underlined the attraction of integration and regional collaboration for many concerned Latin-Americans. This is heightened even more by arguments revolving about the state of international affairs.

Today's highly stratified international system is seen by many Latin-Americans as being divided into two identifiable camps— the developed and the underdeveloped, the modern and the traditional. In terms of power, prestige, and economic status, Latin America finds itself grouped with the Asian and African states at the lower levels of international achievement. Traditional emphasis upon the uniqueness of its historical experience, and of its racial and ethnic blending of European and indigenous cultures, is unable to obfuscate the low international stature of the region. The "integrationists" therefore argue for the creation of common social, economic, and political structures on a regional basis. This, it is contended, holds out the only rational hope of ameliorating the present high degree of international inequality, while raising the status of Latin America and obtaining adequate participation in the decision-making process of the world. Only by integrating its diffuse and varied forces into a single bloc can Latin America make its voice heard within the councils of the nations that have affected its destiny.[1]

Many of these considerations are sternly persuasive, and the common ethnic, cultural, and psychological heritage furnishes the indispensable spiritual and human foundation for the process of integration. Formidable obstacles nonetheless exist, and problems of a physical and technical nature appear nearly insurmountable. The advocates of integration recognize and accept the existence of such problems, willingly undertaking the task of removing or overcoming them through a variety of economic and political actions. Aware of the dangers of pursuing impractical

1. Gustavo Lagos, *International Stratification and Underdeveloped Countries* (Chapel Hill: The University of North Carolina Press, 1963). See also "La Integración de América Latina y su influencia en il sistema internacional," in *La Integración Latinoamericana* (Buenos Aires: Instituto para la Integración de América Latina, 1965), pp. 157-68.

visionary goals, they envisage a broad conception of integration that extends beyond the purely economic sphere to matters of social and political development. The conviction has grown that integration in Latin America demands structural and institutional changes which have the broadest of connotations; economic change must be accompanied by decisions set within the appropriate political framework.

PROBLEMS AND OBSTACLES

Just as the positive arguments for integration are multiple, so are the obstacles both varied and complex.[2] While many of the difficulties are fundamentally economic in nature, others are more closely tied to geographic, social, or political conditions. In the first of these, natural barriers are present in such forms as mountains, jungles, deserts, and vast, trackless expanses. Such environmental circumstances, sometimes worsened even further by uncongenial climatic extremes, have helped to prevent the development of a transportation and communication infrastructure. Existing routes of land communication were originally built to satisfy the needs of export trade, and are inadequate for the incorporation and development of new areas. Region-wide roads, with the exception of the Pan-American Highway, are practically non-existent; only 3.2% of the world's permanent highways are in Latin America. The rail system (80% of which is found in three countries—Argentina, Brazil, and Mexico) is also grossly underdeveloped, the region having only 8% of the world's network. Merchant-marine fleets transport only 6% of the maritime freight, resulting in a $650 million deficit in the balance of payments for transportation and handling charges.[3] Air transportation, relatively more advanced than its fellow media, is nonetheless handicapped by the impossibility of meeting the expense of technological advances and by the competition of powerful foreign enterprises.

Among the many social problems is the over-all fragmentation

2. See Felipe Herrera, "Obstáculos y avances par a una comunidad económica latinoamericana." Speech delivered at the inauguration of the Instituto para la Integración de América Latina (Buenos Aires, Argentina: August 24, 1965).

3. Herrera, "Perspectivas de la integración de América Latina," in La Integración Latinoamericana: Situación y Perspectivas (Buenos Aires: Instituto para la Integración de América Latina, 1965), p. 173.

represented in several countries by class tensions and rivalries. Although the gradual emergence of the middle sectors has added a new dimension to the class structure of politics,[4] the historical dualism of society has survived to such an extent that the interests of propertied landholders and those of the rural masses continue to clash sharply. The latter, living at bare subsistence levels and on the margin of national life, are yet tied to land-tenure systems based upon inequitable *latifundios* and unproductive *minifundios*. While two out of every three Latin-Americans are undernourished, the control exercised by minority groups still approaches a monopoly of social and economic power. Conservative landowners and businessmen reject change as inimical to their own private interests, and the idea of regional integration is treated in similar fashion. The depressed living conditions of the masses are further aggravated by illiteracy, which is roughly 50% for the area as a whole. Until this can be remedied, the possibility of mobilizing the masses in the direction of integration will continue to be remote.

Educational shortcomings go far beyond sheer illiteracy, to be sure. To begin with, Latin-American education retains the formalistic orientation of preceding centuries, and is often largely unrelated to practical national needs. The shortage of the professionals and technicians demanded by the process of development has by no means been overcome by the advances of recent years. Even today, only 3.5% of Latin-American children who enter primary school ever reach the university level. By the year 1960 university student enrollment was in the vicinity of 900,000, which represented barely 4.2% of the population between the ages of 19 and 24. Illustrative of such deficiencies is the fact that some 26,000 agricultural engineers were active in 1962, but that by 1970, agrarian reform programs will require a minimum of 60,000. All Latin-American universities combined are producing only 2,000 agricultural engineers annually.[5] Moreover, the lack of uniformity of the educational programs in general has rendered effective inter-university co-ordination impossible. The systematic collection and evaluation of data pertaining to matters

4. For an analysis of the political rise of the middle class see John J. Johnson, *Political Change in Latin America: The Emergence of the Middle Sectors* (Stanford: Stanford University Press, 1958).

5. Herrera, "Antecedentes y perspectivas de la integración latinoamericana," *Mensaje*, Special Issue, June, 1965, p. 251.

of a regional nature are also sadly lacking, and the misinformation which is occasionally disseminated and accepted can reach appalling proportions.

Institutional and political needs are also a part of the over-all fabric of prerequisites for integration. The present set of structures is less than adequate for even the intermediate stage that lies between tentative co-operation and the anticipated goal of full-fledged integration. At least one promising step was the creation by the Inter-American Development Bank, in 1965, of the Institute for Latin-American Integration (INTAL) in Buenos Aires, which is intended to provide the training required for specialists who must lead and direct the march toward regional development. With the solution of many pertinent questions requiring political decisions at the highest levels, the strength of commitment must be supported additionally by the expertise of the small, if expanding, number of technocrats and intellectuals devoted to integration. In the meantime, resting in the background are such sentiments as the virulently destructive xenophobia. The evolution of nationalism through the past century-and-a-half can only be regarded as another roadblock in the path toward integration. The force of such deep-seated attitudes must be projected into regional channels, for an explicit doctrine of integration is becoming a genuine necessity. The plans for such regional development can have only limited application and validity in the absence of an emotional or psychological commitment such as that sometimes engendered by political ideology. It is scarcely an overstatement to suggest that the average Latin-American needs to be convinced of the convenience and lasting benefit which may accrue once integration can be effectuated in his own country.

In the final analysis it is the economic pattern which overrides all other considerations. The familiar prevalence of the region's historical trade pattern continues to survive in the midst of the general change which characterizes so much of politics and society in contemporary Latin America. Raw materials exported to the outside world continue as the basic economic prop, while manufactured goods are brought in from outside. Although industry in certain countries has moved at a rapid pace under the stimulus of the substitution of imported consumer goods, it has by no means resolved many basic economic problems. Agriculture continues as the fundamental economic activity of the majority of the Latin-American working force; yet the trough of stagnation and low productivity into which it fell, long ago, has continued to exist. With the pattern of trade still revolving around raw-material exports in exchange for manufactured imports, foreign trade has progressively weakened. One of the many indices is the fact that Latin America's share of world trade has diminished from 12.3% in 1950 to 7.9% by 1963. Not only is trade with the outside world suffering from imbalances of various sorts, but the inter-hemispheric trade so vital to the integrationists has been practically nil. The experience of three centuries of colonial rule set the early patterns of foreign trade, in which individual regions dealt with non-continental economic interests; even today, the amount of Latin-American trade that is conducted among the various countries of the hemisphere is miniscule.

The sharp unevenness in development among the individual nations—as well as differences among regions and sectors within the same set of national boundaries—is a further handicap. The situation is anything but homogeneous, for at least moderately-developed countries or regions coexist alongside those characterized by archaic conditions. Existing national structures are internally heterogeneous while lacking significant regional complementarity, and domestic markets are poorly organized in view of the disruptive dichotomy between the urban and rural areas. Technological backwardness continues to plague the entire area; given the inordinately demanding requirements of contemporary modernization and change, Latin America must achieve in one huge leap the stage which industrial nations reached only after a century of evolution. None of the nations singly has a justified cause for optimism, and even the most sanguine commentaries have emphasized the unavoidable necessity for multi-national, regional, collaborative undertakings, which might put to the best and most efficient use the present small supply of expertise and technological competence.[6]

Fiscal aspects of the economic situation are both more complex and more potentially destructive than can be indicated here.

6. A good case for Latin-American integration is made in Roger E. Vekemans, "Economic Development, Social Change and Cultural Mutation," in W. D'Antonio and F. B. Pike, eds., *Religion, Revolution and Reform: New Forces for Change in Latin America* (New York: Frederick A. Praeger, 1964).

The lack of co-ordination of broad currency policies throughout the hemisphere detracts from the intended drive toward integration. Many countries have essentially defective systems, themselves suffering from an insufficiency of public savings. Moreover, there is precious little contact and co-ordination among the financial and investment sources within the various countries. Both the past scarcity of truly multi-national projects and the absence of a system of rational priorities judiciously established on the basis of regional rather than particularistic development serve to detract further from projected future policies and events. Domestic public resources have customarily been unavailable for the goals envisaged by integrationists, and various other factors also restrict drastically the mobilization of existing wealth. The ascending inflationary spiral and socio-political instability discourage the holders of private capital, and the historical reluctance to invest one's capital except in land and tangible material property has by no means been dissipated. Non-governmental investment from abroad is likewise concerned over the same conditions, as well as the lack of a uniform policy through which similar conditions and guarantees might be given by all the Latin-American nations.[7] In summary, these as well as additional structural weaknesses suggest that the movement for integration, if not presenting insuperable obstacles, gives little cause for more than highly guarded optimism.

INDICATORS OF PROGRESS

During the past half-dozen years the inter-American system has been marked by a perceptible evolution in economic relations. The multilateral approach has been strengthened by the creation of new continental and subregional economic and commercial schemes. These have facilitated the march toward many of the integrationist goals, while psychological impetus has been derived from the apparent success of the European Economic Community (EEC), a customs union contemplating increased economic integration and ultimate political unity. The efforts of the Western Europeans have been highly suggestive and inspiring, but are not wholly adaptable to the Latin-American situation because of the inherent differences between the two regions.

7. Herrera, Mensaje, Special Issue, June, 1965, pp. 250-51.

The Europeans have been building upon a highly developed system of communications and a large productive capacity, something lacking in Latin America. Moreover, a sense of political urgency in economic integration has not pressed upon the Latin-Americans; neither have considerations of defense and of peace-keeping responsibilities weighed upon them as they have upon Europeans. There is also in Europe an immeasurably greater backlog of technical expertise and of trained personnel, and a wealth of accurate, detailed socio-economic data on which integration programs may be based. Such conditions are not widely found in Latin America. A final word should point to differences in the orientation of United States policy, for in Europe the direction has been toward the co-ordination of policies and the integration of markets by the Europeans themselves, in contrast with the essentially bilateral emphasis on the approach to Latin America.

Of the variety of efforts which have evolved in recent years, two in particular have been outstanding as integrationist undertakings: The Latin-American Free-Trade Association (LAFTA) and the Central American Common Market. The former is a free-trade organization which seems on the way to becoming an economic union without major political overtones, while the latter is a burgeoning customs union with intentions of increased political collaboration. Before examining these programs in detail, however, one should note the major instrument for regional integration, the Inter-American Development Bank (IDB).

The Inter-American Development Bank.

Constituted by nineteen Latin-American countries and the United States on December 30, 1959, the IDB began formal operations in October of 1961, pledged in its charter to objectives which included the acceleration of "economic development, both individual and collective. . . ." Its short history can be described in terms of three periods, the first of which was devoted to the financing of specific projects judged on their individual intrinsic merits. This gave way in due course to a time of wider and more rational economic planning. The Latin-American states committed themselves at Punta del Este to the formulation of national plans of development; for the Bank, this meant the consideration of individual projects as fundamental parts of an over-all national program. The integrationist stage came third, in which projects and proposals were appraised at least partly on the basis of their relation to regional integration.

Pursuant to this evolution of its financial activities, the Bank has come to be oriented toward integration in several ways. Among the most significant have been (a) the study and financing of regional projects and programs; (b) the financing of national industrial projects with regional ramifications; (c) technical and financial assistance to works improving economic infrastructure; and (d) the study of possibilities of so-called frontier integration (*integración fronteriza*).[8] Pertinent examples include the series of loans in 1963 and 1964 to the Central American Bank for Economic Integration, in the support of both industrial and infrastructural projects within the framework of its subregional integration. Commitments related to the concerns mentioned in (a) and (c) have been the Bank's technical assistance to Bolivia, Colombia, Ecuador, and Peru for studies on the projected highway skirting the edge of the eastern jungles in those countries. A recent illustration of programs under (d) is the creation and support of a special mission to explore the possibilities of regional integration in the neighboring Venezuelan and Colombian border region, as well as funds for a Colombian electricity station in that area which would service nearby communities in both countries.[9]

Latin-American Free-Trade Association.

The antecedents of today's Latin-American Free-Trade Area can be traced back to studies conducted in 1956 by the Economic Commission for Latin America (ECLA). Separate technical groups studied both the possibilities of a regional market and the problems of multilateral payments. The project of a Latin-American common market was formulated along with the idea for a payments union. When the general response proved unfavorable, ECLA turned to other approaches, including the creation of

8. R. Alberto Calvo, "El Banco Interamericano de Desarrollo y el Processo de Integración," in *La Integración Latinoamericana*, p. 80.

9. "Posibilidades de integración económica de las zonas fronterizas colombo-venezolanas," *Informe* presentado por el Banco Inter-Americano de Desarrollo a los Gobiernos de Colombia y Venezuela, Washington, 1964.

a common market for certain groups of products and the alternative of a subregional common market, as later evolved in Central America. The genesis of LAFTA technically dates from the 1960 signing of the Treaty of Montevideo, the fundamental charter which at this writing is subscribed to by Chile, Argentina, Paraguay, Uruguay, Brazil, Peru, Ecuador, Colombia, and Mexico.[10] The organizational structure included the Conference as deliberative body, and, as permanent organs, the *Comité Ejecutivo Permanente* (CEP) and the Secretariat. The CEP is formed of designated representatives of the member governments, while the Executive Secretariat is elected by the Conference itself. A small and underworked staff of about a dozen permanent officials serves in the Secretariat. Additional technical committees and working groups also function sporadically on an *ad hoc* basis.[11]

The specified goal of the Montevideo Treaty is the creation of a free-trade zone. The principal instruments for achieving the objective include (a) a general program for the reduction of tariffs; (b) a special treatment for the countries with the lowest status in terms of development; and (c) special agreements and resolutions to serve in a complementary fashion. The Treaty provides for a pattern of action on tariffs which will lower them by a minimum of 8% annually for 12 years, culminating in a total reduction of at least 96%. A complicated set of procedures for implementing the projected annual reductions has been developed after extensive maneuvering and quiet negotiations. Once a commodity is accepted by all parties through negotiations, it is placed on so-called national schedules (*listas nacionales*). In addition, there are common schedules (*listas comunes*) which contain items that have been moved there from the national schedules. Every three years, 25% of the goods traded among LAFTA members is transferred to the *lista común*. Tariff reduc-

10. By 1966, Venezuela appeared on the verge of joining. With the earlier LAFTA members, the participating countries represented some 220 million people, 82% of the region's total population, and 85% of Latin America's domestic gross product.

11. Miguel Wionczek, "La Historia del Tratado de Montevideo," in *Integración Económica de America Latina* (Mexico: Fondo de Cultura Económica, 1964). Also see Rómulo Almeida, "Origen, estructura, funcionamiento y problemas de la Asociación Latinoamericana de Libre Comercio," in *La Integración Latinoamericana: Situación y Perspectivas.*

tions already negotiated on these commodities become irreversible. There is, however, a wide range of escape clauses, especially in matters related to agriculture.[12] It is also generally true that the poorer states, notably Paraguay, Ecuador, and Bolivia, are entitled to preferential treatment as "relatively underdeveloped." This permits them to retain certain tariffs for the protection of domestic industries. LAFTA founders intended such treatment as an encouragement for the small nations to join.

The original founders of LAFTA hoped that a pattern of complementarity would emerge, especially in the case of manufactured goods. Despite the advantages of regional specialization, the negotiation of complementary agreements has proved exceedingly difficult. Beyond this, however, LAFTA offers broad possibilities for progress in regional industrialization. The removal of trade barriers will be accompanied increasingly by the improvement of transportation facilities and the relative standardization of monetary systems. Whether or not the anticipated free-trade area will truly exist at the end of twelve years remains an open question at present. Much depends upon the spirit in which participating countries respond to and fulfill the actual treaty provisions. The early record has not been promising; during the first two years intra-regional trade grew more than 40%, but the total value of such trade represented only 8.5% of the international trade of LAFTA members. Moreover, 80% is constituted by products which have been traditionally exchanged by the nations in question. And thus, although a final verdict would be premature, the evidence suggests that tariff reductions thus far have done little more than speed up traditional trade in cattle and agriculture.

Central American Common Market.

The true customs union that has evolved as the Central American Common Market (CACM) has proved in many ways a greater and more rapid success than LAFTA. As early as May and June of 1951, an ECLA meeting in Mexico City formally passed Resolution 9-IV inviting the Central American governments to send representatives who would set up a Committee for

12. Wendell C. Gordon, *The Political Economy of Latin America* (New York: Columbia University Press, 1965), pp. 329-30.

Economic Co-operation. Such a group met for the first time in 1952, when the Central Americans began to lay down their early plans for sub-regional integration. Intense study continued for the next five years, during which time a variety of United-Nations and inter-American agencies provided technical advice and assistance. A series of studies included such topics as industrial integration, public administration training, research in industrial technology, finance and development banking, and transportation and electric power. An additional set of bilateral treaties was also worked out during 1952-57, and the culmination of regional efforts came with the signing of the Multilateral Treaty of Free Trade and Central American Economic Integration on June 10, 1958. On that same date a further convention was adopted for the purpose of encouraging the development of regional and sub-regional industry. From that time until December of 1960, a total of eight separate trade agreements was signed in the implementation of economic recommendations. The historic document was signed in Managua on December 13, 1960, with the creation of the Central American Common Market.[13] It went into effect in June of 1961 upon ratification by Guatemala, Nicaragua, and El Salvador. By the close of 1962, Costa Rica and Honduras had also fully committed themselves.

The treaty established the free trade of all products originating in the area, excluding certain listed items which have been subject to special conditions for a period of five years or less. The latter provision was designed to avoid undue dislocations in individual economies. The common market was scheduled to be fully effective by June of 1966. Subsequent developments will include such matters as a standardized tariff arrangement, common economic and industrial nomenclature, and total mobility of capital and labor. Two of the outstanding features of CACM have been the stress on integrated industries and the creation of the Central American Bank for Economic Integration, situated in Tegucigalpa. Among the broader objectives of the treaty is the promotion of new industry that will serve the entire region rather than individual countries.[14] The Bank is charged with seeking

13. Among the most useful journalistic treatments was the extended discussion of Costa Rican Minister of Economy Jorge Borbón Castro, which appeared in San José's *La Nación* in a series beginning January 10, 1961.

14. John P. Powelson, *Latin America: Today's Economic and Social Revolution* (New York: McGraw-Hill, 1964), pp. 209-10.

long-term projects in industries of a regional character. Its capital of $20 million, provided by equal contributions from the five Central American republics, is expected to seek and attract loan capital from other international agencies.

In structural terms the general treaty of 1958 provided for the existence of three major agencies: the Central American Economic Council (composed of the five ministers of economy), the Executive Council, with a representative plus alternates from each country, and the Permanent Secretariat (SIECA) situated in Guatemala City, headed by a secretary-general chosen by the Economic Council for a three-year term. The additional agencies affiliated with the integrationist movement in Central America can be summarized briefly. The *Instituto Centro Americano de Investigación y Tecnología Industrial* (ICAITI) was founded in Guatemala in 1956 with the support of the United Nations Special Fund, and has devoted particular attention to research, industrial services, and scientific documentation. Two years earlier the *Escuela Superior de Administración Pública para la América Central* (ESAPAC) was opened in San José, Costa Rica, also enjoying assistance from the United Nations. Of no small importance is an additional integration-oriented institution, the *Consejo Monetario Centroamericano*. This regional monetary council grew out of periodic meetings held by the five Central Banks and was formally created in 1964. Delegates drafted and adopted a gradual and progressive program aimed toward monetary integration. It is being developed at the present by three organs of its own—the *Consejo Monetario Centroamericano*, composed of the presidents of the five Central Banks; the Executive Secretariat; and an accompanying Advisory Committee.

The concern over the regional unification cause in Central America is traditional and deep-seated.[15] On at least six major occasions in the past century-and-a-half, the Central Americans have made a serious and determined, if generally futile, effort to reunite the regional federation that collapsed in 1838. Thus the renewed concern in contemporary times is hardly startling, and there has been a proliferation of interested agencies within the past few years. For example, the rectors of the five national uni-

15. For a detailed historical description, see Thomas L. Karnes, *The Failure of Union: Central America, 1824-1960* (Chapel Hill: University of North Carolina Press, 1961).

versities formed the *Consejo Superior Universitario Centro-americano* (CSUCA) as a step toward greater regional co-operation and unification of Central American higher education. In the private sector one finds such pro-integration organizations as the journalists' *Federación Centroamericana de Periodistas* and the businessmen's *Federación de Cámaras y Asociaciones Industriales Centroamericanas* (FECAICA). Efforts to unify legislative attacks on food and animal sanitation are the concern of the *Organismo Internacional Regional de Sanidad Agropecuaria* (OIRSA). Perhaps the best-known of the region's multi-national organs is the Organization of Central American States, or *Organización de Estados Centroamericanos* (ODECA). Concern with a possible evolution toward political union, it was founded by the 1951 signing of the Charter of San Salvador, and after several years' hiatus it has recently revived in activity. As common economic progress is achieved concomitant political improvement also becomes more probable.[16]

In comparing the responsibilities and achievements of the Central American Common Market with those of LAFTA the former plainly enjoys clearer objectives. It has also moved much further in terms of an institutional and juridical framework for the systematic execution of a decisive development policy. In less than a decade the Central American Common Market has fully liberated from taxes a sizeable list of products; a common *arancel* has been set up; tax incentives for foreign investors have been systematized and rationalized; and by the close of 1966 all but a few agricultural products were to be covered by the effects of the common market. In spite of such accomplishments in the coordination and freeing of trade and exchange, the Central Americans are realistically aware of certain program limitations. Steps are being taken to develop technical instruments which can program all regional economic activities and promote the coordination of national development plans. Early results from the economic effects of the common market have been notable. Intraregional trade increased in value from $3.6 million in 1950 to $32.7 million a decade later; in another three years it had

16. For a slightly dated but useful account, see James L. Busey, "Central American Union: The Latest Attempt," *The Western Political Quarterly*, XIV, No. 1 (March, 1961), 49-93.

mounted to $66 million. Furthermore, 75% of this intra-regional trade is now for industrial exports.

Causes for this relative success in Central America are not hard to identify. With an area of some 167,000 square miles—approximately the size of France—Central America nonetheless has a population of only some 12 million, 65% of the active population being devoted to agricultural pursuits. Foreign trade is based upon the exports of four products (coffee, cotton, cacao, and bananas), which combine to earn 90% of such income. Moreover, the five Central American nations have followed at least loosely similar historical development, sharing many of the same characteristics and traits. Frequently differences are only a matter of degree. Industrial development has been retarded for so long that there were fewer difficulties than with LAFTA in adopting automatic liberalization of import taxes. In short, by all the usual economic and commercial indices, the Central American Common Market continues to appear far more appropriate than does LAFTA for the over-all progress and potential integration of its member states.

CONCLUSIONS

On January 6, 1965, Chilean President Eduardo Frei addressed a letter to four of Latin America's leading economists: Raúl Prebisch, José Antonio Mayobre, Felipe Herrera, and Carlos Sánz de Santamaría. In it he requested a proposal for measures whereby the Latin-American nations might at the earliest possible date institutionalize economic integration. The following excerpt is suggestive: "In the matter of institutions I would like to make this suggestion: labor as well as managerial forces, either on an individual or cooperative basis, should be given clear participation in the movement for integration. The integration of Latin America, as is the case with the entire process of structural changes, demands essentially a broad popular base. Narrowing integration exclusively to official technical and financial circles regardless of how competent these may be would only lead to failure."[17] Precisely one week later the four economists re-

17. *Carta del Presidente de Chile, Eduardo Frei, a los Srs. Raúl Prebisch, José Antonio Mayobre, Felipe Herrera y Carlos Sánz de Santamaría* (mimeo), January 6, 1965.

sponded to Frei's request. Somewhat later they presented a series of recommendations, in which stress was placed upon the necessity for adopting important political decisions; among their specific proposals were a regional investment policy, revised commercial agreements, and monetary and fiscal measures. Specific institutional mechanisms for the creation of a fully viable Latin-American common market were several, including a Council of Ministers, an advisory committee of specialists, a *Junta Ejecutiva*, and a Latin-American Parliament.

The Council of Ministers, composed of one cabinet minister from each country, was to meet at least twice annually. Alternate delegates could meet more frequently to exchange information and facilitate broad implementation, while decisions were to be taken by majority vote. An advisory committee of specialists would assist the Council, as would a separate body composed of representatives of workers, *empresarios*, universities, and technical and professional organizations. An executive board (*Junta Ejecutiva*) would include a president and from four to six members designated by the Council. The latter would not be affiliated with their own governments, and thus would be free to act independently, being responsible only to the community of member nations. Its functions would include the implementation of recommendations, attention to the application of the principle of reciprocity, the proposal to the Council of steps to accelerate the integrative process, the sponsoring of appropriate studies, the adjudication of conflicts over interpretation, and the co-ordination of tasks in such fields of policy as commerce, investment, international payments, and monetary matters. The proposed Latin-American Parliament was subsequently created by charter in Lima in August of 1965.[18] Providing a regional forum for the discussion of general problems of integration, it is presently intended as an additional mechanism to help provide an atmosphere favorable for the adoption of major political decisions. It is not intended as a supranational legislative assembly.

In the field of regional investment policy, the economists proposed an agreement between the *Junta Ejecutiva* and the Interamerican Development Bank to establish a special instrument for

18. For a brief overview of current developments, see Harry Kantor, "The Latin-American Parliament: A New Attempt to Stimulate Economic and Political Unification," *South Eastern Latin Americanist*, IX, No. 3 (December, 1965), 1-3.

the promotion of studies and projects of regional scope. It would be designed as part of the Bank's structure, to be directed by representatives of both the Bank and the *Junta*. Conflicts of interpretation could be solved by the *Junta* in the first instance and, if no accord were forthcoming, might then be submitted to an *ad hoc* committee of conciliation formed by members drawn by lot from a list of individuals designated by member countries. This arrangement, it was hoped, might lead in time to the creation of a court of regional character.[19]

Thought about the approach to Latin-American integration has evolved through several different phases in recent years. The over-all process, it is believed, should be achieved through a series of successive stages leading from the present situation to a higher plane of co-ordination and broad integration. There is general agreement that genuine progress can be achieved only if the Latin-American countries individually make serious political decisions, setting goals and procedures for the achievement of specified objectives while providing the necessary institutional framework. Economic regional integration is no longer advocated merely as an alternative to national integration; on the contrary, it is seen as helping to co-ordinate the efforts in each country to gain a measure of social justice by renovating and reformist forces. Progress toward regional cohesion is increasingly identified with socio-economic reforms, so that the fruits of integration may be shared equitably by both the rural and urban masses. Regional action is therefore seen not as an alternative to national action, but rather as something which must rest solidly upon national development as well.

There is a growing realization that the institutions required by the drive for integration are by no means solely economic or financial. Instead, appropriate institutions should necessarily be capable of making decisions at the regional level without the need of depending in every case upon negotiation and reciprocal concessions. The commitment to such a belief is perhaps *the* crucial political decision. Cultural and educational systems must be co-ordinated, while the accelerating requirement for advanced scientific and technological research must be met. Overriding all

19. The text of these proposals is found in an annex entitled "Perspectivas para la creación del mercado común latinoamericano," in *La Integración Latinoamericana: Situación y Perspectivas*, pp. 189-217.

substantive political and socio-economic decisions, finally, is the importance of an identifiable integrationist ideology. Whatever the future of the integrationist movement may be, it must be solidly founded upon an intangible psychological commitment that stands without reservation or qualification. Integration is no longer seen as a magical panacea promising immediate resolution of all economic and social problems, but it represents a significant and expanding approach to great promise. Only with steady and unwavering support can it hope to achieve the common aspirations of all Latin America for social justice and economic prosperity.[20]

20. As already indicated, the literature on integration is thin. For a very brief over-all assessment, see Chapter 10, "The Integration of Latin America," in Victor L. Urquidi, *The Challenge of Development in Latin America* (New York: Frederick A. Praeger, 1964), pp. 124-36. A useful discussion of Latin-American economic problems and the evolving ideology of the United Nations Economic Commission for Latin America is contained in Albert O. Hirschman's "Ideologies of Economic Development in Latin America," in Albert O. Hirschman (ed.), *Latin-American Issues: Essays and Comments* (New York: The Twentieth Century Fund, 1961), pp. 3-43.

IV. BEHAVIORAL DIMENSIONS

Technological Change and Higher Defense Organization: A Comparative Analysis*

by Frederic N. Cleaveland and Raymond H. Dawson

The structure and organization of military systems, and national patterns of civil-military politics, arise from the interaction of two sets of variables: the aggregate domestic political demands upon the political system, and the objective military requirements acting upon the military sub-system. The first set of variables consists of the substance of the policy choices which determine the level of resource allocation to the national military establishment, the sub-allocations within the military establishment to service components and particular missions, and the utilization of the capabilities procured; and the policy-making process in which these choices are made. The choices and the process of making such choices will reflect a complex structure of attitudes, preferences, expectations, and institutions. From these domestic political demands are derived the unique, or at least the distinctive, attributes of national military establishments, and through classification of political systems the military sub-systems can be typed and categorized. Thus, using "levels of political culture" ("minimal," "low," and "developed,") as the controlling variable, Professor S. E. Finer has constructed a series of models of civil-military relations, building on this his analysis of the modes, methods, levels, and outcomes of military involvement in domestic politics.[1] The American military establishment is unlike any other, and American civil-military politics are unlike those of any other nation. Both have more in common with the same phenomena in Great Britain than with those in the Soviet Union, but even less with those in Pakistan.

The objective military requirements consist of the functional demands operative upon military sub-systems generally. From

* The authors are grateful to their colleagues, Professor Andrew M. Scott and Mr. William A. Lucas, for their stimulating comments on earlier drafts of this paper.

1. S. E. Finer, *The Man on Horseback: The Role of the Military in Politics* (New York: Frederick A. Praeger, 1962).

these are derived the common attributes of military organizations in any national system, making them distinctive from all other bureaucratic systems and professions. The military establishment —"regardless of its societal context—has a unique character because the threat of violence is a permanent reality to its leaders";[2] it necessarily "builds its routines on the abnormal, its expectations on the unexpected."[3] Since it exists to manage violence, or to manipulate the instruments and symbols of violence, it is a peculiarly centralized, hierarchical, disciplined organization, isolated and self-sufficient. The American, British, Soviet, and Pakistani military all have this in common.

Within advanced industrialized national societies, which can be categorized as major military powers, technological change is generating new military and political requirements and demands which it has been impossible to absorb within traditional institutional and policy patterns. The extent and pace of this technological change have brought exponential increases in the cost of weapons, in the complexities of operation and maintenance of weapons and supporting systems, and in the societal risks implicit in the resort to military measures as an instrument of policy. Because of their novelty, adaptive responses to these pressures have set in motion a trend toward similar kinds of organizational responses, both within national military systems and in the external relationships of those systems with civil authorities. A comparative analysis of relevant developments in Great Britain and the United States over the past two decades provides suggestive data in support of this hypothesis of "standardization" of military systems and civil-military politics, in terms of the kinds of policy questions generated and the political pressures that result (domestic political demands), and in terms of the military requirements to be met.

AMERICAN MILITARY ORGANIZATION, 1940-1949

As the United States moved from isolationism to involvement in the world crisis of 1940-41, and then to a position of world

2. Morris Janowitz, *The Military in the Political Development of the New Nations: An Essay in Comparative Analysis* (Chicago: University of Chicago Press, 1964), pp. 26-27.
3. A. K. Davis, "Bureaucratic Patterns in the Navy Officer Corps," *Social Forces*, XXVII (1948), 145.

leadership, it was immediately apparent that neither its diplomatic nor its military establishment was organized to meet these increasing burdens of responsibility. From the outset it was assumed that the U.S. would fight the war—if and when it became involved—in tandem with Britain. Joint planning at the strategic level was under way by January, 1941, in the ABC₁ military staff conferences.[4]

Such encounters underscored the necessity for improving the effectiveness of the command and staff structures of the U.S. military. The British armed forces participated within much clearer frames of political reference that were developed in a functioning machinery of political-military consultation, and the three British services confronted their American counterparts with prepared and agreed positions. Corresponding preparations by the Americans were mandatory. Certainly these, and all the problems of global war, meant that institutions like the Joint Chiefs of Staff had to be invented, since they did not exist. But in the context of necessity one can discern a pattern of creative adaptation, impelled by the requirements of war but drawing on the experience and practice of the principal ally, an ally long acknowledged as a world power of the front rank.[5]

The very fact of alliance prompted additional innovative responses on the part of both Britain and the United States, while changing military technology quickened the process. New logistical demands and the rapid tactical advances in amphibious operations combined to erode roles and missions for ground and naval operations derived from historic environmental factors. The new significance of air power added another powerful environmental element while weakening still further all the environmental boundaries. Combined—*i.e.*, inter-allied—and joint—*i.e.*, army,

4. For a detailed account of these secret conferences, see Maurice Matloff and Edwin S. Snell, *Strategic Planning for Coalition Warfare, 1941-1942* (Washington: Office of the Chief of Military History, 1953), Ch. 3.

5. Major-General Otto L. Nelson, Jr., remarks, for example, that "The Joint Chiefs of Staff organization emerged because some agency of the sort was essential in our dealings with the British—and in determining quickly over-all military policy and strategy" (*National Security and the General Staff* [Washington: Infantry Journal Press, 1946], p. 397). See also J. D. Hittle, *The Military Staff: Its History and Development* (Harrisburg, Pa.: The Military Service Publishing Co., 1949), pp. 266-67. The most comprehensive account of British defense policy machinery is by Franklyn A. Johnson, *Defense by Committee: The British Committee of Imperial Defense* (New York: Oxford University Press, 1960).

navy, air—commands and staffs were formed for every major theater of operations, and in the higher headquarters.

The American military, and American political leadership in the executive and in Congress, became convinced that major re-organization in defense was essential, but the aspirations and interests of the actors varied widely. At war's end, however, these problems could no longer be avoided, and for two years—until the summer of 1947—organizational questions dominated Ameri-can civil-military politics. Like the Royal Air Force, the U.S. Army Air Forces sought formal independence and equality, after having won *de facto* autonomy during the war. The Army, reversing its post-World War I position, supported its restless, powerful offspring, while seeking a tight, centralized general staff system over all the armed forces, in which the direct access to the President enjoyed during the war would continue. The Navy resisted both, fearing loss of its own air arm to the Air Force, and fearing isolation as a permanent minority of one in the Army-proposed staff system. Congress pressed for a settlement which, in the name of efficiency and economy, would encompass both Air Force independence and tri-service unification and would preserve its own access to the defense establishment.[6]

Secretary of the Navy James V. Forrestal, faced with the need to offer a constructive proposal which would satisfy the political demands for reorganization while safeguarding Navy interests, called upon his friend Ferdinand Eberstadt to muster a task force and develop a specific plan for submission to Congress.[7] The Eberstadt Report, and the ultimate National Security (or Unifica-tion) Act of 1947 which it so profoundly influenced, sought, in a key sense, to dilute the prescription of unification by broadening the scope of the issues. What was necessary, Forrestal told Eberstadt, was to look not only at the organization of the military services but also at the organization and relationships of all de-

6. On the unification debate of 1945-47, see especially Walter Millis (ed.), *The Forrestal Diaries* (New York: The Viking Press, 1951), Ch. 4; Paul Y. Hammond, *Organizing for Defense: The American Military Establishment in the Twentieth Century* (Princeton: Princeton University Press, 1960), Ch. 8; John Ries, *The Management of Defense: Organization and Control of the U.S. Armed Forces* (Baltimore: The Johns Hopkins Press, 1964), Chs. 4 and 6.

7. On Forrestal's role in the reorganization debate, see Millis (ed.), *The For-restal Diaries*, pp. 126 ff; and Robert G. Albion and Robert H. Connery, *Forrestal and the Navy* (New York and London: Columbia University Press, 1962).

partments and agencies concerned with national security, to explore the broad questions of co-ordinating military with foreign policy, strategic with logistical planning, procurement with mobilization.[8]

For the purposes of this discussion, the striking element of the Eberstadt report and much of the subsequent legislation was the conscious, deliberate attempt to model the higher defense and security organization of the United States on that of Great Britain.[9] In part this was done, we must assume, because the Navy was looking for a means of promoting its own autonomy, and the British system offered a convenient tactical model. It is certainly true, however, that the British system commended itself to Forrestal and many others on its merits, as a highly effective system for the co-ordination and control of foreign policy and its military adjunct. It had been seen in operation, and it "worked." This was an impressive tribute to the performance of British officials and officers, and to the War Cabinet, the Chiefs of Staff Committee, and the Committee on Imperial Defense as policy-making bodies. It should be noted that the British model of politics had long commended itself to American academicians, beginning at least with Woodrow Wilson. As late as 1960 a distinguished student of the American military was pointing to the advantages of the British method and system of political debate of military policy.[10] Forrestal, Eberstadt, and the other architects of the National Security Act were in a long and distinguished tradition.

The most important aspect of the American debate on military organization from 1945 to 1947, however, was the extent to which compromise and settlement were the outcome of political demands overshadowing the functional requirements of defense. Furthermore, the structure emerging from that debate followed organizational patterns well established in American public administration. The resulting structure of the Department of Defense resembled nothing more closely than it did the con-

8. Millis (ed.), *The Forrestal Diaries*, p. 63.

9. Forrestal told Winston Churchill on one occasion that "the germinal basis of his [Eberstadt's] plan was the minute by Lord Hankey on the operations of the Imperial General Staff in England" (*Ibid.*, p. 145). The *Diaries* abound with references to Forrestal's admiration for the British Cabinet system.

10. See Morris Janowitz, *The Professional Soldier: A Social and Political Portrait* (Glencoe: The Free Press, 1960), pp. 354-55.

federative or "holding company" type of organizational framework typical of such existing agencies as the Department of the Interior and the Federal Security Agency. The service components of the Department had rich traditions, well-established bureaucracies supported by their own networks of organized interests and carefully protected channels of access to Congress. The office of the Secretary represented a kind of superstructure presiding over the constituent units and designed to provide a semblance of co-ordination but never too much. The impact of domestic political considerations and the traditional structural patterns represented the dominant influence of environmental or political system variables upon the debate over national security organization. It is the thesis of this analysis that in 1945-47 those "external" variables overshadowed the functional demands of the military sub-system.

Eberstadt's report spoke of a need for "a complete realignment of our governmental organizations to serve our national security in the light of our new world power and position, our new international commitments and risks and the epochal new scientific discoveries."[11] The last phrase was only added to the report after Hiroshima. But for all the statements of grand designs, the debate was—in W. W. Rostow's words—"a struggle of bureaucratic politics and of men—not of military ideas."[12] And the product of that debate—in the words of the Hoover Commission, less than eighteen months later—was a National Military Establishment that was "perilously close to the weakest type of department."[13] So heated was the struggle to produce this modest result that, in fact, it delayed for almost two years critical discussion and analysis of military ideas while the world situation went from bad to worse.

AMERICAN DEFENSE ORGANIZATION SINCE 1949

Although one of its principal architects—Forrestal—was placed at its head as the first Secretary of Defense, the system

11. Quoted in Albion and Connery, Forrestal and the Navy, p. 264.
12. W. W. Rostow, The United States in the World Arena: An Essay in Recent History (New York: Harper and Brothers, 1960), p. 175.
13. The Commission on Organization of the Executive Branch of the Government, The National Security Organization, A report to the Congress . . . , February, 1949 (Washington, D.C.: Government Printing Office, 1949), p. 8.

constructed in 1947 was not workable. At least, it was not made to work.[14] Forrestal was given "general direction, authority and control" over the three service departments, but those departments were to be "separately administered," and powers and duties relating to those departments "not specifically conferred upon the Secretary of Defense shall be retained by each of their respective Secretaries." The Secretary of Defense could appoint no more than three special assistants "to advise and assist him." Forrestal's position was indeed like that of others among the Department heads at the Cabinet table, reduced to negotiating with bureau chiefs in their own Departments to whom Congress had granted direct statutory authority for program administration, leaving the Departmental Secretary vaguely responsible but without effective means to direct and control. Forrestal could bargain and negotiate through the elaborate system of interservice and interdepartmental committees, but he could do little more; while President Truman immediately made it clear that the National Security Council emphatically was no "War Cabinet."

The Hoover Commission and its Task Force studying National Security Organization—headed, incidentally, by Ferdinand Eberstadt—rejected the notion that these deficiencies could be accounted for by the "newness of the operation" and concluded that they reflected "serious organizational defects." These defects—"lack of central authority," "rigid statutory structure," and "divided responsibility"—were found by the Commission to exist in a number of executive departments and agencies. And their prescription for correction in the Department of Defense followed general principles established for improved departmental management throughout the executive branch: ". . . we have urged that the foundation of good departmental administration requires that the Secretary have authority from the Congress to organize and control his organization, and that separate authorities to component subordinates be eliminated."[15]

In 1949, Forrestal asked for major changes in the system in

14. John Ries, in *The Management of Defense*, contends that the 1947 system was an effective solution, placing "*real* authority" where it was needed, but that "few recognized it" (p. 121). Certainly Forrestal was not able to recognize it, and he was not unique.

15. The Commission on Organization of the Executive Branch, *The National Security Organization*, p. 6.

order to enhance the authority of the Secretary of Defense over the three services.[16] His request was reinforced by the report of the Hoover Commission. The resulting amendments to the National Security Act of 1947 moved away from the loose confederative structure towards more unified departmental control through a strong Secretary. Up to this point efforts to build an efficient defense establishment continued to reflect centralizing forces at work throughout the Federal executive structure at least as much as they reflected the special demands of the military subsystem.[17] But in the implementation of this reorganization, the peculiarly urgent requirements of national defense have stimulated innovation and creative adaptation in organization and administrative management within the military establishment. Indeed, the Department of Defense has now emerged as a prime source of leadership and demonstration within the federal executive branch for new organizational patterns and techniques of management.[18]

First, the political stature of the individual service departments has been steadily reduced, beginning with the removal of the service secretaries from the National Security Council and their loss of Cabinet-rank in 1949, and continuing through the Eisenhower Reorganization Plan 6 of 1953 and the Department of Defense Reorganization Act of 1958. The corollary has been a tremendous growth in the size and political power of the Office of Secretary of Defense, and the accompanying centralization of management and control around that office. Through creative

16. ". . . I must admit to you quite frankly that my position has changed," he told the Senate Armed Services Committee. Quoted in Hammond, *Organizing for Defense*, p. 239.

17. The whole series of departmental reorganizations growing out of the work of the Hoover Commission and accomplished through statute or reorganization plan followed the same principles underlying the 1949 amendments to the National Security Act. The dominant principle was centralization, transferring to the Secretary full authority over all departmental programs and operations, this authority then to be delegated by him to subordinates at sub-department levels.

18. Morris Janowitz suggests that this leadership of the military establishment in administrative management is at least in part the product of America's brand of civil-military politics, in other words response to political system variables. "Because so much of civilian control is oriented toward management forms, the military has developed greater sensitivity to these problems than to the political consequences of their policies. In many fields—cost budgeting, work measurement, statistical controls, automation—officials in the military establishment are 'out in front,' in the professional judgment of administrative experts." Janowitz, *The Professional Soldier*, p. 348.

adaptation of functional patterns of organization, successive secretaries of Defense have largely transformed the Department from the 1947 model of three highly autonomous components with a loosely co-ordinating superstructure to a relatively cohesive and unified organization. The military departments have increasingly become facilitating or service agencies responsible for procurement, training, and logistical support,[19] while the direct line combat forces are lodged under unified and specified commands. In public administration terms, these commands[20] are field organizations in a direct chain of command running from the President and the Secretary of Defense to the line commander in the field, rather than being under particular service chiefs or military department heads.[21]

In place of the three assistants authorized to Forrestal there are ten assistant secretaries of defense, a number of them assigned responsibilities for specified functions (such as supply and logistics, or manpower and personnel), cutting across the military services and thus adding to the centripetal pull of the

---

19. While these changes in role may have helped to reduce the political stature of the three services, they have probably also enhanced the capacity of the services to survive organizationally. As Samuel Huntington observes, "Diversification of function also gave the services organizational flexibility and balance by freeing them from identification with and dependence upon any single strategic concept or functional mission. . . . The new role of the services was formally recognized in the Reorganization Act of 1958: the interservice and functional commands became clearly responsible for combat, the services for personnel, training, and logistics. By reducing the combat functions of the services, the act insured their continued existence" ("Interservice Competition and the Political Roles of the Armed Services," *The American Political Science Review,* LV [March, 1961], 52).

20. The commands are Alaska, Atlantic, Southern, Continental Air Defense, Strike, Strategic Air, European, and Pacific.

21. The Defense Department's innovation does not lie in having created anew this complex organizational pattern involving both functional components and line components at headquarters and field level. Counterparts of this pattern have existed for years in a number of federal agencies at bureau level, administering relatively specialized and technical programs, involving a number of different functions and the necessity of integrating performance of these specialties into a unified whole, through a field organization operating often far from headquarters e.g., the U.S. Forest Service of the Department of Agriculture and the Bureau of Reclamation of the Department of Interior. The creative dimension of the Defense Department's performance lies in its innovative adaptation of these patterns to an entire department of vast size and complexity, containing three highly autonomous components each with its own rich and distinctive tradition reinforced by powerful political allies. This is an organizational achievement of truly heroic proportions!

Department's top management.[22] Interservice support and supply functions have been consolidated around central agencies such as Defense Supply, which is directly under the Secretary; and Defense Intelligence, Defense Communications, and Defense Atomic Support, all of which are under the Joint Chiefs of Staff. Many functions originally handled by interservice committees, such as the Research and Development Board, have been assigned to such offices as the Advanced Research Projects Agency which operates under an Assistant Secretary of Defense (the Director of Defense Research and Engineering).

The structure and role of the Joint Chiefs of Staff have also been basically altered. The 1947 Act first provided a statutory base for the Joint Chiefs of Staff, but in keeping with the general structure of unification the plan was simply for a committee of service chiefs with no chairman. The 1949 amendments and resulting reorganization created a chairman for the Joint Chiefs, but he was to have no "vote." In 1953, Reorganization Plan No. 6 plus the manner in which President Eisenhower personally dealt with the Chiefs converted the chairman into a full-fledged executive for the organization. Since then the pre-eminence of the Chairman over the service-affiliated members of the Joint Chiefs of Staff has been pronounced.[23]

22. When these new Assistant Secretaries of Defense were first established by the 1953 reorganization plan, and assigned functional responsibilities, they were given no direct command authority over the military department. In practice, however, their access to the Secretary of Defense and their near monopoly of information about their function in all services enabled their recommendations to prevail often despite service department objectives. See Gene M. Lyons, "The New Civil-Military Relations," *The American Political Science Review*, LV (March, 1961), 55. Hanson Baldwin puts the present situation bluntly ". . . all of the Assistant Secretaries of Defense have become, not de jure, but de facto, line *operators* as well as *staff* assistants. By virtue of authority delegated by the Secretary, they can and do cut across service lines and intervene at the lowest echelons." Hanson W. Baldwin, "Slow-Down in the Pentagon," *Foreign Affairs*, XLIII (January, 1965), 274.

23. Similar organizational changes were occurring at this same time (1949-1953) in a number of regulatory commissions and other collective bodies, such as the Civil Service Commission and the Council of Economic Advisers. The Hoover Commission has uniformly recommended that in agencies headed by boards or commissions one member should be designated chairman and given executive authority to act for the group. President Eisenhower helped to reinforce these changes by his personal style of handling administrative matters. In contrast to President Truman who, for example, had preferred to see members of his Council of Economic Advisers individually to insure hearing varied points of view, Mr. Eisenhower looked to one man, the chairman, as spokesman for the

Significant innovations in defense decision-making have accompanied these organizational changes. The most conspicuous advance has come in the development of sharper analytical tools, revolutionizing the process of budgetary planning and control since the 1940's. Throughout the 1940's and the 1950's, effective budgetary controls were exercised over the military departments through the imposition of expenditure ceilings. The Secretary of Defense might support the particular ceiling—or even strive to lower it, as in the case of Louis Johnson—or he might become the armed forces' advocate in pressing for greater spending authority, but the ceiling represented the crucial mechanism of higher political control. The process was simplicity itself. The Budget Bureau provided the President "with certain factual information as to where certain policies would lead. From that the President set a ceiling on the armed forces. . . ."[24] But if such ceilings provided an unambiguous determination of aggregate allocations to the military sector on a year-by-year basis, they were of no assistance to the policy-maker in providing criteria for choosing among alternative programs within the ceiling limits. In this basic sense, ceilings failed to provide the means for coming to grips with crucial policy choices. Secretaries of Defense were left to make "major decisions without adequate information," as Charles J. Hitch has remarked, and ". . . every year the plans and programs of each of the services had to be cut back severely to fit the budget ceiling, by program cancellations, stretch-outs, or postponements—but only for that year. Beyond the budget year, unrealistic plans continued to burgeon—perhaps next year the ceiling would be higher."[25]

The response to this problem has been the development of functional or program budgeting, and the elaboration of what former Defense Department Comptroller Hitch calls the three-phase process of planning–programming–budgeting.[26] Employ-

---

group. He expected differences of opinion to be thrashed out and resolved before recommendations, proposals, or advice, were given to him. In this setting the chairman of an advisory body, including the Joint Chiefs of Staff, acquired special status among his colleagues.

24. From congressional testimony of Budget Director Frank Pace in 1949, quoted in Charles J. Hitch, *Decision-Making for Defense* (Berkeley and Los Angeles: University of California Press, 1965), p. 24.

25. *Ibid.*, p. 26.

26. For an excellent short description of the development of this "planning-

ing systems analysis and cost-effectiveness criteria, programs are projected in terms of end-product alternative capabilities, such as continental air defense or strategic retaliatory forces, rather than being grouped under descriptive categories—such as "personnel" or "procurement"—according to service origin. Planning and budgeting become explicitly joined together, and military forces and their costs are related to the mission they are required to fulfill.[27]

This system of program budgeting that developed in the Defense Department to cope with the exploding problems of military technology is already having a profound effect upon budgetary practices throughout the Executive Branch. In October, 1965, Federal Budget Director Charles L. Schultze, acting for the President, directed departments and agencies outside the defense establishment to draw up program budgets for their operations—"McNamara-style"—by May 1, 1966.[28]

The fact that the Defense Department has pioneered in the development of these tools for decision-makers is significant. This creative achievement is a product of, and illustrates well, the tremendous intellectual ferment that has characterized the whole area of strategic studies over the years since World War II. Rec-

programming-budgeting" process, and the role of cost effectiveness studies, see Chapters 2 and 3, *ibid.*, pp. 21-60.

27. See *ibid.*; William W. Kaufmann, *The McNamara Strategy* (New York: Harper and Row, 1964), Ch. 5; and E. S. Quade (ed.), *Analysis for Military Decision* (Chicago: Rand McNally and Co., 1964), especially Chs. 2, 3, 16 and 17.

28. Robert S. Boyd writing in *The Washington Post* for Sunday, November 14, 1965, under the heading "Managerial Reform Spreads," says in part: "Defense Secretary Robert S. McNamara's managerial revolution has burst out of the Pentagon and into other parts of the Government.

"Twenty-one non-defense departments and agencies are under presidential orders to adopt fundamental McNamara-style innovations by May 1. . . .

"What McNamara did at the Pentagon four years ago—and what is being tried now throughout the Executive Branch—is to focus officials' attention on ends instead of on means. . . .

"Once the Government's many missions are identified officials are under orders to prepare a detailed 'program memorandum' for each one. The papers are due at the White House May 1.

"These memorandums will spell out what the agency is trying to accomplish, what methods it proposes to use, and what it will cost over five years. The cost and effectiveness of using alternate programs—or no program at all—must also be included in the memorandums."

See also "U. S. Agencies Get Order: Join McNamara's Band," *Business Week*, November 13, 1965.

ognizing the novelty of the problems faced, and acknowledging the requirements for continued large-scale scientific and technical support in planning and operations, the military establishment itself provided the initial impetus for this trend in the founding of such defense-research organizations as the RAND Corporation.[29]

The American defense establishment of the 1960's bears little resemblance to the system envisaged by Forrestal and Eberstadt in 1945—or, for that matter, to the form of unification advocated by their opponents in the War Department during 1945-46. While the Defense Department reorganizations of 1949-1953 largely resembled reorganization occurring during the same period in numbers of other federal agencies, the creative adaptation to the requirements of changing mission and continuing technological revolution has now set the Defense Establishment apart as the Executive-branch pioneer in new management techniques and organizational patterns.[30] This drive somehow to institutionalize the process of innovation is a direct response to the peculiar urgency of stresses and strains in the military sub-system.

29. Gene M. Lyons speaks of the creative efforts of the Department of Defense to bring the best technical skills to be found in the nation to bear upon the problems of national security:
". . . a series of innovating techniques have therefore been developed to bring professional competence to bear upon matters of public policy where neither political nor career executives can fully meet the demands. They include *ad hoc* and standing advisory committees, contractual arrangements for consultative services, the assignment of broad investigations or actual operations to outside institutions, and government-financed independent agencies set up outside the formality of the bureaucracy." "The New Civil-Military Relations," pp. 59-60.

30. Dr. Clarence Danhof of the Brookings Institution has directed a major study of government contracting which is nearing completion. In his book on the subject, soon to be published by the Brookings Institution, Danhof characterizes the growth of the contract system and its application, especially by the Defense Establishment, in the field of research and development as "a new form of public administration" which has evolved over the past two decades. He deals extensively with the pioneering role of the Defense Department in the design of organizational structure and administrative process for research and development. In this administration of innovation, as he calls it, the Department of Defense has found in the contract system an efficient way to tap the enormous technical capabilities of the private sector—especially industry and the universities. Here again requirements of the defense sub-system have stimulated the creative adaptation of old forms and techniques, this time to enable the Department to capitalize on national capabilities in research and development. Its progress serves as a continuing demonstration to other governmental agencies, and increasingly they, too, are drawing selectively from Defense Department experience in research and development. See Chapter IV, "Government Contracting and the New Public Administration," in Clarence Danhof's forthcoming book on Government Contracting.

British Defense Organization since 1946

The same kind of observation can be made about the direction of higher defense organization in Britain since the close of World War II. More gradually, but quite decisively, the United Kingdom has in several vital respects moved away from the kind of system which many Americans for years regarded as a model, and, like its American ally, it has moved in the direction of increasing centralization of decision-making and control. Technological change has compelled new forms of adaptive response, and, reversing the process of the 1940's, in more recent years Britain has tended to look to its American ally as a model worthy of some imitation in meeting the new requirements—despite the very different natures of the defense obligations and problems which confront the two governments and despite their different administrative traditions.

First, the authority and "independence" of the British service departments, and the political standing of their civilian chiefs, have been steadily eroded, especially since the reorganization beginning in the late 1950's. Conversely, the power and status of the Minister of Defense—now the Secretary of State for Defense—has just as steadily been enhanced.

In 1946 it was announced that a Minister of Defense would be named. Although the Prime Minister would retain "supreme responsibility for defense," the new Minister would be responsible for the allocation of resources among the services, for general policy on research and development, and for the administration of interservice agencies. The service ministers, however (the Secretaries of State for War and for Air, and the First Lord of the Admiralty), would answer to the Cabinet and to Parliament for their own programs—*i.e.*, for the utilization of the resources allocated. In this context, the Minister of Defense would "coordinate" policy, but he would not "run" the service departments—to use one of Forrestal's favorite phrases. The Chiefs of Staff would continue to have direct and immediate access to the Cabinet and its Defense Committee, and the elaborate committee structure which had developed since the founding of the Committee of Imperial Defense continued as the vital arena of policy development.[31]

31. *Central Organisation for Defence* (London: H. M. S. O., 1946), Cmnd.

For over a decade this system functioned without major change, although there was constant criticism of "interservice rivalry," of the absence of unified strategic plans, and of "sterile arguments" between the "great military interests" which obstructed rationality and efficiency[32]—the counterpart of American complaints of service "parochialism." After the Suez debacle Prime Minister Harold Macmillan and his Minister of Defense, Duncan Sandys, set in train measures for greater centralization, comparable in scope and substance to the 1958 Defense Reorganization Act across the Atlantic in the aftermath of Sputnik. The "central theme," as Franklyn Johnson has observed, was the "transfer of authority over, and representation of, the armed forces to the Ministry of Defense."[33] The Minister of Defense was given authority over all policy questions affecting force levels, organization, equipment, supply, and deployment of the services. Additionally, a chairman of the Chiefs of Staff Committee was established (the Chief of Defense Staff), who would be the principal adviser to the Minister of Defense.[34]

The 1963 Defense White Paper carried these trends toward centralization, and derogation of service authority, even further.[35] The Minister of Defense was elevated to the rank of Secretary of State, while the heads of the air, war, and naval ministries became Ministers of State for Defense. The Cabinet Defense Committee was supplanted by a Committee on Defense and Overseas Policy, and the three service members were dropped from its membership. The new Ministry of Defense and its secretary were vested with all statutory authority previously lodged in the service ministries, while the air, naval and general staffs were merged into a single Defense Staff lodged in the Ministry of

6923. On this and subsequent developments in British defense organization, see Ries, *The Management of Defense*, pp. 73 ff.

32. See William P. Snyder, *The Politics of British Defense Policy, 1945-1962* (Columbus: Ohio State University Press, 1964), pp. 154-55; and the excellent analysis by Laurence P. Martin, "The Market for Strategic Ideas in Britain: The 'Sandys Era,'" *American Political Science Review*, LVI (1962), 23-41.

33. "Politico-Military Organization in the United Kingdom: Some Recent Developments," *Journal of Politics*, XXVII (May, 1965), 343.

34. *Central Organisation for Defence* (London: H. M. S. O., 1958), Cmnd. 476.

35. *Central Organisation for Defence* (London: H. M. S. O., 1963), Cmnd. 2097. See also Ries, *The Management of Defense*, pp. 80-82, and Snyder, *The Politics of British Defense Policy*, pp. 151-57.

Defense. The Ministers of State for the three services, moreover, have been assigned certain functional areas of responsibility comparable to those of the American assistant secretaries of defense. These responsibilities are inter-service. Thus, the Minister for the Army is charged with overseeing "matters of international policy for defense" (Assistant Secretary, International Security Affairs), while the Minister for the Air Force is to co-ordinate all research and development.

Particularly noteworthy also in the new British defense organization is the cognizance taken of the need to apply sharper, more exacting cost and other criteria as aids to decision-making. A Defense Secretariat has been established, and in that secretariat, which reviews and co-ordinates the work of the scientific, administrative, and military staffs, is vested responsibility for the review of "the full scope and content of the defence programme and the Defence Budget." As Snyder points out, the office conducts "systems analysis" comparable to that done by the Assistant Secretary (Systems Analysis) in the Pentagon.[36] Moreover, the new Labor Government, continuing in this vein, placed great stress in its 1965 Defense White Paper[37] on "cost-effectiveness studies," and accorded "high priority" to the development of the "essential tool" of "functional costings." It was announced that a defense-wide "operational analysis" establishment had been formed to conduct systems analysis and related work, and to build a staff of scientists, mathematicians, engineers, and economists. An American firm which specializes in such work for the Department of Defense was providing advice. As one commentator expressed it: "For a moment, a visitor to the Ministry of Defence . . . might have thought himself in Robert S. McNamara's Pentagon."[38] *The Economist* went so far as to remark: "It is still both true and welcome that the cost-effectiveness approach, for the very first time, has been firmly nailed to the masthead of this new team [the Labor Government of Harold Wilson]. If it sinks, they drown."[39]

36. Snyder, *The Politics of British Defense Policy*, p. 153.
37. *Statement on the Defence Estimates, 1965* (London: H. M. S. O., 1965), Cmnd. 2595.
38. "Defence Costs: The Candle-End Fallacy," *Sunday Times* (London), February 28, 1965.
39. "Defending Which Interests," *The Economist*, CCXIV (February 27, 1965), 863.

John C. Ries, whose study of U.S. defense management profoundly admires the British committee system and deplores
trends in U.S. defense organization, expressed the view after the
1963 White Paper that "the major change involves a new name
and a new building."[40] This appraisal no longer seems tenable.
The change in direction in British military organization seems, on
the contrary, to have been undertaken in deadly earnest. As the
1965 White Paper points out: "The changes, already decided or
now contemplated, in organisation and procedures both at Headquarters level in the Ministry of Defence and in the field . . . may
lead, in due course, to more fundamental changes in the structure of Service administration as a whole."[41] Former Congress-
man Carl Vinson's pointed remark that the Office of the Secretary of Defense had become a "fourth service department" can
be made with no less appropriateness about the new Ministry in
Whitehall.

TECHNOLOGY AND ORGANIZATIONAL AND POLITICAL
CHANGE

The movement of defense organization in Britain and the
United States along such closely parallel lines, particularly since
1958, must be construed as the adaptive response, within two
similar yet distinctive systems, to the same kinds of stimuli.[42]
These stimuli are generated by the almost unbelievable rate of
change in military technology, which has in turn produced objective military requirements that neither system could altogether
manage within previous organizational and political frameworks.
Civil-military politics in both systems appear to be evolving along
lines of greater similarity as a consequence.

The first incentive has been that of economic cost. Technology offers an almost endless array of feasible weapons, all very
expensive and most foredoomed to rapid obsolescence. Miscal-
culations, for whatever reason, are immensely expensive, as
demonstrated in Britain in the "Blue Streak" episode and the

40. *The Management of Defense*, p. 82.
41. Cmnd. 2592., p. 41.
42. For a discussion of common problems which stresses differences in management, see Michael Howard, "Organisation for Defence in the United Kingdom
and the United States, 1945-58," in *Brassey's Annual: The Armed Forces Year-
Book, 1959* (New York: The Macmillan Co., 1959), pp. 69-77.

more recent cancellation of the TSR-2. The United States, by reason of its greater wealth, has a relatively wider margin of error, but the necessity for choice has been no less pressing. In such a context, political leadership necessarily searches for greater precision in the guidelines which must shape these choices.

Second, enormous risks are attendant upon such choices. Political control may be exercised—and is exercised—after the fashion so candidly recounted by a former British Minister of Defense. Speaking in 1958, Emmanuel Shinwell described how the £6 billion program submitted by the service chiefs in 1951 was reduced to £ 4.7 billion. "Who did it? I did it. How was it done? Let us take the War Office as an example. The War Office put in a programme amounting to many hundreds of millions of pounds. . . . We cut it, just like that, and the War Office had to accept the cut."[43] The same declaration could be made—with modification only in details—by some former American secretaries of Defense. They also "cut it, just like that," or they presided over the cuts directed by the President and his budgetary advisers. Although it is effective, and exercised by politically accountable officials, in a context of great military danger the potential hazards of such decision-making are obvious.

It is the search for more exacting criteria, in an effort to diminish such hazards, which has undermined much of the traditional autonomy of the armed services, and which has prompted wider utilization of these new approaches to decision-making by the armed services themselves. Over twenty years ago B. H. Liddell Hart remarked: "The way that decisions are reached on questions of strategy, tactics, organisation, etc., is lamentably unscientific."[44] Despite systems analysis, cost-effectiveness studies, and similar devices, that observation is undoubtedly still a valid one. Charles J. Hitch has pointed out that it is difficult to believe "that any significant military problem will ever be wholly susceptible to rigorous analysis," but, as he goes on to observe, "analytical techniques can allow us to make significant choices with a very real increase in confidence."[45] It is not a matter of substituting exacting analysis for judgment. The question, rather,

43. *Parliamentary Debates (Commons)*, 592, col. 1000; quoted in Snyder, *The Politics of British Defense Policy*, p. 156.
44. *Thoughts on War* (London: Faber, 1944), p. 125.
45. Quoted in Quade (ed.), *Analysis for Military Decisions*, p. 326.

"is whether those judgments have to be made in the fog of in-adequate data, unclear and undefined issues, and a welter of conflicting opinions, or whether they can be made on the basis of adequate, reliable information, relevant experience, and clearly drawn issues. In the end, analysis is but an aid to judgment."[46] Discussing pressing policy decisions confronting British defense officials in this vein, *The Economist* has recently remarked that cost-effectiveness and related techniques "expose in their naked-ness many issues that have hitherto been fudged over," but the political choices—such as whether to procure military aircraft in Britain or elsewhere—are not thereby made easy choices.[47] But for all these limitations, one fact remains: for the first time in history weapons and the means of employing them are subjects which can be—and are—studied by the methodology of science to such an extent that these studies substantially influence vital defense decisions. This is the development, and the achievement, which recent trends in higher defense organization both in Britain and the United States most vividly reflect.

At another level, the quest has become urgent for more effective control over the military instrument and over the shaping of that instrument. This urgency becomes compelling with the exponential rise in societal risks involved in the application of military means in the context of a nuclear confrontation. A resort to violence or to the threat of violence may place the very life of the nation in the balance in the most literal sense. The increasing emphasis upon deterrence as the prime function of armed force is the most obvious manifestation of this changed dimension, and deterrence has evoked incentives for continuing, explicit control unknown in pre-nuclear diplomacy.

Finally, the trends in defense organization have been shaped by the changing dimensions of routine military operations. New requirements, far removed from the traditional areas of military expertise, have transformed defense organization and the military profession itself. Innovation of weapons, large-scale research, and development programs are the routine requirements confronting military establishments which aspire to front-rank, or nearly front-rank, status. The weapons themselves, and the supporting systems, require a wide range of technical skills for their

46. Alain Enthoven, as quoted in *Business Week*, November 13, 1965, p. 15.
47. "McNamara's Bandwagon," *The Economist*, CCXI (May 9, 1964), 574.

deployment and operation. A modern air defense system consists of a visible military element (interceptor aircraft, surface-to-air missiles, and the base complex from which they operate), but the effectiveness of this military element is dependent upon early-warning systems, data-processing centers, and a communications network. The operation of these components, to say nothing of their design and development, entails a heavy scientific and technical input. Indeed, it was the air defense problem confronting Britain in the 1930's which prompted a remarkable series of innovations in scientific-military collaboration, and so facilitated the development of operations ("operational," in British terminology) research. In an important sense, this was the forerunner of modern military analysis.[48]

The transfer of military institutions and practices is not novel, nor is it peculiar to Anglo-American relations. It is a practice both ancient and universal. However, such transfer is always facilitated and quickened by the existence of similarities in domestic political demands within the political systems, from which have historically developed, in the British and American nations, similar patterns of civil-military politics. Both are "developed political cultures," both are "civil-military polities," and both are systems of "open equality"—to cite three recent typologies of military systems.[49] And the transfer has been channeled through an alliance relationship which is undoubtedly unique. The Anglo-American coalition of 1940-1945, as Kent Roberts Greenfield has said, "was the closest and most effective partnership that two great powers have ever achieved"—an "unprecedented achievement in the history of nation-states."[50] The same observation is probably applicable to the "special relation-

48. An excellent history of these developments is in U. K. Air Ministry, *The Origins and Development of Operational Research in the Royal Air Force* (London: H. M. S. O., 1963); and see also Basil Collier, *The Defence of the United Kingdom* (London: H. M. S. O., 1957), pp. 36-40 on early developments in the air defense preparations.

49. Cf. Finer, *The Man on Horseback*, especially pp. 141-45; David C. Rapoport, "A Comparative Theory of Military and Political Types," in Samuel P. Huntington (ed.), *Changing Patterns of Military Politics* (New York: The Free Press of Glencoe, 1962), pp. 74-77; and M. D. Feld, "A Typology of Military Organization," in *Public Policy VIII* (Cambridge: Harvard University Press, 1958), pp. 3-40.

50. *American Strategy in World War II: A Reconsideration* (Baltimore: The Johns Hopkins Press, 1961), pp. 24, 43.

ship" between the two nations which has taken form over the years of cold war.

The fact remains, however, that the impact of contemporary technological change was brought about in such rapid developments along such closely parallel lines in the civil-military politics and the military systems of both nations that the present process of transfer suggests a phenomenon significantly different. Historically the rate and scale of change have been gradual, and the adaptive responses, in the interaction of domestic political demands and objective military requirements, have been incremental. By contrast, contemporary developments in military technology have been drastic and intense, whether measured in terms of societal risks, economic costs, or other criteria. Comparative analysis of the Anglo-American experience indicates that it has been so drastic and so intense that assimilation has broken traditional response patterns within both sets of variables. Military professions are becoming more and more technically and managerially oriented, and political leadership presses for more effective, more exacting, and more dependable forms of control. The military function assumes a status of prime importance and urgency in national policy, but that function is increasingly oriented toward the management of deterrence, rather than of violence, in a context of perpetual and unprecedented danger rather than in the fluctuations of war and peace.

Defense reorganization in the United States in 1947, while extensive in scope and purpose, was certainly incremental in nature. It consisted of a series of compromises which, in some degree, did little more than formalize much that had already been done informally during the war. Probably in a normal political environment, with gradual changes in military technology, the compromise of 1947 would have endured over a considerable period of time—at least until another major war or crisis. But crisis was endemic, and by the mid-1950's the rate of change in the defense organization was becoming more drastic. Similarly, higher defense organization in Britain was relatively stable throughout the period from 1946 to 1957, but then began to enter into a stage of quite drastic change. The direction of that change was along lines strikingly similar to those being followed in the United States.

No less suggestive are parallel developments in other ministries of defense. The West German Ministry of Defense, for example, is clearly moving in the direction of adapting for its own use the procedures and techniques developed in the Pentagon, and to this end it has signed a five-year contract (early in 1965) with the Stanford Research Institute for assistance and support in establishing this capability.[51] A remark of Charles Hitch is directly to the point:

There is [he has written] a sort of inevitability about the trend toward unified Defense management ever since the end of World War II—here and in the military establishments of other major powers. . . .

In the Western World, some of our allies, notably the British, Canadians, and Germans, are also introducing programming and systems analysis into the management of their defense establishments. Although their problems are somewhat different from our own because of the nature of their national security objectives and the size and composition of their military forces [and, we should add, because of the nature of the domestic political demands], they believe that these techniques can contribute to the more effective management of their respective defense efforts.[52]

Engels long ago noted that armies were mirrors of the national societies which supported them, and that truism is implicit in most of our classifications of civil-military politics. The Anglo-American data suggest that armies are more and more the mirrors of the state of technological development and that, beyond a certain "take-off point," the level of technology infuses increasing uniformity into the organization of military establishments and into the patterns and issues of civil-military politics.

51. See Maximilian Smidt, *Frankfurter Allgemeine Zeitung*, January 26, 1965.
52. *Decision-Making for Defense*, p. 77.

Negro Political Participation in the South: An Overview*

by Donald R. Matthews and James W. Prothro

Recent changes in the political position of the southern Negro are among the most dramatic and important events in American history. The white primary and other "legal" devices for barring Negroes from the polls have all but collapsed before an increasingly insistent Supreme Court, a vigilant Justice Department, and a more recently insistent Congress. The social and economic pressures which have contributed heavily to the southern Negro's *de facto* disfranchisement in the past are weakening with the industrialization and urbanization of the region. Three federal civil-rights acts have been passed, aimed primarily at ensuring Negro access to the polls. The number of Negroes registered to vote in the region has increased by more than 600 per cent since *Smith* v. *Allwright* was decided in 1944. Negro political organizations, political candidates, and office-holders are no longer uncommon in southern cities. The "sit-ins," "freedom rides," consumer boycotts, and other forms of mass protest by southern Negroes indicate a growing impatience with the rate of progress towards "first-class citizenship" and a willingness to resort to extra-legal (if generally non-violent) tactics in order to achieve this goal.

These events have received very little systematic attention from professional students in politics. Myrdal's *American Dilemma*[1] was published shortly before the white primary was outlawed. V. O. Key, Jr., devoted only 4½ pages of his *Southern Politics*[2] to Negro political activity—the book's primary concern was with the impact of a large and politically inert Negro minority on the shape and quality of the white man's politics. Most

___

* The study upon which this chapter is based was supported by principal grants from The Rockefeller Foundation and additional grants from the Social Science Research Council. The major report of the findings is the authors' book, *Negroes and Southern Politics: Participation and Its Consequences* (New York: Harcourt, Brace and World, Inc., 1966).

1. G. Myrdal, *An American Dilemma* (N.Y.: Harper and Brothers, 1944), 2 vols.

2. V. O. Key, Jr., *Southern Politics* (N.Y.: A. A. Knopf, 1949).

168 COMPARATIVE POLITICS AND POLITICAL THEORY

political scientists seem willing to leave the description and analysis of the revolutionary changes since the appearance of these two classics to today's journalists and tomorrow's historians.[3]

This essay represents part of an effort by the authors to subject Negro political participation in the South to systematic examination. Just as the generalizations of American political science need testing for their true generality in other political systems, so may they be tested in the peculiar political subculture of the South. Our study is concerned not merely with Negro voting and non-voting, although these modes of political participation have a particular significance to southern Negroes, but with all forms of behavior through which people directly express their political opinions. A basic argument of this chapter is that the act of voting is best understood within the context of other, often more continuous, ways of participating in political life and of influencing public policy.

Our analysis is based primarily upon interviews with samples of both Negroes ($N = 618$) and whites ($N = 694$), chosen by strict probability methods from all citizens of voting age living in private households within the eleven former Confederate states.[4] In order to examine differences in Negro participation within the region more thoroughly than can be done with the usual sample survey, four intensive community studies also were conducted, one in an entirely rural Mississippi County (Crayfish County), another in an urban, deep-South area (Camellia County), another in a rural, upper South community (Bright

3. The major exceptions are Alexander Heard, A Two-Party South? (Chapel Hill: University of North Carolina Press, 1952); H. D. Price, The Negro and Southern Politics: A Chapter in Florida History (N.Y.: New York University Press, 1957); Donald Strong, "The Future of the Negro Voter in the South," Journal of Negro Education, XXVI (Summer, 1957), 400-7; John H. Fenton and Kenneth M. Vines, "Negro Registration in Louisiana," American Political Science Review, LI (1957), 704-13; Bradbury Seasholes, "Negro Political Participation in Two North Carolina Cities" (unpublished dissertation, University of North Carolina, 1962); Alfred Clubock, John De Grove, and Charles Farris, "The Manipulated Negro Vote: Preconditions and Consequences," Journal of Politics, XXVI (February, 1964), 112-29; James Q. Wilson, Negro Politics (Glencoe, Ill.: The Free Press, 1960).

4. For a description of the field phase of the study, and especially for the difficulties resulting from the exclusive use of Negro interviewers for Negro respondents, see M. Axelrod, D. R. Matthews, and J. W. Prothro, "Recruitment for Survey Research on Race Problems in the South," Public Opinion Quarterly, XXVI (Summer, 1962), 254-62.

Leaf County), and still another in a city in the upper South (Piedmont County).[5]

This essay attempts to present a descriptive overview of Negro political participation in the South, to compare Negro rates of participation with those of southern whites and, where possible, with those of Negroes and whites outside the region. Although detailed analysis of these findings is left for a later, larger study, the descriptive details imply much about the factors which encourage and inhibit Negro political participation in the American South today.

TALKING POLITICS

The most ubiquitous form of participation in the governmental process is "talking politics." Everyday political discussions, gossip, and arguments between ordinary citizens should not be dismissed as meaningless chatter. Rather, this political talk—even of the most superficial and ill-informed sort—is an important part of democracy in action.

Asked if he ever talked with friends about public problems, a sixty-four-year-old retired farmer, a Negro with a first-grade education, responded:

> The conditions and changes of things as compared to what it had been. It is so different now that it is like a new world. You know, I spent my young life working for little of nothing. I have worked for 50¢ a day. Now that you can git something for working I' most too old to do any of it. And then we talks 'bout how things have changed for our people, how different that be. Well, we talk about all these war businesses. 'Course now I think that's all fulfilling the Bible. God say the world would grow wiser and wickeder. And I 'bout to live to see it.

A white mechanic with four years of schooling also reported talking with his friends about the changes taking place around him, more briefly if no less philosophically: "The Negro situation. I

5. The study also includes a multiple correlation and regression analysis of Negro voter registration figures (reported in D. R. Matthews and J. W. Prothro, "Social and Economic Factors and Negro Voter Registration in the South" and "Political Factors and Negro Voter Registration in the South," *American Political Science Review*, LVII [March and June, 1963], 24-44 and 355-67) and a sample survey of Negro college students in the southern states. Neither body of data will be utilized in this paper.

feel I'm right. If God A'mighty would mean us under one household, he wouldn't a' made America in one place and Africa in another." These exchanges of facts and prejudices, hopes and fears, help to form the climate of opinion within which politicians and public officials make political decisions.[6] Political activists can and do attempt to shape the content of the nation's political talk—indeed, this is a major purpose of all electoral and pressure-group campaigns—yet the task is so enormous that even the most absolute dictator must settle for limited success.

One might reasonably expect southern Negroes not to be active participants in the political conversation of the region. Politics has been "the white man's business" in most of the South for well over half a century. Why should a man who has never voted bother to discuss public problems he can do so little about? Political participation of all sorts is positively associated with education, occupation, and social status: the more educated and the more highly placed a person is in the social structure, the more likely he is to take an active part in the political process. Southern Negroes tend to have received relatively little education at inferior schools, and to have been lumped in an undifferentiated mass at the bottom of the southern social scale. A domestic servant with a fourth-grade education in Camellia County fits these expectations:

I don't have time for talk. I have to work so hard I don't even see them [friends] 'til I git a chance to go to church. Then we don't be talking 'bout things like that. Ain't you talking 'bout things like the wars and prices and stuff? Well, I ain't got no money and talking won't git me none. I ain't got no son to go to the army, so I don't worry none 'bout the war taking 'em; and if we was to ever have a war and they shoot one of them bombs I hear people talking 'bout, we gonna all be dead and gone anyhow, so why talk 'bout 'em and worry 'bout 'em 'fore they get here? I just cross my bridges as I come to 'em.

Lack of leisure even to talk with friends presents an extreme example of lack of the "role dispensability" necessary to active political participation.[7] And low levels of education can be ex-

6. The recognition of the political importance of informal conversation stems from P. F. Lazarsfeld, Bernard Berelson, and Hazel Gaudet, *The People's Choice* (N.Y.: Columbia University Press, 1948).

7. Max Weber, "Politics as a Vocation," in H. Gerth and C. W. Mills, *From Max Weber* (N.Y.: Oxford, University Press, 1946).

pected to produce a feeling of inability to cope with "wars and prices and stuff."

On the other hand, enforced disfranchisement of southern Negroes might be expected to produce a high level of political activity in whatever ways are permitted. Granted that the entire structure of segregation was imposed by governmental force,[8] government has extraordinary importance for the Negro; and ethnic groups in a number of countries have been found to participate more actively in politics if they are the targets of punitive government action.[9] Denied the ballot because of his skin color but still exposed to ordinary American values about democratic citizen participation, the southern Negro might seek other outlets for political self-expression. Hyper-activity might therefore be expected outside the proscribed realm of voting and elections. "We talk about the affairs of wages, and socialism, and what's going to become of us," said a Mississippi farm Negro who has never voted. "We [in this county] don't have no jobs much and what jobs we do have the whites have them. We stand around and look at them work." Here is "role dispensability" with a vengeance!

To what extent does the peculiar importance of politics for Negroes overcome their low levels of education and encourage political activity? So far as talking about public problems is concerned, the amount of public discussion varies widely for both races depending upon the situation (Figure 1). Most political discourse takes place among friends, members of the family, and fellow workers. Relatively few members of either race in the South talk about public problems with community leaders, members of the other race, politicians, or government officials.

On the whole, southern whites talk about public problems somewhat more often than Negroes do. Eighty-four per cent of the whites say they talk politics with friends, as compared to 76 per cent of the Negroes; 76 per cent of the whites but only 64 per cent of the Negroes report talking about these matters with their families. The gap between Negro and white rates of political discussion grows larger as the forum for the discussion becomes

8. C. Vann Woodward, *The Strange Career of Jim Crow* (N.Y.: Oxford University Press, 1955).

9. S. M. Lipset *et al.*, "The Psychology of Voting," in G. Lindzey (ed.), *Handbook of Social Psychology* (Cambridge, Mass.: Addison-Wesley Co., 1954), II, 1127-75.

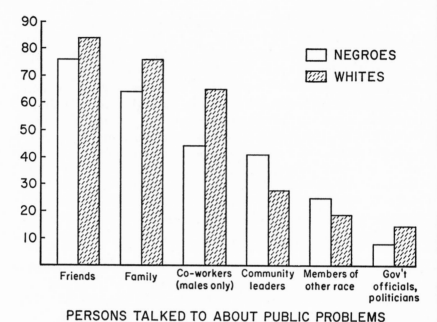

90
80
70
60
50
40
30
20
10

☐ NEGROES
▨ WHITES

Friends   Family   Co-workers   Community   Members of   Gov't
                     (males only)   leaders   other race   officials,
                                                                politicians

PERSONS TALKED TO ABOUT PUBLIC PROBLEMS

FIGURE 1. *Per Cent of Negro and White Southerners Ever Talking About Public Problems (by persons talked to).*

more public. The need for Negroes to secure government action may be great but the rewards from approaching public officials are typically small. In Crayfish County, for example, an elderly Negro farmer explained: "We talk about the road that leads to our house—you can't even get in. When I was sick a car couldn't even get here. That's the main problem I talk about. I've talked to the road superintendent about five or six times. I even asked some of his friends, and the superintendent said he doesn't give a damn about a Nigger road." Three whites report talking about public problems with co-workers for every two Negroes who do; almost twice the proportion of whites talk with politicians and public officials.

But there are two exceptions to this trend. First of all, Negroes report talking about public problems with Negro community leaders much more frequently than whites talk to their leaders. This deviation from the normal pattern probably reflects the subordinate social and political position of the Negro in the South. The southern Negro, typically suffering from severe and cumulative deprivations, often does not feel that he can effectively take his problems directly to the white power-wielders of the community. Instead, he often works through Negro intermediaries. These leaders may be of considerably higher status than the average Negro, yet they can hardly isolate themselves physically from the black ghetto, for they cannot join white leaders in the flight to the suburbs. The *social* distance between a Negro community's leaders and followers is also likely to be very small when compared to the gap found in the white community.[10] No matter how successful, wealthy, or esteemed a Negro leader may be, he is a Negro first. Leaders are therefore more necessary and accessible in the Negro community than in the white.

About a quarter of the voting-age Negroes in the South say they have talked directly with whites about public issues and problems, while only 19 per cent of the whites report having had such discussion with Negroes. The disparity between the two figures again probably reflects status differences between the two races—Negroes are more likely than whites to remember and, perhaps, to exaggerate the extent of political communication across race lines.[11] But more important than these small differences is the substantial agreement between Negroes and whites that almost all political talk takes place *within* racial groups and very little *between* them.

A young Negro maid in Florida put the point quite succinctly when asked if she discussed public affairs with the people where she works: "I don't talk to them because they are Crackers!" A twenty-eight-year-old white laborer in North Carolina represents the opposite side of the coin. Asked if he ever talked about public problems with "any colored people," he said: "I've always called them *Niggers* and I'll keep on calling them that. I call them that to their faces. Might get knocked down one day for doing it, but that won't stop me. I just ain't got no use for them." These are not ideal attitudinal conditions for the democratic dialogue.

The kinds of public problems discussed by southerners are presented in Figure 2. The Negroes discuss racial problems more than any other issue. Race ranks either first or second among public problems Negroes discuss with everyone—friends,

10. Cf. Wilson, *Negro Politics*, pp. 101 ff.

11. Cf. R. E. Lane, *Political Life* (Glencoe, Ill.: The Free Press, 1959), pp. 86 ff., for a summary of the literature on political discussion across status lines.

family, co-workers, community leaders, white people, government officials, and politicians. Economic problems (jobs, unemployment, the cost of living, taxes, and the like) and community problems (schools, housing, etc.) are next most often discussed. Since these "economic" and "community" problems have heavy racial overtones, the southern Negroes' concern for race appears to be all pervasive. Other areas of public affairs— "politics" narrowly defined; international politics; "style" issues such as corruption, efficiency, communism, individual freedom— make up less than one-third of the public problems southern Negroes talk about.

Southern whites are somewhat less preoccupied with race and its consequences. The public problems they most frequently discuss are local community problems (especially the public schools), economic problems, "politics," and government. However, a full 15 per cent of the problems they mention are clearly racial ones, as large a proportion of all issues as international affairs. Since southern community, economic, and political problems are so heavily influenced by racial concerns, race represents a major topic of discussion among southern whites; yet the political interests of southern whites—at least as reflected by their talk —are broader, more cosmopolitan, and less bound by the immediate and personal problems of existence in a segregated society than is true for southern Negroes.

Considerable variety from one community to another is concealed beneath this south-wide pattern of political communication. From the finding that Negroes talk more than whites with community leaders, for example, we drew the inference that Negro leaders are more accessible than white leaders. Since this inference is in keeping with other lines of explanation no less than with our data, it can be entertained with considerable confidence. But the four communities selected for detailed examination indicate that the factual situation varies from one community to the next. In both Crayfish and Piedmont counties, whites are as likely as Negroes to have discussed public affairs with community leaders, such as club or church leaders, but the rates for both races in Crayfish are about twice as high as in Piedmont.[12] In

12. In Crayfish County, 61 per cent of the whites and 58 per cent of the Negroes report such conversations; in Piedmont County, 31 per cent of both races report inter-racial discussions.

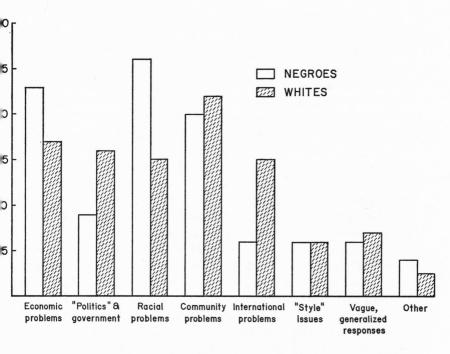

FIGURE 2. *Types of Public Problems Talked About by Negro and White Southerners (in % of all public problems discussed).*

the rural environment of Crayfish, white community leaders share with their Negro counterparts the characteristic of physical and social proximity to their followers. Indeed, Crayfish residents more frequently talk politics with people they regard as community leaders than with their fellow workers. In the urban environment of Piedmont, on the other hand, whites talk with community leaders at about the same rate as Southerners in general. Where Piedmont differs is in the fact that its Negroes' rate of contact with leaders is lower than for southern Negroes in general, at about the same rate as for whites. The more highly differentiated Negro community in Urbania, the central city of Piedmont County, apparently leads to a pattern of leader-follower communication about politics similar to that of southern whites. Rather than negating the descriptive generalization applied to the South as a whole, then, community variations lend additional credence to the generalization by suggesting the conditions under which it holds.

As in the South as a whole, very few Negroes in our four community study areas ever talk about public affairs with government officials or politicians. In Piedmont County 8 per cent, exactly the same as in the South as a whole, report such conversations. Since Negroes hold public office in Urbania, and are active and articulate political participants, one might expect even more Negroes there than in the South in general to contact public officials. But the unusual permissiveness of the environment may be balanced by the greater size of the population. With about the same number of officials as a small town, a relatively large city offers less mathematical chance for any one member of its population to have talked with an official. The proportion of Negroes ever having talked with an official drops to 4 per cent in Camellia County, to 3 per cent in Bright Leaf, and to 2 per cent in Crayfish. The elderly Negro farmer who lamented the road supervisor's lack of interest in a "Nigger road" suggests why. None of the other three counties has a single Negro who holds an important government or party office. To talk with an official, then, is to talk with a white person who is quite likely to be unsympathetic and perhaps insulting as well. This lack of contact with public officials clearly does not stem from a lack of problems —all three of these counties have higher rates of discussion than Piedmont with Negro community leaders, and Crayfish has the highest of all.

What kinds of public affairs do Negroes talk about in different communities? In Piedmont County, even more than in the South as a whole, racial problems dominate discussions in which Negroes take part. Race accounts for 46 per cent of all the topics mentioned by Piedmont Negroes, almost twice the frequency for the entire South and much higher than in Camellia (32 per cent), Bright Leaf (19 per cent), and Crayfish (16 per cent) counties. In the least repressive county, Negroes talk much more about race problems than in most repressive areas, not because they have more race problems but because they have some chance to alleviate the ones they do have.

An elderly doorman in Urbania, out of a job, offers some insight into the discussions there. Asked what he talked about with his friends, he said: "Well, just first one thing and another. Mostly about the picketing of Piedmont Theater. They shot me out of a job. (Who is that?) The young folk what picket the theater. I had worked there sixteen years and they closed the

colored balcony. Course it's all right though." The picketing led
to the integration of the theater. In this environment of open
differences and accommodation of differences, talk about public
affairs between Negroes and whites deals principally with race,
making up an even larger proportion of the topics reported by
Negroes (61 per cent) than by whites (51 per cent) when the
talk is across racial lines.

Camellia, Bright Leaf, and Crayfish counties offer sharp contrasts to Piedmont. Race remains the most common public problem discussed by Negroes in Camellia, where vigorous but largely unsuccessful efforts have been made to end public segregation.
In Bright Leaf and Crayfish counties, however, economic problems emerge as the number one topic among Negroes. In these
primarily rural counties, basic problems of food and clothing are
so pressing for Negroes, and the attainment of status needs so
unlikely, that discussion focuses primarily on such things as jobs
and pay. In talking with white people, Negroes in these counties
are much less likely than in Piedmont to bring up racial problems.
The frequency with which Negroes mention race as the topic of
conversation with whites drops from 61 per cent in Piedmont to
36 per cent in Camellia, and on down to 21 per cent in Bright
Leaf and 24 per cent in Crayfish. Moreover, all three of these
counties differ from Piedmont in that more whites than Negroes
report race as a topic of inter-racial conversation. A retired
farmer in Crayfish (explaining why he had never known a white
person well enough to talk to him as a friend) suggests the
extreme difference between his environment and that of the doorman in Urbania: "I am scared of them (laugh). They'll get you
and try to make you talk and go tell their friends you're one of
them 'Niggers' that's got big ideas. Then they'd want to run you
out of town or beat you up and will even kill you!" For people
who have never visited Crayfish, who number in the millions, this
may sound like an old man's hyperbole; for the few people who
have visited the place, however, it appears within the realm of
the possible.

No precise comparison can be made between the amount and
content of political talk in the North and South. However, 33
per cent of the northern Negroes reported talking to someone
during the 1960 presidential election in an effort to influence his

vote.[13] Thirty-four per cent of the northern whites said they engaged in this form of political talking. In this respect, at least, Negroes in the North participate almost as much as whites. In the South, the gap between whites and Negroes is considerably larger. But it is also far smaller than might be assumed from differences in white and Negro rates of registration and voting.

VOTING

The picture of relatively modest differences in rates of political participation between southern whites and Negroes changes drastically when the focus shifts from talking politics to voting. Eighty-six per cent of the voting-age whites in the South have voted in at least one election; only 41 per cent of the adult Negroes have ever voted. This 2-to-1 ratio is maintained when current status as a registered voter is examined: 66 per cent of the voting-age whites but only 33 per cent of the voting-age Negroes were registered to vote at the time of our survey.[14] In the non-southern states, there is almost no difference in the rates at which Negroes and whites register to vote—80 per cent of the voting-age whites and 78 per cent of the voting-age Negroes were registered to vote in 1960.

When the frequency of voting in presidential elections by Negroes and whites is plotted graphically for both the North and South (Figure 3), the southern Negroes stand out in stark contrast to the three other groups. The frequency with which institutionally or normatively approved behavior is performed tends, when presented graphically, to take the shape of a "J," and this is the shape of the curves representing turnout in presidential elections for northern Negroes and for both southern and northern whites. Most people act in the approved way—in this case, vote regularly—so the highest point is to the right of the graph. But the frequency of Negro voting in the South completely reverses the pattern. Judging from these findings alone, one would conclude that the institutionally-approved behavior

13. This and all subsequent references to the 1960 presidential election are based on data for that election collected by the University of Michigan Survey Research Center.

14. Since not all southern states and localities have registration systems, this figure is based on the respondents' belief that they have met all the state and local qualifications for voting.

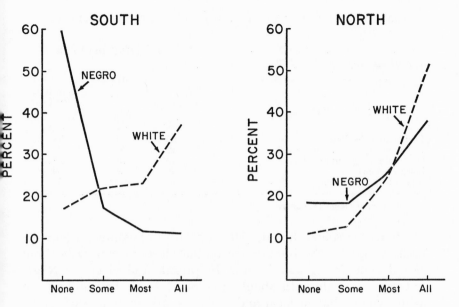

FIGURE 3. *Frequency of Voting in Presidential Elections, by Region and Race.*

for southern Negroes is abstention from voting, and that the least approved behavior is regular participation.

The northern whites are the most regular voters in presidential elections—52 per cent report having voted in "all" presidential elections since they were old enough to vote, and only 11 per cent report participating in none. The northern Negroes and southern whites have almost identical records: 38 per cent of both groups say they have voted in "all" presidential elections, and 17 or 18 per cent in none. Only 11 per cent of the southern Negroes, on the other hand, report voting in "all," and another 11 per cent in "most" presidential elections since they became of voting age; 60 per cent have never voted in an election for president of the United States. The same general picture emerges when the voting for other offices is examined.

Not only are most southern Negroes non-voters, but those who do vote turn out with less regularity than do southern whites (Table 1). The less important and visible the office, the more intermittent becomes the voting of southern Negroes. Thus 55% of the Negroes who have ever voted participated in "all" or "most" presidential elections, yet only 28% voted in "all" or "most"

TABLE 1. *Percentage of Southern Voters Participating in All or Most Elections, by Race and Type of Election*

Type of Electoral Contests	Negro (%)	White (%)	Negro Rate as Per Cent of White Rate (%)
Presidential elections	55	71	78
Gubernatorial primary elections*	42	61	69
Gubernatorial general elections	40	61	66
Local elections	39	66	59
School-board elections	28	48	58

*Registered Democrats only.

elections for school board. The regularity of white turnout decreases, too, as the importance of the elections diminishes, but the decline is far less severe. In presidential elections Negro voters participate with about three-quarters of the regularity of white voters, but in local and school-board elections their regularity of voting is only about half that of their white neighbors.

So far as voting is concerned, then, the participation of southern Negroes is a great deal less than that of whites in the South or North and of Negroes living outside the former Confederate states. This disparity holds up in all four of the communities we studied in detail, but it almost disappears in Piedmont County and it reaches its most exaggerated form in Crayfish County. In Piedmont, three-fourths of the Negroes have voted at one time or another, and 69 per cent are currently registered; compared with the whites in Piedmont, Negro voting is at 91 per cent and current registration is at 95 per cent of the white rates. In Crayfish, on the other hand, only 6 per cent of the Negroes have ever enjoyed the experience of voting, and that was while they lived somewhere else! Not a single Negro is registered in the county; indeed, white residents boast that no Negro has *ever* voted in Crayfish. Negroes in Camellia County participate much more, and in Bright Leaf County somewhat less, than in the South as a whole.[15]

The varying gap between Negro and white participation is revealed by current Negro registration as per cent of white registration: Piedmont, 95 per cent; Camellia, 89 per cent; Bright

15. The proportions ever voting and currently registered in Camellia are 61 and 55 per cent, respectively; in Bright Leaf the respective figures are 27 and 23 per cent.

Leaf, 32 per cent; Crayfish, o per cent. While Camellia Negroes have not attained the extremely high levels of voting that set off Piedmont County, they are closer to Piedmont than to the South in general. A fifty-five-year-old lumber-grader, a man with a third-grade education who had never voted, suggested something of why Camellia County approaches the Piedmont model: "Well, I hadn't given much thought [to voting] 'til here lately. You know, you can live in a place where everything is at a standstill, nobody doing nothing, and you will be in the rut with them. But there ain't nothing that's keeping us from it, so the next time they be voting, I'll be there, too. I been thinking 'bout it seriously here of late. This is all our problem, and if some is going to jail, the least I could do is vote."

When attention is confined to those who have ever voted, additional community differences appear. Whereas Piedmont County has far more Negroes registered to vote than the other counties, Camellia County has the largest proportion of regular voters among those Negroes who are registered. Defining a regular voter as one who has voted in all or most elections since reaching voting age, Camellia has more regular Negro voters for every type of contest—presidential elections, gubernatorial primaries and general elections, local elections, and school-board elections. The number of regular voters among white participants in the two counties is about the same, but roughly 10 per cent more of the Negro voters in Camellia vote regularly. The difference is smallest for presidential elections (47 per cent regular Negro voters in Piedmont to 53 per cent in Camellia) and greatest for local elections (28 per cent to 45 per cent). The unusually high registration of Negroes in Piedmont has apparently reached the point where it includes more voters with low motivation than are found in Camellia. In other words, the smaller proportion of Negroes who are registered in Camellia may represent a more select group. But Bright Leaf County suggests that a more complex explanation will be required: although only 23 per cent of its Negroes are registered, this small group includes few regular voters (30 per cent for presidential elections, 5 per cent for local elections).

The white voters in these counties, as in the South as a whole, tend to vote more regularly than do the Negroes. The difference is greatest, of course, in Crayfish, where no Negroes vote; but it is also extreme in Bright Leaf. Only in Camellia does the regularity of turnout by Negro voters approach that of whites. Crayfish is further distinguished by a tremendously high frequency of voting in local elections—86 per cent of its white electorate vote in all or most local or county elections, and 77 per cent can make the same claim for school-board elections. Voters in the other three counties turn out much less regularly for local elections, although they equal or surpass Crayfish in regularity of voting in presidential elections. The peculiarity of Crayfish is seen in the fact that its voters participate more regularly in local than in presidential elections. This extreme provincialism is not simply a product of rurality. Bright Leaf County is predominantly rural, but for local elections it has the smallest proportion of regular voters, both white and Negro, to be found in our four counties.

PARTICIPATING IN POLITICAL CAMPAIGNS

Americans probably spend more time, lung power, and money "campaigning" than any other democratic people. The vast size of the American electorate, the large number of elective offices, the system of holding elections at fixed intervals without regard to the existence of crises or issues, the nomination of candidates through primary elections—all help explain why. Political campaigns and general elections for state office may be waged less extensively in the South, as a predominantly one-party region, but the flamboyant, no-holds-barred battles in the Democratic primaries may make up for that lack. Indeed, some writers maintain that the South is peculiarly politicized, that Southerners take to politics as naturally as to hominy grits and black-eyed peas.

Despite the elaborate nature of American campaigns, most of the activity comes from a small proportion of the citizenry. In the heat of the 1960 Kennedy-Nixon battle, for example, only 12 per cent of the adult citizens in America engaged in one of the most common forms of campaign participation—attending campaign meetings or rallies. Most Americans are sufficiently aware of politics to mention it occasionally in casual conversation, and most of these go to the trouble of voting on election day; but campaign participation is a more demanding form of activity.

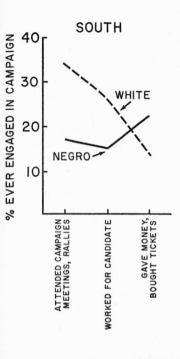
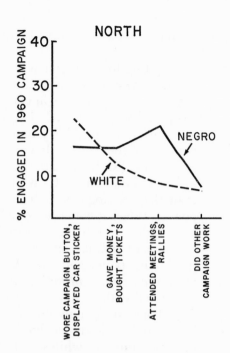

FIGURE 4. *Participation in Political Campaigns, by Region and Race.*

Only a minority of Americans take any part in a campaign, even when participation is very broadly defined.

Granted that only a minority of southern Negroes (41 per cent) have ever voted and that even fewer (33 per cent) are currently registered, one would expect to find an infinitesimal number ever to have participated in campaigns. This expectation is reinforced by the findings on southern whites: although 86 per cent have voted and 66 per cent are currently registered, only 45 per cent have *ever* taken any part in a political campaign. When we remember, however, that the low voting rates of southern Negroes may stem from a repressive environment rather than simply from lack of interest, a contrary expectation becomes possible—especially as applied to less visible forms of participation. The data support the latter expectation: 35 per cent of southern Negroes report that they have engaged in some kind of campaign participation. Whereas Negroes vote at only 48 per cent of the rate of whites, their campaign participation is 78 per cent as high as that of whites. Rather than widening, the gap between Negro and white participation thus decreases startlingly with the shift from voting to campaign activity as the measure of participation.

As Figure 4 indicates, the greatest difference between southern whites and Negroes in campaign participation is found in the most visible form of activity, and the smallest difference in the least visible form. Thirty-four per cent of the whites but only 17 per cent of the Negroes have attended campaign meetings, rallies, barbecues, fish-fries, and the like. In terms of volunteer work for a candidate or party, white participation drops more sharply than that of Negroes, reducing the difference to 11 percentage points. When it comes to giving money or buying tickets to help a candidate, white participation drops still more sharply while Negro participation increases. The difference is reduced to 9 percentage points and, even more impressive, *Negroes participate more than whites in giving money.* Giving money is an activity associated with high income, and southern Negroes are one of the lowest income groups in the country. When this consideration is added to the knowledge that southern Negroes vote at only half the rate of whites, the rate at which they give money becomes the more impressive. As suggested above, however, monetary contributions are a relatively anonymous form of participation that may be feasible for a subordinate minority whose right to a voice in politics is not universally recognized.[16] People who think government action is needed to improve their lot will normally participate more actively than those less directly dependent on government. Anonymous participation may permit this normal tendency to work in the case of some southern Negroes.

This description gains added credence from non-southern data and from the community studies. During the 1960 presidential election, non-southern Negroes participated more than whites in almost every aspect of the campaign—more gave money, attended meetings or rallies, engaged in direct campaign work, and were contacted by a party worker. Only in wearing campaign buttons or displaying car stickers did white participation exceed that of Negroes in the North—and fewer Negroes have automobiles. The contrasts between Piedmont and Camellia counties,

16. Organized criminal elements, for example, can sometimes participate in politics by way of monetary contributions, although more open participation would be out of the question. Cf. A. Heard, *The Costs of Democracy* (Chapel Hill, N. C.: University of North Carolina Press, 1960).

on the one hand, and Bright Leaf and Crayfish, on the other, add
to the picture. In the two rural counties, campaign rallies are for
"whites only," so few Negroes have ever attended. In the two
urban counties, Negroes are not excluded from rallies. Indeed,
any candidate for office in Urbania must actively seek Negro
support; somewhat more covertly, candidates in Capitol City also
attempt to establish Negro support, and the entire slate of candidates will appear at special Negro rallies. Accordingly, a fourth
to a fifth of the Negroes in Piedmont and Camellia have attended
political meetings, compared with less than 10 per cent in Bright
Leaf and Crayfish. But the highest proportion of campaign
contributors (29 per cent) is found in Crayfish, where no Negro
is allowed to vote!

Granted the inhibitions in Crayfish against Negro voting—
such as getting slugged with a pistol—and the uniformly anti-
Negro position of local candidates, the meaning of this finding is
not immediately clear. Campaign participation normally means
a high level of political involvement. But Crayfish is a peculiar
place where the most accommodative Negroes might be required
to contribute by their white superiors, in which case campaign
contributions would represent "Uncle Tomism" rather than
independent political action. A comparison of contributors and
non-contributors indicates that, at least in this respect, Crayfish
is not peculiar. Negro campaign-contributors are more likely
than non-contributors to have talked politics in the family, with
friends, and with Negro leaders, but they are less likely to have
talked politics with whites. In view of the nature of the inter-
racial discourse in Crayfish, the contributors look less like Uncle
Toms than the non-contributors.

These findings suggest that the low voting rate of southern
Negroes may not adequately reflect their political participation.
Negro and white differences are less acute in talking about
politics and in taking part in campaigns. But what about the
most demanding forms of political participation?

BELONGING TO POLITICAL ASSOCIATIONS, HOLDING
PARTY OR PUBLIC OFFICE

Opportunities for Southerners to vote or to participate actively in political campaigns occur regularly but at widely-spaced

intervals, according to the electoral calendars of their respective states. While sometimes very demanding of time, emotion, and money, these forms of political participation are still intermittent. Talking politics is more nearly a continuous process—although it, too, tends to reach a peak during election season—but talking represents a minimum investment of political interest and involvement. The forms of political participation to which we now turn our attention are both more taxing and more continuous than any we have considered so far. They are, therefore, the least common ways in which both whites and Negroes take part in the political processes of the South.

Southerners may be "different," but they are joiners as often as are other Americans. All but 9 per cent of the Negroes and 15 per cent of the whites belong to some kind of association, club, or formal group. Most of the groups to which Southerners belong are not explicitly "political." Churches, fraternities, lodges, PTA's, business and professional groups are the most popular types of groups (in that order) among both races. While these non-political associations may, at times, have important political consequences, their effects are sufficiently indirect or infrequent that it would be absurd to consider belonging to them to be a form of political action. Membership in groups like the Young Democrats or Young Republicans, the League of Women Voters, the NAACP, White Citizens Councils, and various Civic Leagues, on the other hand, represents a clear-cut and conscious involvement in the world of politics.

About 10.5 per cent of the voting-age Negroes in the region belong to political organizations and associations—most commonly the NAACP. Only 2.5 per cent of the whites are similarly involved. Thus we find, at this extremely demanding level, that Negroes in the South participate more than southern whites! Moreover, this seems to be the case in a wide variety of southern locales. In Piedmont County, for example, 18 per cent of the Negroes but only about 4 per cent of the whites belong to the wide range of political organizations existing there. In Camellia County, 6.5 per cent of the Negroes and 1.5 per cent of the whites report membership in political associations. For once, the picture remains the same in Bright Leaf and Crayfish counties— 5 and 9 per cent of the Negroes are members of political groups while not one white respondent in either county reported an analogous membership. The rich and active associational life of American Negroes has often been noted. Less widely recognized is that their group activity carries over into the explicitly political arena, despite the low rate of Negro voting.

Office-holding in political parties and government is quite another matter. The holding of party and public office has been almost entirely a white prerogative since the turn of the century. While this situation is gradually changing, Negro office-holding is so rare that not one Negro in our sample had ever held a public office of any kind, while 1.6 per cent of the whites had been federal, state, or local officials at some point in their lives. The situation is almost as one-sided so far as political party office is concerned. One Negro respondent (0.2 per cent of the whole) was a precinct committeeman. Six white respondents (0.9 per cent) held office in the Democratic or Republican parties. On this level, southern politics is still a white man's game.

THE POLITICAL PARTICIPATION SCALE

So far, we have separately discussed the different ways in which southern whites and Negroes participate in the political process. In this concluding section we shall demonstrate that talking politics, voting, taking part in electoral campaigns, belonging to political organizations, and holding party or public office are not only related to one another but are, in fact, different degrees of the same phenomenon.

If these different forms of action can all be considered as different amounts of political participation, then they must be related to one another in a cumulative way. Those who engage in the most "difficult" form of participation also should participate in the less demanding ways, just as a strong man who raises a 300-pound weight above his head should be able to do the same thing to a 299- or a 123- or a 47-pound weight as well. The maximum number of pounds the strong man lifts tells us—assuming that he is not exhausted in the process of experimentation!—that he can lift everything which weighs less than that amount.[17]

17. The Guttman Scaling procedure described here in layman's language has been the subject of a large technical literature. For more details see S. A. Stauffer, *et. al., Measurement and Prediction* (Princeton, N. J.: Princeton University Press, 1950), Chs. 3-9. It should be pointed out that the construction of a single Guttman Scale to describe the behaviors of two populations as different as

The most infrequent—and therefore the "hardest"—form of activity we have examined is that of holding party or public office; the next most uncommon form of behavior is belonging to political groups. These are followed by taking part in electoral campaigns; voting; and talking politics, the most ubiquitous form of behavior described above. An ideal cumulative pattern of these behaviors—lumping together office-holding and membership in political groups since such a small number of Southerners do either—would be as follows:

Talks:	Votes?	Participates in Campaigns?	Holds Office or Belongs to Political Group?
Yes	Yes	Yes	Yes
Yes	Yes	Yes	No
Yes	Yes	No	No
Yes	No	No	No
No	No	No	No

In this ideal "cumulative scale," the "highest" form of participation an individual engages in always perfectly predicts both the "lower" and "higher" forms of his participation. Thus if Mr. "A" holds a public office or belongs to a political organization, he *also* participates in political campaigns *and* votes *and* talks politics. If Mr. "B" does not hold an office or belong to political groups but does participate actively in electoral campaigns, he also votes and talks politics. All those who vote also talk about political events and problems. If, on the other hand, Mr. "C" does not even talk about politics—the "easiest" and most common form of participation—he does not participate in any other way. If the facts conform to this logical scheme or "model," then our confidence that all these actions tend to "measure" the same thing— political participation—is increased. If the facts conflict with this model, we can be certain that no single concept such as "political participation" underlies all the behavior we have described so far.

In order to examine the closeness with which southern realities conform to an ideal cumulative scale, each person interviewed was classified as to whether or not he (1) had ever talked about politics or public problems, (2) had ever voted, (3) had

southern Negroes and whites requires the sacrifice of some technical refinements in the interests of comparability. A technically more elegant scale might have been constructed from our data, but not one which would accommodate both races.

ever participated in political campaigns, or (4) now held office or belonged to a political organization. Since each person was defined as a participant or non-participant on four different questions, there are sixteen logically possible combinations of actions. Only the five patterns listed above are consistent with a cumulative scale. Ninety-five per cent of the Negro responses and 98 per cent of the white responses fell into one of the five "pure" scale types. Any batting average over 90 per cent is, by convention, considered an adequate demonstration of the existence of a scale. That is, such a high rate of conformity to the expected pattern of behavior indicates that the different tests are indeed measuring the same thing and that they differ only in being harder or easier to pass. This means we can safely say that people who vote but do not take part in campaigns *will* also talk politics but *will not* hold office or belong to a political organization. At least we can "safely" say this in the sense that we will be correct over 90 per cent of the time. Such a scale is of great theoretical utility, then, because it permits us to talk about political participation as a general phenomenon rather than being forced to discuss each discrete political act in unique terms.

The small number of "errors"—or behavioral patterns which deviate from the ideal scale—are often the result of interviewer mistakes or quixotic interpretations of questions by a few respondents. A respondent, for example, who says that he is the mayor of his home town but has never talked about public problems or campaigned is either a congenital liar or has misunderstood the questions. Thus the 2 per cent of the white and 5 per cent of the Negro answers which did not conform to one of the five ideal patterns were assigned to the "pure" pattern which they most closely approximated, a standard procedure in scaling analysis. As we shall see below, some of the scale "errors" are large enough and regular enough to suggest that something more than clerical or perceptual mistakes was involved. These deviations from a "pure" scale pattern will be shown to be of great importance in understanding differences between Negro and white political participation in the South.

A comparison of the over-all rates of political participation of Negro and white Southerners is presented in Figure 5, using the political participation scale described above. Along the bottom of the figure the different scale types are arranged, from those

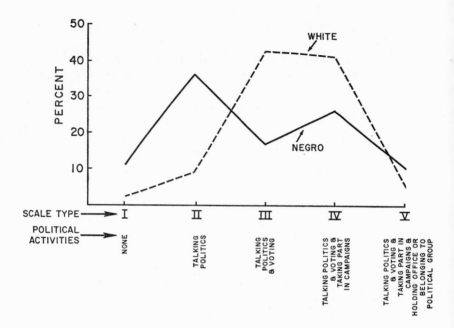

FIGURE 5. *Political Participation Scale Frequencies, by Race.*

who engaged in none of the political actions making up the scale (Type I) to those who engaged in all (Type V). The vertical axis represents the per cent of the Negro and white adult populations found in each participation type.

The most obvious and immediately apparent difference between Negroes and whites is the most important: the *over-all pattern* of political participation is very different for the two races. Very few whites are completely inactive (2 per cent), or content merely to talk about politics and public problems (9 per cent). An equally small number of whites are extreme political activists (5 per cent). Thus, about 84 per cent of the whites talk politics and vote (43 per cent), or talk politics, vote, and occasionally take part in political campaigns (41 per cent). The line representing the level of white participation approximates a bell-shaped, normal distribution curve—the same shape of curve which one would find if the heights of Southerners were plotted on a graph (most people are clustered near the average height, and very few are potential basketball stars or circus midgets).

The pattern for Negroes is startlingly different. The curve for Negroes has two peaks separated by a deep valley at the voting

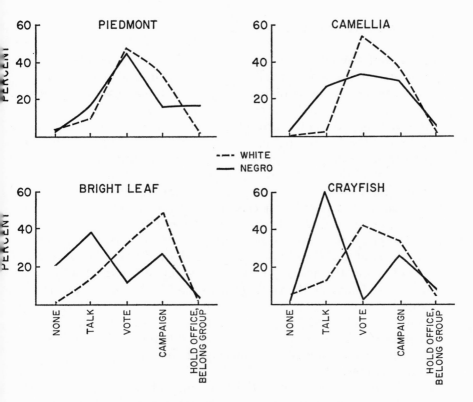

FIGURE 6. *Political Participation Scale Frequencies, by County and Race.*

stage. Political participation rates are far less uniform among southern Negroes than among southern whites. A large number of Negroes are politically inert or nearly so—11 per cent have never talked about politics or public affairs, and 36 per cent have talked but never voted. On the other hand, twice the proportion of Negroes as whites are thorough-going political activists. And 26 per cent of the Negroes report taking part in some way in political campaigns. Most Negroes who become registered voters do not restrict themselves to that form of political participation alone but *also* become active in political campaigns and organizations, at least occasionally. The most common degree of white participation, on the other hand, is to vote but go no further.

Additional insight into these peculiar racial differences is gained by shifting our attention from the South as a whole, to the four counties we have studied in some detail (Figure 6). In

Piedmont County—no racial utopia by anyone's standards and yet one of the least racially repressive counties in the South—there are few if any significant differences in patterns of participation between the two races. Both the Negro and white curves are bell-shaped. The sharp dip at the voting level and the bifurcation of the Negro population is entirely absent. Apparently, in Piedmont County, "people are people" so far as participating in government is concerned. The picture is slightly different in Camellia County. Both racial curves are roughly bell-shaped, but the Negro population contains many more inactive persons than the white while also containing about the same proportion of campaign participants and activists. The two rural counties—Bright Leaf and Crayfish—possess the sharp division between the inactive and the active Negro that we found for the South as a whole. In Crayfish, the void between the Negroes who have never voted (62 per cent) and those who have campaigned (23 per cent) or belonged to political groups (4 per cent) is almost incredible. Underscoring these wide differences in patterns of Negro participation is the similarity of the white patterns in the four counties.

A mere examination of the frequency of scale scores for the South as a whole and for our four counties suggests, *without any further analysis*, that major barriers to Negro voting exist, which are not operative for whites and which have less effect upon other forms of Negro political participation. Becoming a registered voter apparently is much more difficult for Negroes than whites—at least in counties like Bright Leaf and Crayfish—and, at least partly as a result of this, a smaller proportion of Negroes ever achieve this level of participation. But those who do become voters are therefore unusually dedicated and determined citizens who participate in other respects to a higher degree than do white voters.

Additional support for this possible interpretation of the data is given by an examination of "scale errors." As was explained above in our brief description of the construction of the Political Participation Scale, a scale is based upon the assumption that the highest and most demanding form of political participation a person engages in predicts perfectly how he will behave for "lower" forms. Thus someone who takes part in campaigns also votes and also talks about politics. While this proved to be the case for a vast majority of Southerners, there were still a few anomalies or "errors." Most of these scale errors for Negroes concerned voting. Specifically, the largest single cause of scaling error was the Negroes who had never voted but who had taken part in campaigns, or belonged to political groups, or held party or public offices.

Table 2 shows the proportion of all Negroes and whites with this apparently anomalous pattern of behavior, for our four counties and for the South as a whole. In Piedmont County only 5 per cent of the Negroes engaged in the more demanding forms of political action without voting—only 2 percentage points more than was true for the whites. In Camellia and Bright Leaf counties, on the other hand, non-voting activists comprised 9 and 15 per cent of the Negro population, respectively, while only a small handful of whites reported such extraordinary behavior. Finally, in rural, deep-South Crayfish County almost a third of the Negroes participated in campaigns (largely through anonymous gifts of money) or belonged to political organizations (usually the NAACP), even though being non-voters.

If the South as a whole included as much "error" as Crayfish County we would have to conclude that it was not mere error but an indication that voting was not part of a Political Participation Scale—that it was a "non-scalar item," not related to the others in such a way as to permit prediction from one form of behavior to the other forms. Since all of these forms of participation are closely related for the South as a whole, however, we conclude that the failure of active Negro participants in Crayfish to vote is indeed a manifestation of error rather than of a defective scale. Those people in scale types IV and V *ought* to be voters in terms of their other political behaviors. Their indication that they have never voted is a defect, not in perception or in the local meaning

TABLE 2. *Percent of Respondents Who Have Held Public Office, Belonged to Political Group, or Participated in Election Campaign But Who Have Never Voted; by County and Race*

County	Negroes	Whites
Piedmont	5%	3 %
Camellia	9%	1.5%
Bright Leaf	15%	4 %
Crayfish	31%	3.5%
Southwide	12%	2 %

of voting but in the local political system. "Artificial" barriers to normal participation for Negroes would seem to account for most of the so-called "errors" in our scale.

CONCLUSIONS

What, then, have we learned about Negro political participation in the South from this essentially descriptive paper? Three major conclusions seem to merit a brief summary.

1. While southern Negroes generally participate in politics less than whites, the gap is far less wide than it is usually assumed to be. When one remembers that southern Negroes are far more often of low socio-economic status than are southern whites, and that low status is associated with political inactivity in all populations, the difference in participation rates between the two races seems relatively small.

2. The rates of Negro participation, and the gap between Negro and white rates, vary widely from community to community in the South. Community-related variables, then, would seem to play a large part in determining how much, and in what ways, southern Negroes take part in the political process.

3. Inhibitions to Negro voting exist, especially in the more rural and repressive communities, which do not exist for whites and which are not as effective in suppressing other modes of political activity among Negroes. If these restraints are removed a substantial increase in Negro voting should occur. Southern Negroes are already surprisingly active in the political life of the region in all other ways.

V. METHODOLOGICAL
DIMENSIONS

Response Set in Political Survey Research on Costa Rican and Panamanian Students: A Comparative Analysis*

by Daniel R. Goldrich

INTRODUCTION

Within recent years there has been a wave of complaints that the study of Latin-American societies lacks a systematic empirical orientation.[1] One of the principal ways in which social scientists have sought to meet the deficiency is through more consciously theoretical research designs, many of which depend on the acquisition of data through the social survey technique. In this situation where so little cumulative information exists and where so few studies have been replicated, the new studies are likely to be widely used and highly influential, and thus it is most important to assess them with regard to the validity of their data. For example, a major problem in the conduct of social surveys where the population is inexperienced with them, unused to the expression of opinion, and/or limited in literacy skills, is submissiveness toward the interviewer. This can result in data the "straight" interpretation of which can lead to substantially unwarranted conclusions.

* Appreciation is hereby expressed to the following agencies for support of one or another phase of the research: the Center for the Advanced Study in Educational Administration, the Institute for Community Studies, and the Institute of International Studies and Overseas Administration, all of the University of Oregon, and the Office of International Programs, Michigan State University. Will Wroth assisted in the development of the response set scales, and he and Robert L. Sandels assisted in the field work. My gratitude is also expressed to the students and administrators of the schools for their co-operation, and to Marshall N. Goldstein for his very helpful criticism.

1. See, for example, "The State of Research and Study in Latin American Government and Politics," in J. D. Martz, *The Dynamics of Change in Latin American Politics* (Englewood Cliffs, N. J.: Prentice-Hall, 1965), pp. 1-6; Merle Kling, "The State of Research on Latin America," in Charles Wagley (ed.), *Social Science Research on Latin America* (New York: Columbia University Press, 1964); J. L. Payne, *Labor and Politics in Peru: the System of Political Bargaining* (New Haven: Yale University Press, 1965), pp. 282-83; and the evaluation of such commentary by K. H. Silvert, "American Academic Ethics and Social Research Abroad; the Lesson of Project Camelot," American Universities Field Staff Reports Service, July, 1965.

There have been extremely few survey-based studies of a political sociological nature on Latin America, and in those few, little apparent attempt has been made to assess the extent of response set, i.e., *the systematic response by the respondent to the format in which questionnaire or interview items are presented rather than to the intended substance of the items.*

The study of political orientations of Panamanian and Costa Rican youth reported herein was based on a survey using a questionnaire as the data-collection device. Inasmuch as this provided a new experience for most of the respondents (and the surveying of these kinds of respondents' opinion was a relatively new experience for the researcher), it seemed incumbent to evaluate the data from the standpoint of how well the questionnaire tapped responses intentionally raised by the items themselves, rather than simply to assume that the high degree of formal co-operation given by the respondents was an acceptable predictor of the validity of the responses.

STUDY DESCRIPTION

This is a comparative study of the political orientations of Panamanian and Costa Rican secondary-school students. The Panamanian data were collected in 1961, the Costa Rican in 1962. Some of the schools have a five-year and some a six-year secondary sequence, and the respondents are drawn from the last two and last three years' classes, respectively, in order that they be old enough to be involved in the student political environment and mature enough to respond to the complex political questions put to them. The schools studied are the same type in the two countries: they are all in the capital city metropolitan area, and include an upper- and upper-middle-class private Catholic school, a middle- and working-class public school, and a vocational-mechanical arts school with students from the lower class. Data on students' social class identification, parents' education, and family possessions independently validate the strong differences in socio-economic status popularly attributed to the set of schools. In all cases, either the entire or a very substantial proportion of the student body in the relevant grades was given the questionnaire.

In all cases, preliminary arrangements involved first contacting the rectors of the schools, explaining the nature of the study, and requesting about one hour of time during a school day for the administration of the questionnaire. It was explained that the research was the endeavor of a professor from a state university in the United States, that it had grown out of a program of cross-cultural political socialization research, and that the particular study was financed by one of the university's research institutes. Co-operation was apparently given readily. The questionnaires were completed in each school during one day. Care was taken to assure that students in different classes and rooms could not discuss the questionnaire among themselves. There were no problems of disorder or overt confusion.

In all cases, the administration of the questionnaire was directed by a student from the national university who had been serving as an assistant on the study. This person stood before the assembled student respondents, explained the auspices, procedures, and purpose of the study, answered preliminary questions, and assured the students that neither their teachers nor administrators nor anyone else, with the exception of the research team, would see the completed questionnaires. Confidence was no doubt the more readily won by the fact that respondents were not asked to sign their names nor otherwise to give identifying information. The university student assistant remained with the students during their completion of the questionnaires, but actually had no problems to resolve. The cover page of the questionnaire also described the auspices, purposes, etc. Briefly, the sponsors were described as a group of North American professors making a study in a number of countries throughout the world of students' opinions on the civic life of the nation. The statement stressed the scientific nature of the inquiry, the importance of student opinion in their countries, the dependence of the study on their free co-operation, and the maintenance of their responses in confidence. Finally, the statement indicated the manner in which the questionnaire should be filled out, etc.; this section was exceedingly short inasmuch as the questionnaire format was straightforward and easily comprehended by students of this level.

A note on the two countries

The two national sets of students have had about the same kind of educational experiences formally, in the sense that the curriculum and quality of instruction have been evaluated as roughly equivalent.[2] Consequently, differences in response to the questionnaire would not seem attributable to these factors. It is conceivable that variation in response set, even for an educated elite group, could result from differences in the national social structure and level of economic development. And in this regard, Costa Rica and Panama have been considered quite dissimilar, the former having been widely characterized as more middle class socially, while the latter's image is of oligarchic domination of wealth, status, and power. Actually, the two countries rank closely together on basic indices of social structure and economic development. Thus the cultural differences that seem to exist may be more a function of different historical experiences (such as early colonization or land tenure patterns) than a direct consequence of present social and economic conditions.

For example, with regard to education, the literacy rates are 80 per cent and 70 per cent for Costa Rica and Panama respectively, ranking fourth and sixth in Latin America; additionally, the proportions of children enrolled in primary, secondary, and higher educational institutions are high and quite similar. The pattern of land distribution, considered a major difference between the two, is similar in gross terms; but ownership is more widespread in Costa Rica, while more Panamanian peasants lack legal title to the land they cultivate. After Canal-related activities, Panama depends as does Costa Rica on exports of bananas and coffee. But politically, the differences are substantial. Panama has been politically stable, in the sense that power has been confined very largely to the commercial and landowning elite group of families; political competition remains on a personalist basis largely within this circle and is characterized by the absence of any programmatic parties. Costa Rica has experienced considerable political change over the past twenty-five years,

2. The evaluator was a U. S. university professor of education who was serving as advisor through the Agency for International Development to Central American ministries of education on vocational education at the secondary level. He had had extensive experience with both the Panamanian and the Costa Rican schools.

having incorporated the middle class into the decision-making process, and having parties that differ ideologically and that serve in some measure to integrate the lower class. Therefore, it seems likely that whatever gross differences in response set may appear vis-à-vis a politically-oriented questionnaire are more usefully to be investigated as a function of the national political differences than of the national differences in economic development and social structure.

THE SCALE OF RESPONSE TYPE

The types of response set under examination here are the tendencies of some people to assent to the propositions made to them in an interview or questionnaire situation and of other people to reject them, in both cases independently of the content of the propositions. (The format of the items containing the propositions is given in Figure 1.)

Unfortunately, the response set problem not having been anticipated, the questionnaire contained few items the substance of which was reversed but the format of which was identical, which items could thereby have served as a check on internal validity. This was a serious deficiency in view of the need to explore the factor of salience in affecting response type. Salience

FIGURE 1. *Section of Questionnaire (in translation), Indicating Format of Types of Items Used in Scale of Response Type*

	Agree Strongly	Agree Somewhat	Agree Slightly	Disagree Slightly	Disagree Somewhat	Disagree Strongly
48. The government should provide work for all who need it.						
49. Violence should never be used to decide political questions.						
50. Democracy is not appropriate for poor countries.						
51. Essentially, the United States and this country are good friends.						

202 COMPARATIVE POLITICS AND POLITICAL THEORY

refers to the extent to which the content of a particular item attracts the attention and consideration of the respondent. Rather than assuming that people exhibit either response set or content sensitivity, it is hypothesized here that some people respond to a questionnaire situation in a set fashion consistently, while others behave in such fashion only occasionally or with regard to certain content areas. In order adequately to assess the extent of consistent and/or partial response set, a relatively large number of pairs of reversed items in different content areas is required. However, only two pairs of reversed items widely dispersed through the questionnaire were available and used as tests of response set.

One pair was common to both the Panamanian and Costa Rican questionnaires. The other pair varied in substance. The pair common to both asked for evaluation of politicians; the other pair asked in Costa Rica for an evaluation of the President, and in Panama for an evaluation of the Christian Democratic movement. All four items had the same general format: a statement with which the respondent was asked to agree, strongly, somewhat, or slightly, or to disagree, strongly, somewhat or slightly. The items were as follows:

The majority of the public officials work in behalf of the people's welfare.
A great number of politicians sell themselves easily.
Costa Rica only:
 Don Francisco Orlich will carry out a job of great value for the country.
 I do not expect Orlich to be a good president.
Panama only:
 Christian Democracy represents the formula for resolving national problems.
 Christian Democracy will be incapable of making the changes the country needs.

There is no logical a priori way of determining reversals in meaning. Meaning is culturally determined and not a universal phenomenon, and thus the respondents' behavior is more usefully conceived as reaction to stimuli than as "rational" or "irrational." Selection of these pairs of items was made on the basis that, of those available in the questionnaire, they were the ones that seemed to be most nearly opposed in meaning and the least ambiguous for the student respondents.

Originally another pair of items in the same format and dealing with an aspect of nationalism had been additionally selected to tap response set. They are cited here as an illustration of the difficulty of constructing post-hoc controls for the problem. The items, in both Costa Rican and Panamanian questionnaires, were:

North American companies should not be permitted to operate in this country.

If the job were good, I would like to work for a North American company here in [Panama, Costa Rica].

Focusing on ideology, it appears at first that the items contradict one another: one cannot oppose local operations of U.S. companies and also accept employment from them, nor vice versa. But this is an imposed "rationality," for the nationalist syndrome may well involve a rejection of foreign corporations in the abstract but an avidity for the income and fringe benefits provided by their employment. Or, a variation on the theme, it may involve a long-term perspective, combining hostility toward the United States with an inclination to take everything one can get from U.S. sources before the "inevitable" seizure or ouster of these enterprises. (There is no even remotely systematic information available on the orientations toward nationalism of local employees of U.S. firms in Latin America.) Similarly, a Latin-American student (particularly conceivable on the part of an upper-class respondent) may logically reject the first statement, thereby affirming the desirability of U.S. firms' operating in the country, while also rejecting the second statement because one personally does not want the types of employment made available therein. In any event, the degree of obviously logical contradiction between these nationalist items from the standpoint of the student respondent seems much less than that for the two previous pairs, and for this reason they were judged unsatisfactory as indicators of response set.

The decision was then made to assess content sensitivity on the basis of response to the two selected sets of items. However, content sensitivity is not an absolute; response types range empirically from an extreme of sensitivity to an extreme of response set. The range was measured as follows: on each item, there were six categories of response, ranging from strong agreement through strong disagreement, as previously described. This range was scored:

Not Ascertained—	0
Strong Agreement—	1
Some Agreement—	2
Slight Agreement—	3
Slight Disagreement—	4
Some Disagreement—	5
Strong Disagreement—	6

The two subscales were based on the following scores per pair of items:

High Acquiescent—	1 or 2 on one item, and 1 or 2 on the other
Low Acquiescent—	3 on one item, and 1, 2, or 3 on the other
Content Sensitive—	1, 2, or 3 on one item, and 4, 5, or 6 on the other
Low Rejector—	4 on one item, and 4, 5, or 6 on the other
High Rejector—	5 or 6 on one item, and 5 or 6 on the other
Not Ascertained—	0 on either item

The respondents were located on the general scale of response type according to the combination of responses on the two subscales, as indicated below in Figure 2. On the general scale, classification as Content Sensitive depended on responding "sensitively" to at least one of the subscales and with less than high acquiescence or high rejection on the other. Classification as Acquiescent resulted from responding in acquiescent fashion to both subscales, or with high acquiescence on one and anything other than high rejection on the other, or with low acquiescence on one and nonresponse on the other. Classification as Rejector resulted from responding in rejecting fashion to both subscales, or with high rejection on one and anything other than high acquiescence on the other, or with low rejection on one and nonresponse on the other. Combinations of responses of equal weights of acquiescence and rejection (for example, high acquiescence and high rejection) were given a "mixed" classification (and were extremely few in number). Only those whose responses were not ascertained on both subscales were classified as Not Ascertained.

FIGURE 2. *Formation of General Scale of Response Type (Matrix shows general scale types, formed by responses on two subscales.)*

		"Politicians" Subscale					
		NA	CS	HA	LA	LR	HR
"Christian	NA	NA	CS	A	A	R	R
Democracy"							
Subscale	CS	CS	CS	A	CS	CS	R
(Panama)							
	HA	A	A	A	A	A	A-R
or							
	LA	A	CS	A	A	A-R	R
"Orlich"							
Subscale	LR	R	CS	A	A-R	R	R
(Costa Rica)							
	HR	R	R	A-R	R	R	R

Key:
NA — Not Ascertained
CS — Content Sensitive
HA — High Acquiescent
LA — Low Acquiescent
A — Acquiescent
LR — Low Rejector
HR — High Rejector
R — Rejector
A-R — Mixed Acquiescent-Rejector

THE FINDINGS

Response set is clearly a problem of substantial proportions in this study. Among the three groups of students in each country, the consistently Content Sensitive (those scored as sensitive on both subscales) were a minority in all cases, ranging from a high of 42 per cent among the Panamanian upper-class students to a low of 18 per cent among the Panamanian lower-class. On the other hand, the consistently Content Sensitive were the modal type in five of six student groups (Table 1). But even where a less stringent requirement for Content Sensitivity is used on the general scale (Content Sensitive on one subscale and something less than a high degree of acquiescence or rejection on the other), Sensitivity is attained by as much as 70 per cent of the group in only two cases, and by only 41 per cent of the Panamanian lower-class students (Table 2). With regard to the two subscales, the Content Sensitive are a minority in five of the twelve instances (Table 3). Sensitivity is attained by 70 per cent in only one case, and by 60 per cent or more in only four cases. The seriousness of the problem for developing political theory is indicated below.

TABLE 1. *Percentage of Consistent[a] Content Sensitivity, Acquiescence, Rejection, and Nonresponse, by Class Background*

Country	Class Background		Consistent			Inconsistent	Total %
		CS	A	R	NA		
	Upper	42	8	0	10	40	100
Panama	Middle	39	9	1	2	49	100
	Lower	18	21	1	12	48	100
	Upper	30	13	0	2	55	100
Costa Rica	Middle	27	10	3	3	57	100
	Lower	26	11	1	3	59	100

Key:

  CS — Content Sensitive
  A — Acquiescent
  R — Rejector
  NA — Not Ascertained
Inconsistent — All other combinations
[a]Consistent means the same score on both subscales.

TABLE 2. *Percentage of Response Types on General Scale, by Class Background*

Country	Class Background	CS	A	R	A-R	NA	Total %	N
	Upper	62	23	4	0	10	99	283
Panama	Middle	71	20	6	1	2	100	219
	Lower	41	41	5	1	12	100	386
	Upper	60	30	5	4	2	101	121
Costa Rica	Middle	70	17	8	2	3	100	100
	Lower	64	25	5	3	3	100	207

Key:

  CS — Content Sensitive
  A — Acquiescent
  R — Rejector
  A-R — Mixed Acquiescent-Rejector
  NA — Not Ascertained

A major focus of the larger study is political legitimacy, defined in part by the evaluation of national decision-makers. Hence the "politicians" subscale was particularly crucial, for it helps the analyst to estimate whether purported evaluations of decision-makers are genuine or a response set. An important Panamanian political problem concerns the extent to which educated sons of lower-class families support, accept, or oppose

TABLE 3. *Percentage of Response Types on Subscales, by Class Background*

Country and Subscale	Class Background	Response Pattern					
		CS	A	R	NA	Total %	N
Panama							
	Upper	53	28	5	13	99	283
"Politicians"	Middle	70	23	3	4	100	219
Subscale	Lower	40	38	4	18	100	386
Costa Rica							
	Upper	39	48	9	4	100	121
"Politicians"	Middle	43	38	11	8	100	100
Subscale	Lower	45	40	3	11	99	207
Panama							
"Christian	Upper	66	18	3	13	100	283
Democracy"	Middle	55	29	10	7	101	219
Subscale	Lower	34	41	7	18	100	386
Costa Rica							
	Upper	66	20	8	7	101	121
"Orlich"	Middle	63	20	6	11	100	100
Subscale	Lower	57	25	8	11	101	207

Key:
    CS — Content Sensitive
    A — Acquiescent
    R — Rejector
    NA — Not Ascertained

their national political system. A potential indicator of evaluation of the decision-makers is reaction to the item, "The majority of the public officials work in behalf of the public welfare." Of the Panamanian lower-class students responding to this proposition, 54 per cent agreed. Controlling on response set, however, one finds that only 25 per cent of the agreers were content sensitive. Of those in strong or substantial agreement, only 14 per cent were content sensitive. *In short, the supportive or legitimate response category was heavily filled by "insensitive" responses. The decision whether or not to control for content sensitivity thus determines in substantial measure what interpretation is made of the data.*

Whether one considers the responses on the subscales or the combined responses on the general scale, it is clear that the major response set problem is acquiescence. The incidence of acquiescence, rejection, and nonresponse for the three sets of students in each country on the two subscales forms a pattern such that acquiescence is the largest problem in each of the twelve instances, and that in all twelve there is more acquiescence than rejection and nonresponse combined (Table 3). In all cases there is more than twice as much acquiescence as rejection, and in ten of twelve there is more than twice as much acquiescence as nonresponse.

Rejection as a set is found most infrequently. The incidence of consistent rejection is 1 per cent or less for five of the six groups of students, and the highest incidence is 3 per cent for the remaining group (Table 1). On the general scale, the range of rejection is from 4 to 8 per cent (Table 2). On the subscales, the highest incidence is 11 per cent, and in eleven of twelve instances rejection occurs in less than 10 per cent of the sample (Table 3).

One significance of this pattern is that it provides further evidence of the generally co-operative response of the students to the project, inasmuch as "indiscriminate" rejection or failure to respond would seem the more likely channels through which to express hostility. In response to the new, politically-focused questionnaire situation, we hypothesize, the general tendency was to co-operate, but where the content was too difficult to comprehend or to permit of decision, or was lacking in salience, the easiest answer—agreement—was given. If it is a correct hypothesis that this is a reflection of co-operativeness toward the study, it suggests the broad possibilities for the collection of data from intellectual groups that are widely considered to be hostile both to North Americans and to scientifically-oriented social research. It also suggests that, because the incidence of response set within the generally co-operative environment of data collection tends to be high, a serious inquiry must be undertaken to illuminate the causes and correlates of content sensitivity.

RESPONSE SET AND SOCIAL BACKGROUND

Studies of response set conducted on U.S. populations have found a relationship between acquiescence and socio-economic status (usually indicated by education). For example, Agger et al., found that in a random-sample survey of a small metropolitan area, 37 per cent of the grade-school educated were acquiescent, compared to 25 per cent of the high-school educated, and 16 per cent of the college-educated. Content sensitivity occurred less among the grade-school educated than the others, and rejection occurred more among the college-educated than the others.[3] This has been theoretically accounted for by the role of education in instilling a more complex orientation toward causation in human behavior (disposing the highly educated to reject categoric statements about society), and by the tendency of lower-status people to agree to propositions put to them by higher-status interviewers or questionnaire administrators as a function of deference. Although the student respondents in the present study are at a common level of education, we hypothesize that the differences among the three sets of students in the two countries vis-à-vis parents' education, status, and general style of life are sufficiently large to result in substantial differences in response set. In addition, the deference factor may reinforce this tendency among the lower-class students. (The reputation of the schools, the students' reports of parents' education, family possessions, and father's occupation, plus the students' own class identification all varied consistently and quite substantially in such a way as to validate the distinctions made here at the outset between upper-, middle-, and lower-class student bodies.)

Variation in response type does not occur in the hypothesized manner in this study. In neither country does acquiescence vary inversely with class background (Table 2). Although the Panamanian lower-class students acquiesce much more than do those of middle- and upper-class backgrounds, the upper-class students acquiesce slightly more than the middle-class. But even the sharp differences found in Panama between lower-class students and their higher-class counterparts do not occur in Costa Rica; there the middle-class students are the least acquiescent, as in Panama, but the lower-class students are close in this regard, and the upper-class students exhibit the most acquiescence. Furthermore, in neither country does rejection vary by class.

In both countries the middle-class students were the most content sensitive. This may be partly a function of the style and substance of instruction in their schools, which is probably more

3. R. E. Agger, M. N. Goldstein, and S. A. Pearl, "Political Cynicism: Measurement and Meaning," *Journal of Politics,* XXIII (August, 1961), 477-506, esp. 503-6. See also Angus Campbell *et al., The American Voter* (New York: Wiley, 1960), 512-15.

oriented to scientific inquiry and modes of explanation than in the religion-based schools of the upper class, and more oriented to the humanities and social sciences than in the vocational schools of the lower class.

A review of the incidence of general content sensitivity among the six sets of students shows similar patterns, then, with one exception: the high score of the Costa Rican lower class and the low score of the Panamanian lower class. This is interesting in view of the similarity in their educational experience, and of the fact that the Costa Rican lower-class students come from less-educated families than do their Panamanian counterparts (though both are, of course, from substantially less-educated families than are the middle-class students). Inasmuch as the questionnaire was heavily oriented toward politics, it is possible that the difference in content sensitivity is a function of the differential politicization of the lower class. Where the lower class has more opportunity to participate politically, and where leaders appeal for support on the basis of needs and policies that relate closely to their conditions of life, the lower class is more likely to perceive the personal relevance of politics and to make considered judgments about political propositions. There seem to be substantial differences between the Panamanian and Costa Rican polities in these regards, though the scope and degree of difference have not been very systematically assessed. Unfortunately, however, it is impossible with the present data to test whether the greater content sensitivity of the Costa Rican lower-class students is a function of their being more politicized than their Panamanian counterparts, because the generally acquiescent students tend also to asquiesce on the measures of politicization, thereby invalidating the use of the responses for this purpose. (Previously, students' responses on their social background were used in confirmation of the strong socio-economic status differences among the schools. The logic of the use of these data despite the widespread fact of response set is that there was available an independent check against the pattern of social differences provided by the responses—in this case, reputational differences relating to the eliteness of the upper-class schools, the general status of liberal arts schools versus vocational-mechanical arts schools, etc., private versus public school tuition costs, the residential areas from which the various student bodies were drawn, etc. With regard to the politicization of Panamanian and Costa Rican lower-class students, no independent validators were available.)

RESPONSE SET AND SUBSCALE CONTENT

We have commented on the relatively high frequency of response set among the Panamanian lower-class students on both subscales. For all of the other groups, however, there is considerable variation in the quality of response from one subscale to the other. The Panamanian middle- and upper-class students are much more sensitive to the "politicians" subscale than are the Costa Ricans (Table 3). Conceivably, the salience of Panamanian politicians is related to their reputation for inefficiency and unresponsiveness, while Costa Ricans, if not elated over the quality of their public servants, evaluate them as intermediate in these regards. In short, salience may vary with cynicism about politics and politicians and with the degree of opposition to the prevailing political system.[4]

The other subscales deal with different matters—the current president in Costa Rica, and the Christian Democratic movement in Panama. The presidency being the key political position in Costa Rica, it is hardly surprising that sensitivity to the content of this subscale increases for all student groups. Since Christian Democracy originated in the "better circles" of Panama, it is similarly unsurprising that the greatest sensitivity to the movement is evidenced by the upper-class students and that the lower-class students are even less sensitized to it than they are to politicians as a general category.

If we want to make statements about general content sensitivity versus partial content sensitivity (sensitivity in some areas of questioning but not others)—the factor of salience—we obviously need at least two subscales. But of our two subscales, only one is really comparable in both Panama and Costa Rica, the "politicians" subscale. Since the "Christian Democracy" subscale in Panama may well have a built-in class bias—salience for

4. Evidence in conformity with this hypothesis is provided by a restudy of Panamanian upper-class students in 1963. A substantial increase in content sensitivity on the "politicians" subscale was associated with a substantial increase in opposition to the prevailing system. See *Sons of the Establishment: Elite Youth in Panama and Costa Rica* (Chicago: Rand McNally, forthcoming).

the upper-class students—we have a limited basis for the analysis of patterns of general versus partial content sensitivity within Panama and between Panamanians and Costa Ricans.

Still, some comparative assessments can be made. For example, the Costa Ricans respond rather uniformly in regard to class: there is little difference between class groups in content sensitivity on either subscale. One of the Panamanian subscales by its very nature particularly elicits differential class sensitivity, and the resulting pattern of class differences must be interpreted with this in mind. The other subscale, however, also shows substantial class differences in sensitivity, without a built-in bias. This indicates the possibility that Costa Rican students of varying class background share a more common political socialization experience in some regards than do the Panamanian students. This seems of particular interest because the level of economic development of the two national societies is relatively similar, a condition that suggests political variation as the source of differential class sensitivity to political questions. Whether this differential degree of social integration in responding to political questions is indicative of differential social integration in the political behavior of students in Panama and Costa Rica is an important question, but it cannot be pursued with the data at hand.

Another comparative assessment can be made despite the class-biased "Christian Democracy" subscale. It can be seen that the Panamanian lower-class students exhibit little content sensitivity on either scale, so that their tendency toward response set cannot be explained away simply on the basis of the differential class appeal of the upper-class-led and -oriented Christian Democracy.

The fact that the "Orlich" subscale in Costa Rica focuses on one of the most salient possible political symbols, and that the items constituting it are about as straightforward and simple as is conceivable, provides a particularly useful basis for assessing the extent of the response set problem. If a large proportion of students fails to demonstrate sensitivity to this content, then the problem would seem to be a substantial one. (A high level of content sensitivity on this subscale would not, however, logically demonstrate the inconsequential nature of the problem.) In fact, content sensitivity on this subscale ranges from 57 to 66 per cent.

This seems to represent considerable evidence that response set is a substantial problem and not just a function of extremely complex or abstruse propositions in a questionnaire.

TABLE 4. *Percentage of Consistent, Partial, and No Content Sensitivity, by Class Background*

Country	Class Background	Response Pattern				
		CS on both subscales	CS on either subscale but not both	CS on neither subscale	Total %	N
Panama	Upper	42	36	22	100	283
	Middle	39	47	14	100	219
	Lower	18	39	44	101	386
Costa Rica	Upper	30	46	25	101	121
	Middle	27	52	21	100	100
	Lower	26	51	23	100	207

Key:
CS — Content Sensitive

The fact is that for five of the six groups of students, partial content sensitivity (sensitivity to one area only) occurs more frequently than general content sensitivity (Table 4). In four of the six cases, partial rather than general content sensitivity is much more widespread. This suggests that the problem of comprehending, minimizing, or making use of response set is extremely difficult, because it includes not only a general way of reacting to questionnaire stimuli—which would be relatively easy to control—but also a reaction to specific content areas. The marked variation in Costa Rica to two subscales both of which dealt with politicians (in the one case the category as a whole, and in the other, the incumbent in the foremost political role) attests among these students to the absence of a general response set, even vis-à-vis the evaluation of politicians. For five of six groups of students, general response set (absence of content sensitivity on both sub-scales) characterized 25 per cent of the group or less. In short, these findings suggest the possibility that similar variations in response type might occur with reference to the whole range of variables comprising a study such as this, and that any attempt to control the problem has to deal with or at least further explore this possibility.

214 COMPARATIVE POLITICS AND POLITICAL THEORY

SUMMARY AND CONCLUSIONS

This paper raises the question of whether response set is a serious problem in survey data collected through questionnaires on political orientations from two sets of Latin-American secondary-school students. The assessment is limited by the fact that indices of content sensitivity were not built into the questionnaire and had to be devised after the fact. The resulting scale, composed of two subscales, included one subscale common to both Panamanians and Costa Ricans, and one the content of which varied but the form and scoring of which were identical.

Response set has been shown by this measure to occur widely. The major type of set is acquiescence; rejection and nonresponse occur much less frequently. A failure to control for response set, at least with regard to the area of evaluation of politicians, could have led to a substantially invalid interpretation of the data and seriously distorted conclusions.

The incidence of response set does not follow the pattern expected from studies done in the United States. Variation was not inverse to socio-economic background of the students, and while the middle-class group in each country scored highest in content sensitivity, the two lower-class groups scored quite differently in the two countries. A hypothesis accounting for the different response patterns of the Panamanian and Costa Rican lower-class students as a function of differential politicization was formulated. It was untestable with available data, however, since the acquiescent as measured by the general scale of response type also tended to acquiesce on items measuring politicization.

The relative infrequence of rejection and nonresponse was taken as an indicator of the high degree of co-operation of students with the study, but the high incidence of acquiescence demands explanation by future inquiry.

Response set varied substantially but inconsistently by content areas, class, and country. Few general propositions are possible given the design of the research, but a major possibility is that response set is substantially a function of specific content areas. More of the students were partially content sensitive (scored as sensitive to only one of the two subscales) than either generally content sensitive or generally acquiescent or rejecting. This would mean that control of the problem would require holding response set constant, area by area or variable by variable, an endeavor that seems extremely costly and complex. Before such an expensive and elaborate design were adopted, it would seem useful to design a study specifically on the nature of response set and the conditions facilitating sensitivity to content. In the interim, checks on response set, at least for the major variables in a social survey, would seem in order.

The present study relied relatively little on open-ended items, but that would seem a promising direction in which to go to increase the validity of the data as well as to ascertain correlates of response set and content sensitivity. A more varied format within interview schedules and questionnaires might provide data permitting greater use of the phenomenon of response set in a theoretically relevant way. For example, response set may occur among those least likely to see the world, the political system, etc., as manipulable. The incidence of response set may under certain conditions of research design be useful as a datum in the same imaginative way that Daniel Lerner and his associates made use of nonresponse and lack of opinion in their study of modernization in the Middle East.[5]

5. *The Passing of Traditional Society* (Glencoe: Free Press, 1958).